The Hermeneutics of Tradition

The Hermeneutics of Tradition

Explorations and Examinations

edited by

CRAIG HOVEY *and* CYRUS P. OLSEN

CASCADE *Books* • Eugene, Oregon

THE HERMENEUTICS OF TRADITION
Explorations and Examinations

Copyright © 2014 Wipf and Stock Publishers. All rights reserved. Except for brief quotations in critical publications or reviews, no part of this book may be reproduced in any manner without prior written permission from the publisher. Write: Permissions, Wipf and Stock Publishers, 199 W. 8th Ave., Suite 3, Eugene, OR 97401.

Cascade Books
An Imprint of Wipf and Stock Publishers
199 W. 8th Ave., Suite 3
Eugene, OR 97401

www.wipfandstock.com

ISBN 13: 978-1-62564-498-5

Cataloging-in-Publication data:

The hermeneutics of tradition : explorations and examinations / edited by Craig Hovey and Cyrus P. Olsen.

xx + 252 pp. ; 23 cm. Includes bibliographical references.

ISBN 13: 978-1-62564-498-5

1. Tradition (Theology). 2. Hermeneutics. I. Hovey, Craig, 1974–. II Olsen, Cyrus P. III. Title.

BS476 .H36 2014

Manufactured in the U.S.A.   Last Update: November 12, 2014

Contents

List of Contributors   vii

Acknowledgments   ix

Introduction   xi

Part One—Tradition: Evangelical, Catholic, and Orthodox

1. Up the Mountain with the Fathers: Evangelical *Ressourcement* of Early Christian Doctrine
   —*Hans Boersma*   3

2. Communion and Catholicity: Nyssa, Augustine, Aquinas
   —*C. C. Pecknold*   25

3. The Hermeneutics of Schism and the Question of "Sister Churches"
   —*Will T. Cohen*   47

Part Two—Tradition: Ancient, Late-Medieval, and Modern Analyses

4. The Holiness of the Church in North African Theology
   —*J. Patout Burns Jr.*   75

5. Martin Luther's Hermeneutics of Christ's Deified Flesh
   —*Adam G. Cooper*   105

6. Alasdair MacIntyre's Hermeneutics of Tradition
   —*Craig Hovey*   144

Part Three—Tradition: Liturgy and Lament

7   Tradition, Truth, and Time: Remarks on the "Liturgical Action" of the Church
—*Robert C. Koerpel*   173

8   Joseph Ratzinger and the Hermeneutic of Continuity
—*Tracey Rowland*   193

9   The Wound of Tradition
—*Jonathan Tran*   226

Contributors

HANS BOERSMA, J. I. Packer Professor of Theology at Regent College

J. PATOUT BURNS JR., Edward A. Malloy Professor Emeritus of Catholic Studies at Vanderbilt University

WILL T. COHEN, Associate Professor of Systematic Theology at the University of Scranton

ADAM G. COOPER, Senior Lecturer in Patristics at the John Paul II Institute for Marriage and Family in Melbourne, Australia

CRAIG HOVEY, Associate Professor of Religion at Ashland University

ROBERT C. KOERPEL, Visiting Assistant Professor of Theology, St. Catherine's University

CYRUS OLSEN, Associate Professor of Theology and Religious Studies at The University of Scranton

C. C. PECKNOLD, Associate Professor of Historical and Systematic Theology at The Catholic University of America

TRACEY ROWLAND, Dean of the John Paul II Institute for Marriage and Family in Melbourne, Australia, and professor of political philosophy and continental theology

JONATHAN TRAN, Associate Professor of Theology and Ethics at Baylor University

Acknowledgments

VERSIONS OF SOME OF these essays have appeared as follows:

Hans Boersma, "Up the Mountain with the Fathers: Evangelical Ressourcement of Early Christian Doctrine," *Canadian Theological Review* 1 (2012) 3–22.

C. C. Pecknold, "'Man Is by Nature a Social and Political Animal': Essential and Anti-Essentialist Relational Ontologies Revisited," *The Heythrop Journal* 54 (2012).

Adam G. Cooper, *Life in the Flesh: An Anti-Gnostic Spiritual Philosophy* (Oxford: Oxford University Press, 2008) 108–30. The excerpt here has been reproduced by permission of Oxford University Press.

The editors are grateful to these journals and publishers for their kind permission to reprint this material.

Introduction

THE HERMENEUTICS OF TRADITION project presented in this volume analyzes Christian methods of understanding traditions and how they are communicated culturally, textually, and liturgically. The following essays strive to avoid simple valorization of traditions while affirming the strength of "tradition" as a category at once uniting and dividing the church.

While hermeneutics is most commonly associated with texts, philosophers and literary critics have expanded our notion of text over the last century, noting the permeation of culture and tradition throughout the process of interpretation. Meaning is derived from the interaction—dubbed a cycle or spiral—among the language, culture, and history of the interpreter, rather than simply exacted by an isolated exegete. In short, the role of tradition has come to the fore. When Jacques Derrida claimed that everything is a text ("there has never been anything but writing"[1]), he meant that nothing falls outside the range of things that must be interpreted using mediating structures, such as language.

The difficulty of turning to shine a light on how one's experience of language, culture, and so on—what Martin Heidegger called fore-structures—condition one's interpretations of everything is a function of the fact that shining a light in this way will itself *also* inevitably be a process of interpretation.[2] Traditions hold us without being wholly transparent to our inspection. We are, as Heidegger said, "thrown" into traditions—they form and surround us. Interpretation thus inextricably depends on a tradition's experienced contingent variables in the very process of identifying its hold. To a thinker like Heidegger, while this is clearly a circle, it "is neither a makeshift nor a defect." Rather, taking part in the circle "is the strength of thought, [and] to continue on it is the feast of thought."[3] Part of the reason is that hermeneutical circles never remain two-dimensional, but rather take

---

1. Derrida, *On Grammatology*, 159.
2. Heidegger, *Being and Time*, 195.
3. Heidegger, *Origin of the Work of Art*, 144.

flight, as it were, or descend, in a spiral fashion among a community of interpreters who actively think and live within it.

The interplay between readers and texts accordingly takes on a three-dimensional spiral structure as the process of interpretation and re-interpretation carries on. The spiral character of the exercise enriches the tradition within which texts are read just as it also undergoes this deepening under the text's control and influence. By now it should be clear that "text" is being used far beyond its strictly literal sense. In the "feast of thought," tradition should be thought of as itself a kind of text that must be interpreted and reinterpreted. When this is done *from within*, the tradition spirals over itself, along the way revealing resonances and depths possibly unheard and unknown previously. One of the key aims of this volume is to follow theological traditions' spiral.

A central concern of many of the essays collected here is the uncertain and unstable interplay between the human and the divine. As a species hungry for meaning, our contributions to the condition of the world are apt to appear all-too-human. After all, are not all the easily-identifiable fore-structures (culture, language) manifestly human creations? Yet assuming that a human contribution limits the range of possible meanings to those that are straightforwardly terrestrial and cultural will lead to suspicion and distrust that is theologically unwarranted. Where religious traditions partially reveal their beauty is in their ability to liberate from the suspicion that all meaning in this world remains *simply* arbitrary human artifice. If only we could unmask the contrived game of power, we might be tempted to say, then we could get beyond G. K. Chesterton's comment about tradition: that it is the "democracy of the dead." Active and intelligent participation in that democracy is among our highest callings, and so should be affirmed as necessary for human flourishing. Indeed theology has found various ways of affirming God's involvement in and with the things that the church carries with it, borne of past struggles to find meaning, while also taking care to avoid confusing those things directly with God.

The crucial task for this aspect of hermeneutics and tradition—namely, the interplay between the human and the divine—is to give some kind of account of what belongs to culture and history and what transcends them. On one such account, the fact that every theology bears the marks of the culture in which it was produced presents an obstacle to the catholicity of the church and an impediment to ecumenical efforts. Theologians of every age will therefore be challenged to make clear distinctions between what belongs to what John Meyendorff calls "holy 'Tradition' as such" and human traditions that vary according to culture, language, and history.[4] Variation

---

4. Meyendorff, *Living Tradition*, 25.

among the things affirmed about holy tradition may be celebrated as the one church's diversity; variation between merely human traditions divide the church by mistaking what is transitory (human) for what is enduring (divine).

Yet how easily is this separation between human and divine tradition accomplished in practice? Can the very attempt to separate them in some sense fail to do justice to the complexity of how the two are intertwined? Consider the many ways this can be seen with Scripture, the words of which are themselves both human and divine. The many texts that make up the Bible often differ by author, century, culture, and language; yet they are all the Word of God. Furthermore, the canon of the Christian Bible was assembled through all-too-human debates that sought both to recognize and attribute authority to some texts and not others; yet the ability to call the resulting collection of texts Christian Scripture depends on recognizing the canonization process as at once also the work of God's Spirit. As it happens, a clear division between the human and the divine in Christian tradition can be maintained only by disregarding the more genuine ways of understanding their interrelations. Tradition understood theologically thus requires the fundamental openness to its (possibly) divine attributes and conditions. A default naturalism in our culture renders that openness difficult to sustain, yet necessary to articulate in order that the leaven of religious tradition may continue its work.

Attention to theology's sources—such as Scripture and tradition—consequently involves the divine-human interplay we here assert is involved in hermeneutics of tradition; these sources shape each other, and not only by way of the Bible's authorship and canonization. In *New Horizons in Hermeneutics*, Anthony C. Thiselton locates "hermeneutics of tradition" largely in relation to pre-modern biblical interpretation and identifies postmodern parallels, noting in particular how the anti-individualism of postmodernity retains points of contact with earlier notions of tradition. He presents a short formula for locating differences between pre-modern, modern, and post-modern hermeneutical tendencies: "On the basis of belief in God, *trust* [characteristic of pre-modern hermeneutics] assumes the kind of methodological role which *doubt* assumes for modernism as exemplified in Cartesian rationalism, and which *suspicion* assumes for post-modernism in socio-critical hermeneutics and in deconstruction."[5] Theologians today struggle to balance these competing methodologies; indeed no interpreter can operate without an interplay among them.

In their essays in this volume, Hans Boersma and C. C. Pecknold both show how doctrines that originated through a particular interpretation of

---

5. Thiselton, *New Horizons in Hermeneutics*, 143.

parts of the Bible then come to function as a rule of faith for reading it as a whole. Boersma investigates the limited nature of doctrinal systems and human finitude by showing how the Church Fathers read Scripture and their cultures according to a Christological and Trinitarian rule of faith. If theology's goal is deification or anagogy (going "up the mountain"), then the finite human struggle to know the infinite Trinity inevitably meets with the ineffable mystery of God. Boersma argues that doctrine's limits are here—in God's mystery rather than in, for example, the many kinds of skepticism that have characterized modern knowing for centuries. It is precisely as we keep in mind the limits of doctrine that we can learn to appreciate once again its anagogical purpose; recognition that we have yet to arrive at full knowledge challenges us to probe deeper and ascend higher. The dialectic of limitation and ascent parallels the simultaneous dependence of doctrine on Scripture and how it must return again and again to fund, repair, and inspire the desire to discover more of Scripture's mysterious author amidst its pages.

Likewise, Pecknold shows how a Trinitarian rule of faith guided theologians Gregory of Nyssa, Augustine, and Thomas Aquinas in interpreting Genesis and the meaning of the *imago dei*. Because it is not immediately clear from the text itself what it means for humans to have been created in God's image, these theologians looked to the relations between the persons of the Trinity in order to draw an analogy with human relationality. It turns out that there are many ways that this human analogy to God's internal differentiation (yet in unity) are displayed. These include friendship, the sexual difference between male and female, and reproduction. The knowledge we have of things that are not like us nevertheless requires communion such that an association between knowing and loving becomes a chief way of coming to terms with the unity of the rational and the relational. Pecknold concludes by holding up Pope Emeritus Benedict XVI as a contemporary inheritor of this Catholic theological tradition. Benedict does not separate relationality (love, friendship, unity) from metaphysics (who we are or who God is by nature) but instead holds them together in much the same way that theology and ethics are properly united within a Trinitarian rule for interpreting all of reality. In this light, Pecknold laments the disunity among Christians who nevertheless confess one, holy, catholic, and apostolic church.

Notice that whether one looks for clear distinctions or complex interplay between human and divine contributions is already a work of interpretation. There are traditions of interpretation that underlie both of these such that our queries might be even further extended. How ought *these* (further back) traditions be considered? Are they "of God" or are they "of ourselves"?

It is possible that if we are unable to say, we will be driven to look more deeply for the hand of God in our lives and work.

It may be this precise uncertainty that holds most promise for ecumenical encounters by refusing to cease asking these kinds of questions. Will Cohen considers the problem of schism in his essay "The Hermeneutics of Schism and the Question of 'Sister Churches.'" He asks about the status of traditions that some have come to think no longer require interpretation. He resists the ideas that "tradition" ought to function like a collection of answers to our questions and that "appealing to tradition" means simply looking back to see what others have said. The difficulty with this approach is the way it neglects temporality and context, embodiment in history and culture. Even when it seems like it, there is no guarantee that the questions we ask are the same as those that our predecessors asked. Cohen appeals to the monumental work of Hans-Georg Gadamer on hermeneutics in order to show that there are two crucial, but often neglected, moves involving tradition. First, we only truly understand the meaning of a question when it is also a question *for us*, when we genuinely do not know the answer. Included in this is, secondly, our not knowing what our forebears meant when they arrived at their answers. Being attentive to temporality is likely to highlight this. Cohen applies these insights to revisiting the schism between the Catholic and Orthodox churches.

Why, Cohen asks, see the schism as a *fact* to which one can appeal rather than as an ongoing *question* that keeps being asked? What would it mean to keep asking it even now? Following Vladimir Lossky, Cohen makes a theological virtue out of the fact that the activity of interpretation is part of the tradition it is seeking to understand. For Christians, this means that God has not abandoned the church to sort through on its own what was previously given, but God sustains in every new moment the Christian struggles to believe what is true. As Cohen puts it, "Interpretation and tradition are one. Both are of God—and both are participated in by man." Rather than function as an anchor tethering a community to intransigence, tradition ever unfurls its lines of continuity through interpretation.

The next three essays demonstrate the hermeneutics of tradition at work in ancient, late-medieval, and modern contexts. Given the ecumenical spirit of unity that characterizes this volume as a whole, Patout Burns's historical and theological account of holiness follows naturally as a case study in addressing the very issue of a wounded church. In "The Holiness of the Church in North African Theology" Burns analyzes the holiness of the church and its power to sanctify in Christian North Africa from the late second century through the middle of the fifth century. During this period, Burns argues, a closely related set of issues was addressed, using an overlapping set of scriptural texts. As circumstances and even techniques of interpretation changed, scriptural texts were used in different ways and combinations to develop theologies which justified practices of admitting, retaining, or excluding sinners from the communion and clergy of the church.

Since second- and third-century justifications were generally known to the fourth- and fifth-century writers, these later theologians were both interpreting the scriptural texts to develop explanations and also criticizing the interpretations (and explanations) offered by their predecessors. For example, using Tyconius' principles of scriptural interpretation, Augustine modified the explanations of Tertullian and Cyprian to identify the saints within the church as the human mediators whose holiness guaranteed the efficacy of the sacramental ministry of the clergy. This African tradition of interpretation was modified as it was subsumed by the Roman church and later by the medieval scholastics. The African insistence on the human mediation of divine grace and its preference for holy mediators survived in the laity's preference for monastic clergy, the cult of the saints, and the honorific titles conferred upon ministers.

Adam Cooper next provides a case study of Martin Luther that shows how the reformer sought to preserve and extend earlier theologies of deification such as those discussed by Boersma. In "Martin Luther: Hermeneutics of Christ's Deified Flesh," Cooper destabilizes all Reformation narratives that place one issue—such as *sola scriptura* or some similarly isolated criterion—at the center of all debate; thereby he respects the spiral mentioned earlier, for Reformation interpretation is multidimensional. Cooper accordingly situates Luther as a theologian deeply immured in the hermeneutics of tradition, especially related to what he calls the "self-localization of God," the varied Old Testament means by which God freely elects to become present to God's people (such as through ark, tabernacle, and temple). Many long-standing interpretations of Luther improperly ignore the deeply sacramental, incarnational, and ontological basis of Luther's biblical realism, all of which cannot profitably be omitted from any attempt to summarize his theology in terms of a single paradigm.

Martin Luther's *Werke* is varied enough to sustain an appropriate sacramentality. Echoing Boersma's essay, Cooper shows how the deified flesh of Christ serves to unite Luther's sacramental sensibilities with his vision for ecclesial reform. Whenever Luther speaks of "Christ" or of our being "in Christ" or of Christ's presence "in faith" or "in us," we should never take the words in a vague, ethereal or immaterial sense, but always as referring to the Son of God in his physical humanity and its word-bound, sacramental presence in the world. Cooper shows how this vision operates in Luther's writings on Scripture, marriage, and social ethics. One discerns a hermeneutics of continuity in Luther when the focus is upon union with the life-giving flesh of Christ. Union with the life-giving flesh of Christ, therefore, takes on corporeal contours in holy works performed within each believer's particular vocation, a cooperative process of willing transformation that necessarily accompanies faith.

The questions this collection asks about the usefulness of tradition as a source for continuing engagement and interpretation have their own context: they arise amid specific modern anxieties about the nature of knowledge. For example, concerned to avoid a thoroughgoing relativism in which every interpretation must be as valid as every other, Wilhelm Dilthey asked, "But where are the means to overcome the anarchy of opinions that then threatens to befall us?"[6] This anxiety is a typically modern one in which the Enlightenment impulse to be free of all tradition is haunted by the specter of its exact obverse. Craig Hovey describes Alasdair MacIntyre's response to this kind of anxiety by giving an account of moral traditions in light of questions raised by genealogical rejections of modern rejections of tradition. MacIntyre's work has been especially important to theologians who share neither the (for example, Kantian) conviction that *a priori* truths will come into reason's view regardless of tradition's contingencies nor Dilthy's unease over whatever bleak alternatives there might be. Meanwhile, Friedrich Nietzsche celebrated the possibility of an alternative, one that would be created by the Übermensch and the culture that produces him. MacIntyre contends that tradition represents a third way. He famously argues that reason itself is "tradition-constituted" and that traditions are arguments throughout time. Hovey shows how the dialectics of tradition (in being both identity-granting and action-enabling, in tying past and future, knowledge and ignorance) comport with the Christian virtues necessary to live as "middle creatures" whose "thrownness" into traditions that were already underway demands constant interpretation of reality and therefore a hermeneutic that negotiates both revelation and mystery. It locates the genuine site for this kind of articulation beyond both Kant and Nietzsche.

The final section—"Liturgy and Lament"—captures the church's timeful participation in the active work of tradition. Just as Cooper's essay accentuates the sacramental self-localization of God central to some Christian hermeneutics of tradition, Robert Koerpel finds a similar voice in the writings of the philosopher Maurice Blondel. Koerpel, however, focuses more directly on liturgy in "Tradition, Truth, and Time: Remarks on the 'Liturgical Action' of the Church." He argues that Blondel must be read as offering

---

6. Dilthey, "Reminiscences on Historical Studies," 389.

a different understanding of history via the ontological realities presented to the world in Christian liturgy. Blondel's account of tradition challenges its readers to consider tradition in terms different than, but still attuned to, the modern practice of historiography. It does so by articulating tradition as the synthetic living reality, the bond (*vinculum*) which mediates the dialectical tension between history and faith, eternity and temporality, receptivity and kenosis, and deposit and development while representing the *vinculum substantiale* (substantial bond) that exists between Creator and creature established by Christ's hypostatic encounter with the world. (Here Koerpel's textual analyses well complement Burn's and Cooper's insights, given that each of these studies note the centrality of the hypostatic union to a hermeneutics of tradition.)

Furthermore, the concrete process by which tradition unfolds God's truth in time is through the faithful action of the church. In Blondel's horizon "faithful action is the Ark of the Covenant" where God's truth represented in doctrine becomes a living reality in the church. Liturgical action embodied in church tradition is not only a representation of revealed truth in human history, but also the church's encounter with and participation in revealed truth in time. The transmission of tradition that takes place from person to person in the church through time is an analogical reflection of the *kenotic* self-giving and the spontaneous receptivity that occurs between the life of the divine persons of the Trinity. In this way the church imperfectly participates in the perfect transmission of Christ that flows from the incarnation and its finality.

Tracey Rowland's essay "Joseph Ratzinger and the Hermeneutic of Continuity" looks at the relationship between cultures and developments in liturgy. She follows Ratzinger/Pope Emeritus Benedict XVI in critiquing attempts to amend the Church's rites to fit changes within wider societies, a move that might be termed a hermeneutics of rupture. Rowland describes Ratzinger's more nuanced approach toward tradition—neither slavishly reproducing it, nor abandoning it at every turn in favor of what is new. For this reason the essay is a striking example of how to speak about the "organic growth" of a tradition with respect to other influences such as language and music, particularly when, within a culture that is in the process of being influenced by Christianity, "baptized" pagan elements are discerned for how they can contribute to Christian practice and doctrine. According to Ratzinger, the office of the Pope itself exemplifies the spirit of restraint he counsels more broadly since the Pope is "not an absolute monarch whose will is law, but the guardian of an authentic Tradition."

Yet since the Church is a living body with which the Holy Spirit dwells throughout history, one should expect a certain amount of liturgical development, particularly since liturgy is one of the chief ways that the church hands on tradition. Rowland argues that it is not the role of the church to constantly update its liturgical rites in order to adapt to changes in the wider culture. Where there is confusion, it often has to do with considering cultures (especially national cultures) to be more autonomous and self-sustaining that they really are, an assumption buttressed by certain commitments of modern philosophy. Rather, as Ratzinger says, "the church is her own cultural subject for the faithful," not dependent on national, historical cultures. For this reason it can therefore be an alternative to them. If some kinds of development are warranted and some are not, it is important to ask whether a proposed development genuinely preserves and extends (rather than simply copies or dismisses) the apostolic tradition. On the other hand, Rowland follows Ratzinger in refusing to bring all rites into uniformity, noting that the pre-Conciliar co-existence of many different Catholic rites signals a salutary richness and diversity. Finally, Rowland calls for maintaining high aesthetic standards when it comes to the liturgy lest the Church cede to pastoral pragmatism and utility what is really part of the Christian witness to the beauty of God.

In the final essay, "The Wound of Tradition," Jonathan Tran leads with a stern caution about placing too much confidence in tradition. Using the work of Willie Jennings, Jonathan Tran critiques recent appeals to tradition that have been inspired by the work of Alasdair MacIntyre. Together they argue that MacIntyre places too much faith in tradition. Tran insists that there is always a gap—often a sizable one—between example and theory; this is normal. But we are misled if we consistently focus on a tradition's triumphs (such as its ideas) rather than its failure to lament how the people the tradition has produced are far less triumphant. A tradition's "wounds" are therefore its failures to live up to its own promises and stated ideals. What is too easily neglected is careful attention to the kinds of lives that a tradition produces, often leaving the impression that the superiority of one tradition over another is something that can be demonstrated at the level of scholarship. Tran pushes our consideration of tradition into the sometimes uncomfortable arena of real history. He claims that we must be aware of how "tradition" can make us blind to people who work with and live out the tradition in ways that are not anticipated by the tradition itself. Accordingly part of any tradition's robustness will be shown in how it is able to abide with the wounds of its own history once these wounds are identified. With the help of Stanley Cavell's work, Tran commends lament as the most appropriate theological response to the church's many "tradition-constituted wounds."

The Hermeneutics of Tradition presents the latest scholarship on tradition as a concept and reality in the development of Christian cultures, specifically as these cultures develop in text and in practice. One aim is to show that traditions are upheld, communicated, and developed within a recognizable set of interpretive guidelines (or rules) and that analysis of these sets both requires and reveals a "hermeneutics of tradition." The work of the authors included here presents the precarious integrity of traditions and the often-tenuous hold upon those traditions exercised by the hermeneutics that drive dynamics of preservation and change. As scholars and religious worshippers continue ancient traditions of receiving strangers with generous hospitality, the coherence of tradition serves conversations about where our true differences lie.

Bibliography

Derrida, Jacques. *On Grammatology*. Translated by Gayatri Chakravorty Spivak. Baltimore: Johns Hopkins University Press, 1976.

Dilthey, Wilhelm. "Reminiscences on Historical Studies at the University of Berlin." In *Hermeneutics and the Study of History*, edited by Rudolf A. Makkreel and Frithjof Rodi, 387–90. Princeton: Princeton University Press, 1996.

Heidegger, Martin. *Being and Time*. Translated by John Macquarrie and Edward Robinson. New York: Harper & Row, 1962.

———. "The Origin of the Work of Art." In *Basic Writings*, edited by David Farrell Krell, 169–212. Rev. ed. New York: HarperCollins, 2008.

Meyendorff, John. *Living Tradition: Orthodox Witness in the Contemporary World*. Crestwood, NY: St. Vladimir's Seminary Press, 1997.

Thiselton, Anthony C. *New Horizons in Hermeneutics: The Theory and Practice of Transforming Biblical Reading*. Grand Rapids: Zondervan, 1992.

Part One

Tradition: Evangelical, Catholic, and Orthodox

1

Up the Mountain with the Fathers
Evangelical Ressourcement *of Early Christian Doctrine*[1]

HANS BOERSMA

THE LAST SEVERAL DECADES have witnessed a fascinating development among evangelicals. More and more, evangelical theologians are developing an interest in the theology of the Church Fathers. Suspicious of the ways in which previous generations of evangelicals approached Christian doctrine—too often, so it is thought, as an abstract and lifeless cataloguing of propositional statements of truth derived from syllogistic argumentation—contemporary evangelicals are turning to premodern modes of doing theology; and they look to the Church Fathers, in particular.[2] This retrieval or *ressourcement* of the Fathers is, for all sorts of reasons, a wonderful thing, and this essay is intended as a small contribution to this burgeoning enterprise.

At the outset, however, I want to insert two caveats. First, a *ressourcement* of the Church Fathers that turns to the early Church in order to recover a putatively ideal era along with a pristine and pure theology is bound to end in failure. As one begins to read the Fathers, it soon becomes evident

---

1. I want to thank Craig D. Allert and John G. Stackhouse for their comments on an earlier draft of this essay.

2. I am thinking of the *ressourcement* project initiated by D. H. Williams, the work of Christopher A. Hall and other evangelical scholars, as well as the increasing proliferation of book series on and by the Fathers, also among publishing companies like InterVarsity Press.

that some of the most revered theologians were perhaps rather acrimonious characters. It also becomes clear that some of the issues that occupied the Fathers tremendously are no longer in the center of attention today, so that to rehash the very same issues may render us, to some extent at least, irrelevant. Simply to go back to the early Church would mean to jettison later developments that we actually value a great deal and that we do not want to go back on. This is not to gainsay that a *ressourcement* of the Fathers can be a wonderful thing. But proper *ressourcement* is never simply a jump from where we are today into the second-century thought world of St. Irenaeus or the fifth-century theology of St. Augustine. A worthwhile retrieval of the Church Fathers both recognizes the limitations of individual theologians in the early Church *and* it acknowledges significant development between the age of the Fathers and our own twenty-first century. So, we have to say "no" to a naïve idealization of the Church Fathers.[3]

Second, while I do understand the negative reaction that many contemporary evangelicals have to what we often call "modern" approaches to theology, I am convinced it would be a mistake simply to play off the Church Fathers' more intuitive, more biblical, more symbolic approach against what we may sense is the far too rational, systematic, and propositional theology of the modern period. Such a broad sketch does have its value. Modernity has indeed encouraged us to do theology in a sometimes strictly rational fashion, which causes serious problems. But we need to keep in mind two things:

(1) The Church Fathers were not averse to deep and careful thought. Whether we analyze Irenaeus's opposition to the Gnostics in the second century, read Gregory of Nyssa's reflections on the nature of human language, or engage St. Augustine's anti-Pelagian writings, in each case, we cannot but be impressed, perhaps even daunted, by the intellectual rigour, the depth of analysis, and the vehemence with which theological statements of truth are proposed and defended. The nearly unanimous conviction of the Fathers is that human reason constitutes the very image of God, which makes it the most highly prized aspect of the human person. In short, the Church Fathers do not excuse intellectual laziness.

(2) The Church Fathers never confused mystery with skepticism. In today's postmodern climate, contemporary evangelicals tend to react against the

---

3. This is not to say that *ressourcement* theologians commonly fall prey to such a naïve idealization. Certainly, thoughtful theologians such as Henri de Lubac and Yves Congar always insisted that retrieval of the Tradition in no way meant simply a return to the premodern period.

certainties of the past that fuelled mutual misunderstanding, fed intellectual pride, and kept denominations apart. We have become impatient with the intellectual boundaries and edifices previous generations erected, and the postmodern climate of our culture has made us skeptical of our epistemic ability to arrive at truth.[4] As a result, we sometimes turn to premodern theological approaches because we mistakenly believe they are more congenial to our postmodern skepticism than the propositionalism of our immediate evangelical forebears. It is true that the Church Fathers would have objected to the rationalist propositionalism of modernity. But we should not confuse their high regard for mystery with a lapse into skepticism. The mystery that the Fathers explored is something fundamentally different from the skepticism that today eats away at the foundations of Western culture.[5]

With those caveats in mind, let me turn to the topic of Christian doctrine in the early Church. In what follows, I will explore five aspects: (1) the purpose of doctrine; (2) the basis of doctrine; (3) the context of doctrine; (4) the development of doctrine; and (5) the limits of doctrine—all of this with reference to the early Church.

The Purpose of Doctrine

With regard to the first aspect, the purpose of doctrine, perhaps I can best illustrate the point I am trying to make by means of the Beatitudes in Matthew 5. Here Jesus pronounces as "blessed" or "happy" eight categories of people. These eight categories ultimately devolve into one. The poor in spirit, those who mourn, the meek, those who hunger and thirst for righteousness, the merciful, the pure in heart, the peacemakers, and those who are persecuted are all one and the same group. As our Lord addresses the crowds, and in particular his disciples (Matt 5:1), he addresses us all, and he holds out the prospect of happiness to everyone.[6]

---

4. It seems to me that this skepticism is evident both among intellectually highly refined philosophers such as Jacques Derrida and Michel Foucault and within a general cultural climate in which people give up searching for truth because they assume it cannot be found.

5. For more detailed exploration of the difference between skepticism and regard for mystery, see Boersma, *Heavenly Participation*.

6. The Great Tradition is remarkably unified with regard to the idea that happiness constitutes our ultimate end. See, for instance, St. Gregory of Nyssa, *The Beatitudes*; St. Augustine, *Confessions*, X.xx (2) (Chadwick, 196); St. Augustine, *Concerning the City of God against the Pagans*, VI.12 (Bettenson, 252–53); St. Thomas Aquinas, *Summa Theologica*, I/II, q.3, a.1 (595–96); John Calvin, *Institutes of the Christian Religion*, III. xxv.11 (1007).

The textual details that stood out for the Church Fathers as they read the Scriptures were at times rather different from the things we tend to notice. Take the word "mountain" (*oros*) in verse 1: "Now when he saw the crowds, he went up on a mountainside [*oros*] and sat down." The mindset of the Fathers was such that for them this word *oros* leapt off the page, as it were. The cause of this is what they regarded as the purpose of theology. Let's listen in on the fourth-century Cappadocian spiritual master, St. Gregory of Nyssa (c. 335–c. 394). In the first of his sermons on the Beatitudes, he immediately honed in on Matthew's "mountain"—a "spiritual mountain of sublime contemplation."[7] "This mountain," said Gregory,

> leaves behind all shadows cast by the rising hills of wickedness; on the contrary, it is lit up on all sides by the rays of the true light, and from its summit all things that remain invisible to those imprisoned in the cave may be seen in the pure air of truth. Now the Word of God Himself, who calls blessed those who have ascended with Him, specifies the nature and number of the things that are contemplated from this height.[8]

For Gregory, the Beatitudes served to unshackle us from our imprisonment in the Platonic cave (the world of the passions), and they placed us in the presence of Jesus ("the Word of God Himself" as Gregory would rather put it), so that we might enter upon the brightly lit-up heights of the mountain and be prepared for contemplation. For Gregory, the mountain was the place of theological contemplation.

St. Augustine, likewise, was drawn to Matthew's reference to a mountain. It triggered Ps 36:6 in his mind: "Thy righteousness is like the mountains of God." Augustine interpreted this to mean that "the one Master alone fit to teach matters of so great importance teaches on a mountain."[9] "For Augustine," comments Robert Louis Wilken, "the reason Jesus went up on a mountain is clear: he wanted to teach them about higher things. Seated on a mountain they were lifted above the quotidian affairs of their towns and villages, the cares and trials of life with family and friends and neighbors."[10] Wilken is quite right, it seems to me. The "mountain," explained Augustine, is a reference to "the greater precepts of righteousness,"[11] and he compared these "greater precepts" to "lesser ones which were given to the Jews."[12]

---

7. Gregory of Nyssa, *Beatitudes*, 85.
8. Ibid.
9. Augustine, *Our Lord's Sermon on the Mount*, I.i.2 (4).
10. Wilken, "Augustine," 43.
11. Augustine, *Our Lord's Sermon on the Mount*, I.i.2 (4).
12. Ibid.

Thus, he contrasted Law and gospel, seeing in the "mountain" a reference to the latter. Next, he identified this contrast with the juxtaposition between the earthly and heavenly kingdoms: "Nor is it surprising that the greater precepts are given for the kingdom of heaven, and the lesser for an earthly kingdom . . ."[13] For St. Augustine, when the Son of God gave instruction on the mountain, we must be dealing with gospel teaching.[14]

Neither Gregory nor Augustine referred explicitly to the purpose of theology. Their preoccupation with the locale of Jesus' teaching is nonetheless remarkable. It shows that when they did theology, they kept in the forefront of their minds the spiritual purpose of "sublime contemplation," as Gregory would put it, or the virtuous aim of the highest possible righteousness, as Augustine would have it. The Fathers' purpose for theology, we could say, is that we join Jesus on the mountain. To put it in the Fathers' own language: the purpose is to "lead up"—*anagōgē*, in Greek. Theology, for the Fathers, had to do with leading people upward in order to join the life of God: the purpose was anagogical. The Church Fathers were never concerned with theological systems for their own sake. To be sure, theological precision and accuracy mattered to them; careful theological thinking was of definite importance. But they always kept an eye on the purpose of approaching the height of the mountain and entering into the life of God.[15]

The battle over the divinity of the Son, which led to the First Ecumenical Council, the Council of Nicaea in 325, and then to the Second Ecumenical Council, that of Constantinople in 381, did not concern abstract, lifeless propositions. What was at stake for theologians such as Athanasius, Basil of Caesarea, and Gregory of Nyssa was our ability to ascend the mountain of God. One of the problems with the common theological textbook approach to the Fathers is that most introductory texts present just a brief run-down of the mere facts of history. Thus, we are given a list of the seven ecumenical councils, from 325 to 787, along with the decisions they made and the theological truths they enshrined. There's a certain value in this, but in the process it is easy to overlook that at stake was the very purpose of theology. The purpose was anagogical; it was to go up the mountain and there to enter into the blessedness of the eternal Word of God.

Let me illustrate the point with St. Basil's well-known booklet, *On the Holy Spirit*. Here, Basil did battle not so much with the Arians who denied

---

13. Ibid.

14. St. Pope Leo the Great (c. 400–61) displays a similar preoccupation with Matthew's reference to the "mountain." See St. Leo the Great, "Sermon XCV: A Homily on the Beatitudes," 202–3.

15. This approach receives its perhaps most classic expression in St. Gregory of Nyssa, *The Life of Moses*.

the full divinity of the Son, but with the so-called Pneumatomachians or Spirit-fighters, who rejected the notion that the Spirit was one of the three Persons of the one God and who saw the Spirit as a lesser force, instead. St. Basil would have none of it: if the Spirit were a lesser force, this would impede his ability to lead us up onto very heights of the mountain. Commented Basil,

> Through the Holy Spirit comes the restoration to paradise, the ascent to the kingdom of heaven, the return to adopted sonship, the freedom to call God our Father and to become a companion of the grace of Christ, to be called a child of light, to participate in eternal glory, and generally, to have all fullness of blessings in this age and the age to come.[16]

We cannot think "highly" enough of what the Fathers regarded as the purpose of Christian doctrine. For Basil, this purpose was a state of "fullness of blessings." One can appreciate that for the Fathers, to reduce doctrine to intellectual juggling of concepts would be to demean terribly the lofty goal of the anagogical ascent of the theologian. The theologian—whether a simple believer or a highly trained academic—was to participate in the very life of God. From the second-century theologian Irenaeus onward, the purpose of theology was participation in the life of God or, to put it differently, the purpose was *theosis*, deification.[17]

The Basis of Doctrine

Of course, one can only reach the purpose of doctrine if a proper basis is in place, as well. Next, therefore, I want to move to a discussion of the basis of doctrine. Evangelicals strongly maintain that Scripture is the basis of doctrine. Properly understood, this approach is right on target and also very much in-line with the Church Fathers. They teach us unambiguously that exegesis and doctrine belong together. When the Fathers were debating the divinity of the Son—articulated at the first two ecumenical councils, Nicaea (325) and Constantinople (381)—it was the exegesis of Scripture that was at stake, perhaps most notably the reference to the creating, founding, and begetting of Wisdom in Proverbs 8.[18] When the next three ecumenical

---

16. St. Basil the Great, *On the Holy Spirit*, 15.36 (68).

17. For discussions of the theology of deification, see Russell, *Doctrine of Deification*; Keating, *Deification and Grace*.

18. For the use of Proverbs 8 in the Arian controversy, see Clayton, "Orthodox Recovery of a Heretical Proof-Text"; Behr, *Nicene Faith*, 123–61; Young, *Biblical Exegesis*,

councils—Ephesus (431), Chalcedon (451), and the Second Council of Constantinople (553)—debated the way in which the human and divine natures of Christ were related to each other—the question was how to interpret the meaning of the Philippian hymn about the humiliation and exaltation of the Son of God (Phil 2:6–11) and the Johannine statement, "The Word became flesh" (John 1:14).[19] When the question came up how to do justice to the oneness of the Person of Christ if he not only had a divine but also a human will—the controversy over monothelitism, which was settled by the sixth ecumenical council, the third Council of Constantinople (660)—the crucial Bible passages were Luke 22:42 ("Father, if you are willing, take this cup from me; yet not my will, but yours be done") and John 6:38 ("For I have come down from heaven not to do my will but to do the will of him who sent me").[20] Finally, when the seventh and last of the ecumenical councils, the Second Council of Nicaea (787), insisted on the appropriateness of the use of icons in the church's liturgy, the debate centerd on the Decalogue's prohibition of graven images (Exod 20:4) and on New Testament references to Christ as the image of God in 2 Corinthians 4:4 and Colossians 1:15.[21] Throughout the period of the ecumenical councils, doctrine was regarded as derived from biblical exegesis.

Our contemporary division between biblical and dogmatic theology would, therefore, have been anathema to the Fathers. For them, there was no dogma without Scripture. Of course, the opposite was true, as well: Scripture had to be read through a dogmatic or theological lens. From a patristic perspective, we are quite right, then, to be fearful of doing theology in the abstract and apart from biblical interpretation. But we should be equally nervous about biblical exegesis that equates the meaning of a biblical passage with its historical origins. After all, for the Fathers, theology was the practice of anagogy. And if, for them, theology and doctrine relied heavily on biblical interpretation, this meant that biblical interpretation, too, was a matter of anagogy, of ascent onto the mountain in order to come into the presence of the very Word of God.[22] The reason, therefore, that the Fathers

---

29–45; Helleman, "Gregory's Sophia," 345–50. For further reflection on the relationship between biblical "wisdom" language and Christology, see Ford and Stanton, *Reading Texts, Seeking Wisdom*.

19. Pelikan, *Christian Tradition*, 1:247, 256–58.

20. Ibid., 2:68.

21. Ibid., 2:96, 107.

22. Charles Kannengiesser points out that "anagogy" or "uplifting" "from the literal to the spiritual sense in the interpreter's mind was the most essential procedure of patristic exegesis" (*Handbook of Patristic Exegesis*, 256). The more restricted eschatological understanding of the anagogical sense entered into the Latin world through John

were never satisfied with a purely historical or literal reading of the text was that they always kept in mind the anagogical purpose of the Scriptures. The mountain was the place where one entered into the great mystery of the ultimate meaning of the Scriptures. The relentless insistence of the Fathers on spiritual or anagogical interpretation was based on their recognition that Scripture was meant not primarily to teach us something about the past, but to draw us into the mystery of Christ, in whose blessedness we could participate if only we would ascend the mountain. "No Christian," insisted St. Augustine in his book on *The Literal Meaning of Genesis*, "will have the nerve to say they [the biblical accounts] should not be taken in a figurative sense, if he pays attention to what the apostle says: *All these things, however, happened among them in figures* (1 Cor 10:11), and to his commending what is written in Genesis, *And they shall be two in one flesh* (Gen 2:24), as *a great sacrament in Christ and in the Church* (Eph 5:32)."[23] Figural or anagogical interpretation was, for the Fathers, the way to do justice to the spiritual reality that one encountered by reading Scripture on the mountain, in the presence of Christ.

When insisting that doctrine must be scripturally based, the Fathers did not mean that Scripture *in isolation* could function as the basis of doctrine. We already saw that they maintained that Scripture be read theologically or spiritually. This meant that one approached Scripture as a Christian believer whose mind was shaped by the newness of the coming of Christ. It was impossible to leave behind one's Christian convictions as one approached the text of Scripture. Michael Fiedrowicz makes this clear when in his introduction to St. Augustine's *Expositions of the Psalms*, he mentions a fivefold christological interpretation of the Psalms among the Fathers. He explains that the Psalms were interpreted as (1) a word to Christ (*vox ad Christum*); (2) a word about Christ (*vox de Christo*); (3) a word of Christ, spoken by him (*vox Christi*); (4) a word about the church (*vox de ecclesia*); and (5) a word of the church, spoken by the church (*vox ecclesiae*).[24]

I want to focus briefly on the first three, the more strictly christological, of these five approaches. First, when the psalmist addressed God, the Fathers had little hesitation in seeing in these words also a prayer addressed to Christ (*vox ad Christum*). No doubt, the rationale was theological. Since Christ had not only a human but also a divine nature, it was entirely legitimate to address him as God in the very words of the Psalms. Thus, when the psalmist appealed to God for help, for forgiveness, for justice, and the

---

Cassian (c. 360–c. 435) and later became common in the Middle Ages (ibid., 257).

23. Augustine, *Literal Meaning of Genesis*, I.i.1 (168).
24. Fiedrowicz, "General Introduction," 44–45.

like, each of these petitions could legitimately be interpreted as petitions to Christ.[25]

Second, for Augustine, the Psalms spoke not just *to* Christ, but also *about* Christ (*vox de Christo*). The opening words of St. Augustine's commentary on the Psalms are Christ-filled words. On "Blessed is the man" (Ps 1:1), the African Bishop commented: "This statement should be understood as referring to our Lord Jesus Christ, that is, the Lord-Man."[26] Augustine then continued by speaking about Christ's faithfulness in contrast to Adam's lack thereof: "*Blessed is the person who has not gone astray in the council of the ungodly*, as did the earthly man who conspired with his wife, already beguiled by the serpent, to disregard God's commandments."[27] Without any hesitation, Augustine began his commentary with a christological reading of the psalm. The psalmist's voice here was a *vox de Christo*, a voice about Christ.

Third, Augustine was convinced that the Psalms also contained words of Christ, spoken by him (*vox Christi*). One of the key elements of patristic exegesis of the Psalms was the determination of who it was that was speaking in the psalm. Fiedrowicz refers to this as "prosopological exegesis," from the Greek word *prosōpon*, meaning "person."[28] Prosopological exegesis asked the question: which *person* is speaking in this psalm? Once one had figured this out, much of the rest of the psalm also fell into place. Understandably, if the person speaking was Christ himself, this would be particularly significant. The passage would then be not a word to Christ (*vox ad Christum*) or a word about Christ (*vox de Christo*) but a word of Christ, spoken by him (*vox Christi*). For example, when in Psalm 22, the psalmist said, "Dogs have surrounded me; a band of evil men has encircled me, they have pierced my hands and my feet" (22:16), the psalm appeared not just to make a prophecy *about* Christ, but to introduce Christ as himself taking on his lips the words of the psalm. Likewise, Christ seemed to be speaking about himself and about his own suffering and resurrection also in Psalm 71:20: "Though you have made me see troubles, many and bitter, you will restore my life again; from the depths of the earth you will again bring me up." All of this is to say that when theologians such as Augustine opened the Scriptures, they already had in mind the christological confession of the church.[29] When

---

25. Ibid., 45.
26. Augustine, "Exposition of Psalm 1," 67.
27. Ibid.
28. Ibid., 50.
29. Cf. Byassee, *Praise Seeking Understanding*, 54–96.

reading the Psalms, they looked for the *vox ad Christum*, the *vox de Christo*, and the *vox Christi*.

We could say that when the Fathers read the Scriptures, they entered it by way of concentric circles. They began with the very center, Christ himself. Christ himself was the measuring stick, the canon, for all interpretation of Scripture. He, the Person of Christ, was the rule of faith or the canon of truth, on which the faith was based and by which all biblical reflection should be measured. As the church grew in her convictions regarding the Person of Christ and the doctrine of the Trinity, Trinitarian doctrine became, as it were, the second concentric circle identifying the heart of the gospel and thereby also the distinct character of the church. Already St. Irenaeus, in the second century, centered his discussion of what he called the "rule of faith" on the triune God. "This then," writes Irenaeus,

> is the order of the rule of our faith, and the foundation of the building, and the stability of our conversation: God, the Father, not made, not material, invisible; one God, the creator of all things: this is the first point of our faith. The second point is: The Word of God, Son of God, Christ Jesus our Lord. . . . And the third point is: The Holy Spirit, through whom the prophets prophesied, and the fathers learned the things of God . . .[30]

The Trinitarian structure of Irenaeus's rule of faith is unmistakable. Already in the late second century, the second concentric circle was firmly in place. Long before the canon of the Bible was recognized as such in the fourth century, the canon of Christ and of the Trinity was already in place, even if many of the details still had to be worked out. To be sure, to point to the lack of a biblical canon in the second century is not to deny that Irenaeus used many of the same books that we today recognize as canonical. His battle with the Gnostics was very much an exegetical battle. But Irenaeus was keenly aware that the christological and Trinitarian starting-points formed the primary circles of authority and, therefore, were the lens through which one had to interpret the Scriptures themselves.[31] The numerous creedal-like Trinitarian statements that individual Church Fathers treated as the canon or rule of faith lay at the basis of all later doctrinal development. They functioned as canonical even in the sense that they were the rule by which one could tell which Scriptures were to be received as canonical and which ones were not. In that sense, the canon of the Bible came to function as a wider circle around the inner circles of Christology and Trinitarian doctrine. For the Fathers, Scripture was indeed the basis of Christian doctrine. But it never

---

30. Irenaeus, *Proof of the Apostolic Preaching*, 6.
31. Cf. Allert, *High View of Scripture?*, 121–26.

functioned as basis *in isolation* from the prior christological and Trinitarian rule of faith.

The Context of Doctrine

It should be clear by now that the Fathers regarded the living Tradition of the church—the growing conviction regarding Christ and the Trinity—as the primary context in which to make sense of doctrine. The Church's primary confession embodying that doctrine was the Creed defined by the Councils of Nicaea and Constantinople in the years 325 and 381. In addition to the Creed itself, we could say that the church's primary constitutional decisions legitimately interpreting this Creed were the seven ecumenical councils of the first eight centuries. This broad ecclesial context constitutes what we may call the consent of the Fathers (*consensus patrum*).

The Fathers' high regard for the ecclesial context of Christian doctrine may initially strike evangelicals, in particular, as odd. The reason, I suspect, is that when as evangelicals we affirm that Scripture is the basis of doctrine, we have a tendency to think of Scripture *in isolation*. When regarded in isolation, the Bible becomes a book that we interpret for ourselves, as individuals. Almost inevitably, such interpretation tends to be historical rather than anagogical. That is to say, when we take the Bible as an isolated document, apart from the church's confession, we end up doing the one thing that we think we can do as individuals: figure out what the human words of the text initially meant. For the Fathers, by contrast, communal or ecclesial reading of Scripture was essential. They even went a step further by insisting that just as one could discern *Christ* in the Scriptures, so one could also recognize there the presence of the *church*. To illustrate this point, I briefly want to return to Michael Fiedrowicz's reference to a fivefold christological interpretation of the Psalms among the Fathers. Fiedrowicz speaks not only about a *vox ad Christum*, a *vox de Christo*, and a *vox Christi*, but also about a *vox de ecclesia* (a word about the church) and about a *vox ecclesiae* (a word of the church, spoken by the church). The Church Fathers could move from a christological reading to an ecclesial reading because they were convinced that Christ and his church were one. An ecclesial reading was ultimately a christological one.

St. Augustine, in particular, never tired of insisting that Christ and his Church should be viewed together as the "whole Christ" (*totus Christus*). Christ's reprimand of Saul—"Saul, Saul, why are you persecuting me?" (Acts 9:4)—meant to Augustine that Christ identified with his Church (see Matt

25:40; 1 Cor 10:16–17; 12:2; Col 1:24).[32] The head and the body, the groom and the bride, together made up the one, complete Christ. Jason Byassee, author of an inspiring book on Augustine's interpretation of the Psalms titled *Praise Seeking Understanding*, makes the comment that Augustine's commentary presents "a 'christo-ecclesiological' form of exegesis, premised on the *totus Christus*, the 'whole Christ,' who speaks throughout the Psalter."[33] Whatever the Psalms said about Christ one could apply to the church and even to individual believers. Conversely, whatever the Psalms said about individual believers, one could also refer to Christ himself.

On such an understanding, it should not surprise us that for the Fathers the primary context of interpretation was that of the church. The Bible was a book that one understood best not within the context of the academy but within the context of the church. The anagogical ascent onto the mountain and into the presence of Christ—the very purpose of theology—was a pilgrimage on which one embarked in the company of the saints. This company, then, ensured the proper interpretation of the Scriptures. We could even say that the unity of the ecclesial company was the very purpose *why* one read the Bible in the first place. Love, insisted St. Augustine, was the purpose of all interpretation of Scripture: "So anyone who thinks that he has understood the divine scriptures or any part of them, but cannot by his understanding build up this double love of God and neighbour, has not yet succeeded in understanding them."[34] For Augustine, once one had achieved the fullness of the virtues in love—or, put differently, once one had reached the top of the mountain—Scripture had fulfilled its purpose. At that point, one no longer needed it. Augustine maintained that "a person strengthened by faith, hope, and love, and who steadfastly holds on to them, has no need of the scriptures except to instruct others."[35] In heaven, Scripture, like all sacraments, will have fulfilled its purpose, and we will no longer need it. True, Scripture is the basis of all doctrine. But the love and fellowship of the church guarantee its proper interpretation.

Some evangelicals may get a little nervous about this strong emphasis on a christological and ecclesial basis of doctrine. And, indeed, while I would not want to back down from what I have just argued, so far I have presented only one side of the coin. The Church may be the main context that shaped Christian doctrine, but it wasn't the only one. Doctrine did not take shape in splendid isolation from the church's surroundings. These surroundings

---

32. Cf. Fiedrowicz, "General Introduction," 53–54.
33. Byassee, *Praise Seeking Understanding*, 63.
34. Augustine, *On Christian Teaching*, I.86 (27).
35. Ibid., I.93 (28).

were, we could say, a second contextual factor that entered into the articulation of Christian doctrine. The theology of the church didn't flourish without interaction with philosophy.[36] Diogenes Allen's helpful book *Philosophy for Understanding Theology* makes the point that the Church Fathers were Hellenic in the sense that they persistently asked about revelation: "How is that so?" Allen then makes a comment that I believe is quite significant for evangelicals:

> There would have been no such discipline as Christian theology without the Bible and without a believing community. But likewise we would not have the discipline of theology without the Hellenic attitude in Christians that leads them to press questions about the Bible and the relations of the Bible to other knowledge. Thus when people call for purging Greek philosophy from Christian theology, unless they are referring to specific ideas or concepts, they are really calling for the end of the discipline of theology itself, though they may not realize it.[37]

Allen recognizes that, although theology's purpose is anagogical, its basis christological, and its primary context ecclesial, theology cannot function without the Hellenic philosophical context—primarily that of Neoplatonism—in which it developed.[38] This context, far from endangering the biblical basis of theology, enabled believers to articulate their faith and thus allowed faith to seek understanding. As evangelicals are more and more turning to the Church Fathers, they do well to recognize that an *authentic* engagement with the Fathers implies a theological reading of Scripture that recognizes the affinities between the Christian faith and at least significant elements of Hellenic philosophy. Without the thought patterns, philosophical categories, and even terminology of ancient Greek thought, creedal Christianity—the kind that wants to live by the church's rule of faith—becomes an oxymoron.

The Development of Doctrine

The twofold context of doctrine—the church and Hellenic culture—implies that doctrine develops over time. My earlier account of the widening concentric circles, too, implies that doctrine develops, beginning with Christ, moving on to the doctrine of the Trinity and from there to the Creeds and

---

36. On this issue, see especially Pelikan, *Christianity and Classical Culture*.
37. Allen and Springsted, *Philosophy for Understanding Theology*, xviii.
38. This point is argued at length in Boersma, *Heavenly Participation*.

the conciliar decisions of the church. The topic of development of doctrine is one that I believe evangelicals need to do some careful thinking about. The notion of development becomes unavoidable, it seems, once we affirm that Scripture, as the basis of doctrine, doesn't function in isolation. Development results from the fact that Christ himself is the primary rule of faith and that Scripture witnesses to the living and ascended Lord. The same Spirit of Christ who inspired the Scriptures lives in the church's ongoing Tradition. In his book *Unity in the Church*, the great nineteenth-century Catholic theologian Johann Adam Möhler (1796–1838) emphasizes the ongoing presence of the Spirit in the life of the church, guaranteeing development of doctrine.[39] "Christianity," writes Möhler, "does not consist in expressions, formulae, or figures of speech; it is an inner life, a holy power, and all doctrinal concepts and dogmas have value only insofar as they express the inner life that is present with them."[40] Möhler's argument about development hinges on the recognition that, at least for the first three centuries, the period he describes in his book, Christianity was not a religion of the book. Christianity was the Spirit-led Church of the apostles that, guided by the Spirit, developed the deposit of faith that was implicitly present in God's self-revelation in Christ. Everything was already there, implicitly, in the great treasure, Jesus Christ. The Fathers saw it as their calling to "cash in" this treasure of Christ.[41] For the Fathers, therefore, Christianity was not a religion of the book. This does not mean that they didn't regard the Scriptures as authoritative or, as I have already indicated, as the basis for Christian doctrine. They clearly did. But they regarded them so highly precisely inasmuch as the Spirit used the Scriptures to clarify for the church the riches of the implications of her faith in Christ.

Let me give an example: the doctrine of the Theotokos. The third and fourth ecumenical councils, those of Ephesus (431) and Chalcedon (451), affirmed as the church's doctrine that the Virgin Mary was Theotokos—God-bearer, that is. In the fifth century, the Antiochene Bishop of Constantinople, Nestorius, refused to give Mary this honorific title. Christokos (Christ-bearer) was an appellation with which he was comfortable, but he rejected the title Theotokos. The reason is that Nestorius wanted to keep Christ's two natures separate to such a degree that there were not only two natures, but actually two persons. Nestorius's theology became known as a "theology of the indwelling Logos"; in his view the eternal Word, the

---

39. Cf. Boersma, *Nouvelle Théologie and Sacramental Ontology*, 41–52.

40. Möhler, *Unity in the Church*, §13 (111).

41. The terminology of *monnayer Jésus* ("cashing in Jesus") is that of Pierre Rousselot and Henri de Lubac. Cf. Boersma, *Nouvelle Théologie*, 219–23.

Logos, the divine Person, simply took up residence in the human person, Jesus of Nazareth. So, when the Bible spoke of Mary giving birth to Jesus or of Christ suffering for us, we should understand that to mean *not* that Mary had given birth to the eternal Logos, but that the Virgin had given birth to the human person, Jesus. The Alexandrian theologians, headed by Cyril, were insistent, however, on honouring Mary with the designation Theotokos. John 1:14 stated, "And the Word *became* flesh," not just "And the Word took up residence in the flesh."[42] Therefore, the union was a close one; so close, in fact, that Mary should be called Theotokos or God-bearer. The close union between the two natures meant that if Mary bore Jesus in the flesh, she could be said to have given birth to God. As I indicated already, the church, in the decisions of her ecumenical councils, largely took the side of the Alexandrians on this issue. This meant that the two councils of 431 and 451 were highly significant for the development of both Christology and Mariology. The church's official doctrine now read the biblical text—in particular passages such as John 1:14 and Phil 2:6–11—in such a way that it maintained a close connection between the divine and the human natures. The corollary was that Mary could and should be honoured with the title of Theotokos. This is but an example of developments that inevitably take place when the Spirit guides the church to think through the implications of the treasure of God's self-revelation in Christ.

Development is not the same thing as revision. It may not be superfluous to make that point. I cautioned at the beginning of this essay against undue idealization of the Church Fathers. But it may be equally necessary to be on guard against the other extreme. I suspect that sometimes evangelicals may be so comfortable with development—or, actually more likely, the modern notion of progress, which is something altogether different—that it doesn't bother us at all if and when our doctrine deviates significantly from that of the Fathers. When we move in quite different directions, we perhaps simply assume that we have better insight than they did. I would argue, however, that such a line of thinking is based on the erroneous supposition that Scripture functions *in isolation*. If it is true that Scripture comes to us by way of the church's rule of faith and by way of Spirit-guided development, then this development necessarily builds on what has gone before. Doctrine that once was false cannot become true at a later point in time, and, vice versa, doctrine that once was true cannot become false at a later point in time. Doctrinal development presupposes continuity. Whenever we face a doctrinal issue, it is a good rule of thumb for us as Western evangelicals to ask ourselves two questions: (1) what was the theological approach on this

---

42. Pelikan, *Christian Tradition*, 1:247.

issue in centuries past? And (2) what is the thinking of the non-Western world on this particular issue? These kinds of questions help, it seems to me, to prevent development from turning into revisionism.

The Limits of Doctrine

The final topic I wish to address seems to me to be of timeless significance. So far, I have highlighted the importance of theology and of Christian doctrine. And, clearly, the Fathers thought Christian doctrine hugely important for anagogical ascent into the life of the triune God. But doctrine had its limits, too. Few people were as keenly aware of the limits of doctrinal statements as the fourth-century Cappadocian, Gregory of Nyssa.[43] The limits of doctrine show up in Gregory's approach in at least three ways: (1) for Gregory knowledge was not just rational in character; (2) it was limited by its inability to grasp the essence of God; and (3) it progressed infinitely. First, then, St. Gregory pointed to the supra-rational character of mystical knowledge by insisting that when Moses ascended onto the mountain, he proceeded by way of three steps. His vision of God began with light, after which God spoke to him in a cloud, and finally Moses saw God in darkness.[44] The first way, the way of light, was the way of purgation, in which the soul struggled against the passions. The second way, the way of the cloud, allowed the believer to come to knowledge of God by means of the senses. The objects of the created order gave access to God himself. Abraham, for instance, "gained a yearning to gaze upon the archetypal Beauty" by observing the beauty of the world around him.[45] Gregory obviously valued the knowledge of God's beauty. In particular, the reflection of God in the purified soul gave a kind of knowledge—albeit obscure in character—of God himself. The soul mirrored the beauty of God:

> So it is that the soul that has been purified by the Word and has put off all sin, receives within itself the circular form of the Sun and shines now with this reflected light. Hence the Word says to her: You have become fair because you have come near to my light, and by this closeness to me you have attracted this participation in beauty.[46]

---

43. For the following paragraphs, I borrow from Boersma, *Heavenly Participation*, 160–63.
44. Gregory of Nyssa, *From Glory to Glory*, 23.
45. Ibid., 120.
46. Ibid., 171.

Gregory's term "participation" is a significant one. It indicates that the soul did not just have an external link with God but was privileged to enjoy real participation in the life of God.

Paradoxically, Gregory described the most intimate union with God (the third way) as an entry into darkness. The soul, explained Gregory,

> keeps on going deeper until by the operation of the spirit it penetrates the invisible and incomprehensible, and it is there that it sees God. The true vision and the true knowledge of what we seek consists precisely in not seeing, in an awareness that our goal transcends all knowledge and is everywhere cut off from us by the darkness of incomprehensibility. Thus that profound evangelist, John, who penetrated into this luminous darkness, tells us that *no man hath seen God at any time* (John 1.18), teaching us by this negation that no man—indeed, no created intellect—can attain a knowledge of God.[47]

Gregory, who had a predilection for paradoxical expressions, spoke of "luminous darkness" to describe the goal of the mystical life. Clearly, this goal was not just intellectual knowledge of God. The goal, explained Gregory, transcended all knowledge because the "darkness of incomprehensibility" meant that the goal lay beyond us. No one was able to attain knowledge of God, asserted the Cappadocian Father boldly.

Second, for Gregory human knowledge was limited because it was unable to grasp the essence of God. We already saw that, in a real sense, for Gregory human discourse was unable to grasp the truth of God. Hence, Gregory observed that the injunction of Ecclesiastes that there was "a time to be silent and a time to speak" (Eccl 3:7) prioritized silence over speech. This observation provided occasion to reflect on the transcendence of God, which far exceeded the human ability to express in words:

> In the present text I think that silence is mentioned first because human speech finds it impossible to express that reality which transcends all thought and every concept, which the soul that has been torn from evil constantly seeks, and to which it yearns to be united once it has been found. And he who obstinately tries to express it in words, unconsciously offends God. For He Who is believed to transcend the universe must surely transcend speech.[48]

---

47. Ibid., 118.
48. Ibid., 126.

For Gregory, the essence of God was beyond human comprehension. This was the ultimate reason for human silence. Observation of the created order and of the purified soul might give some degree of knowledge of God. But the truth of God himself remained beyond human ken. Gregory thus had a real sense of humility with regard to the human ability to know God. Gregory, the French patristic scholar, Jean Daniélou, explains, was ultimately a negative or apophatic theologian, for whom positive speech about God finally had to give way to negation.[49] For Gregory, "the man who thinks that God can be known does not really have life; for he has been falsely diverted from true Being to something devised by his own imagination."[50] While Gregory (an ardent defender of Nicene Trinitarian theology!) in no way discouraged the positive naming of God, he always reminded his readers that such naming must be rooted in the humble acknowledgment of the infinite otherness of the incomprehensible God.

Third, Daniélou highlights especially Gregory's doctrine of *epektasis*, which resulted from his insistence that human knowledge was participatory in character and that it was inadequate because of the incomprehensibility and infinity of God's essence. Gregory took the notion of *epektasis* from Phil 3:13, where St. Paul wrote that he was "straining" (*epekteinomenos*) toward what lay ahead. To Gregory, this meant that the soul's ascent into God would never cease. The infinity of God implied that despite our growth in knowledge, God remained beyond our understanding. Thus, according to St. Gregory, Phil 3:13 meant that

> in our constant participation in the blessed nature of the Good, the graces that we receive at every point are indeed great, but the path that lies beyond our immediate grasp is infinite. This will constantly happen to those who thus share in the divine Goodness, and they will always enjoy a greater and greater participation in grace throughout all eternity.[51]

The infinity of God implied, insisted Gregory, that no matter how much we might progress in virtue and so in the knowledge of God, God always remained greater. In fact, the journey of heavenly participation in no way lessened the distance that still separated the soul from her goal: "Thou art always to the same degree higher and loftier than the faculties of those who are rising."[52]

---

49. Ibid., 30.
50. Ibid., 146.
51. Ibid., 211–12.
52. Ibid., 212.

Daniélou, clearly attracted to the mystical approach that the doctrine of *epektasis* represented, explains that there are two aspects to the soul's progression, both of which are implied in the Greek expression:

> On the one hand, there is a certain contact with God, a real participation, a divinization (Greek *epi*: "at" or "towards"). The soul is, in a true sense, transformed into the divine; it truly participates in the Spirit, the *pneuma*. But God at the same time remains constantly beyond, and the soul must always go out of itself (Greek *ek*: "out of")—or, rather, it must continually go beyond the stage it has reached to make a further discovery.[53]

Gregory's approach to human truth claims about God implied real participation in the life of God, while at the same time it retained infinite divine transcendence.

Gregory's approach is a wonderful example of the sense of mystery that characterized the theology of the Fathers. Gregory had a great stake in the Trinitarian controversies of the fourth century. It should be abundantly clear that Gregory's sense of mystery and of humility in the face of God is something altogether different from postmodern skepticism. Contemporary evangelicals are right to question the rationalist overconfidence that characterized a great deal of modern theology. The best way to counter it, however, is not by way of a lapse into skepticism but by means of a return to theology as anagogy.

Conclusion

In this essay, I have tried to make a small contribution to a *ressourcement* or retrieval of the Church Fathers. Perhaps the most significant contribution that patristic theology can make to contemporary evangelical theology is to re-instil an awareness of the importance of anagogy. The conviction that theology had to do with "going up the mountain," or with entering into the life of God, undergirded much patristic thinking. While the Church Fathers undoubtedly had their limitations, they were right to think that theology had to do with spirituality, and that this spirituality ought to center on otherworldly realities. With such an anagogical mindset as a starting-point, there are a number of implications that follow with regard to Christian doctrine. The purpose of doctrine, on an anagogical understanding, is not to construct rational systems of thought, however biblically based they may be; the purpose is deification or entry into the life of God.

---

53. Daniélou, "Introduction," 59.

Although Scripture forms indeed the basis for theology, the Fathers were rightly convinced that Scripture was meant to be read through a dogmatic or theological lens. The christological and Trinitarian convictions of the church are, as it were, the "rule of faith," by which truthful interpretation is distinguished from error. This implies that as evangelicals we need to relearn that, although Scripture is the basis of doctrine, the Bible does not function in isolation from the church's basic beliefs and practices. The Church, then, is the primary context for all Christian doctrine. Of course, the Fathers recognized that the church functioned in a cultural and philosophical context—especially that of Neoplatonism—that had to be taken seriously. As a result, the Christian doctrine of which we today are the heirs stems from the fruitful dialogue between the early Church and its Hellenic context. It seems to me a *sine qua non* for the future of creedal Christianity that biblical interpretation continue to take seriously this original Christian encounter between faith and reason.

If Scripture does not function in isolation but serves its anagogical purpose in an ecclesial and philosophical context, this means that Christian doctrine develops over time. Christ, the Fathers rightly saw, is our primary rule of faith, and development is—as Henri de Lubac phrased it—the "cashing in" of this christological treasure. Development, we could also say, constitutes an anagogical journey that both begins and ends with Christ. Since this doctrinal development takes place within a christological and ecclesial context, it will inevitably be characterized by a great deal of continuity. When individuals read the Scriptures, they are meant to read them in continuity with the way in which the church's tradition has developed over time.

One of the most beautiful aspects of the anagogical approach of the Fathers is the keen sense of mystery that it preserved. Surely, there is a point of contact here with the yearning for mystery among many contemporary evangelicals. St. Gregory of Nyssa's insistence that knowledge is not just rational, that theology can never grasp the essence of God, and that our knowledge of God progresses infinitely is a wholesome reminder to us that our ability to articulate doctrine has its limits. To be sure, we ought not to confuse this patristic respect for mystery with postmodern skepticism; the horizontal focus of such skepticism leaves little or no room for anagogy. Nonetheless, doctrine does have its limits, ultimately because theologizing remains a human, and hence finite, enterprise. It is precisely as we keep in mind the limits of doctrine that we can learn to appreciate once again its anagogical purpose; for it is only by recognizing that we have not yet arrived at full knowledge that we are challenged to probe deeper and ascend higher. Then we can go up the mountain again, there to learn from the mouth of the eternal Word what it means to participate in the ineffable mystery of the life of God.

Bibliography

Allen, Diogenes, and Eric O. Springsted. *Philosophy for Understanding Theology*. 2nd ed. Louisville: Westminster John Knox, 2007.

Allert, Craig D. *A High View of Scripture? The Authority of the Bible and the Formation of the New Testament Canon*. Grand Rapids: Baker Academic, 2007.

Augustine, Saint. *Concerning the City of God against the Pagans*. Translated by Henry Bettenson. London: Penguin, 1984.

———. *Confessions*. Translated and edited by Henry Chadwick. Oxford: Oxford University Press, 1998.

———. "Exposition of Psalm 1." In *Expositions of the Psalms 1–32*, translated by Maria Boulding. The Works of Saint Augustine: A Translation for the 21st Century III/15, edited by John Rotelle. Hyde Park, NY: New City, 2000.

———. *The Literal Meaning of Genesis*. In *On Genesis: A Refutation of the Manichees; Unfinished Literal Commentary on Genesis; The Literal Meaning of Genesis*, translated by Edmund Hill, edited by John E. Rotelle. The Works of Saint Augustine: A Translation for the 21st Century I/13. Hyde Park, NY: New City, 2002.

———. *On Christian Teaching*. Translated by R. P. H. Green. Oxford: Oxford University Press, 1997.

———. *Our Lord's Sermon on the Mount*. Translated by William Findlay, revised by D. S. Schaff. In vol. 6 of *The Nicene and Post-Nicene Fathers*, Series 1. Edited by Philip Schaff. 1886–1889. 14 vols. Reprint, Peabody, MA: Hendrickson, 1994.

Basil the Great, Saint. *On the Holy Spirit*. Translated by Stephen M. Hildebrand. Popular Patristics Series 42. Crestwood, NY: St Vladimir's Seminary Press, 2011.

Behr, John. *The Nicene Faith*. Formation of Christian Theology 2. Crestwood, NY: St. Vladimir's Seminary Press, 2001.

Boersma, Hans. *Heavenly Participation: The Weaving of a Sacramental Tapestry*. Grand Rapids: Eerdmans, 2011.

———. *Nouvelle Théologie and Sacramental Ontology: A Return to Mystery*. Oxford: Oxford University Press, 2009.

Byasse, Jason. *Praise Seeking Understanding: Reading the Psalms with Augustine*. Grand Rapids: Eerdmans, 2007.

Calvin, John. *Institutes of the Christian Religion*. Edited by John T. McNeill. Translated by Ford Lewis Battles. Library of Christian Classics 21. Philadelphia: Westminster, 1960.

Clayton, Allan Lee. "The Orthodox Recovery of a Heretical Proof-Text: Athanasius of Alexandria's Interpretation of Proverbs 8:22–30 in Conflict with the Arians." PhD diss., Southern Methodist University, 1988.

Daniélou, Jean. "Introduction." In *From Glory to Glory: Texts from Gregory of Nyssa's Mystical Writings*, translated and edited by Herbert Musurillo. Crestwood, NY: St. Vladimir's Seminary Press, 2001.

Fiedrowicz, Michael. "General Introduction." In Augustine, *Expositions of the Psalms 1–32*, translated by Maria Boulding. The Works of Saint Augustine: A Translation for the 21st Century III/15, edited by John Rotelle. Hyde Park, NY: New City, 2000.

Ford, David F., and Graham Stanton, eds. *Reading Texts, Seeking Wisdom: Scripture and Theology*. Grand Rapids: Eerdmans, 2003.

Gregory of Nyssa. *The Beatitudes*. In *The Lord's Prayer; The Beatitudes*, translated and edited by Hilda C. Graef. Ancient Christian Writers 18. New York: Paulist, 1954.

———. *From Glory to Glory: Texts from Gregory of Nyssa's Mystical Writings*. Edited and translated by Herbert Musurillo. Selected and introduced by Jean Daniélou. Crestwood, NY: St. Vladimir's Seminary Press, 2001.

———. *The Life of Moses*. Translated and edited by Abraham J. Malherbe and Everett Ferguson. New York: Paulist, 1978.

Helleman, Wendy Elgersma. "Gregory's Sophia: 'Christ, the Wisdom of God.'" *Studia Patristica* 41 (2006) 345–50.

Irenaeus. *Proof of the Apostolic Preaching*. Translated and edited by Joseph P. Smith. Ancient Christian Writers 16. New York: Paulist, 1952.

Kannengiesser, Charles. *Handbook of Patristic Exegesis: The Bible in Ancient Christianity*. Leiden: Brill, 2006.

Keating, Daniel A. *Deification and Grace*. Naples, FL: Sapientia, 2007.

Leo the Great, Saint. "Sermon XCV: A Homily on the Beatitudes." In *Nicene and Post-Nicene Fathers* 2.12. Translated and edited by Charles Lett Feltoe. 1895. Reprint, Peabody, MA: Hendrickson, 1994.

Möhler, Johann Adam. *Unity in the Church, or, The Principle of Catholicism Presented in the Spirit of the Church Fathers of the First Three Centuries*. Translated and edited by Peter C. Erb. Washington, DC: Catholic University of America Press, 1996.

Pelikan, Jaroslav. *The Christian Tradition: A History of the Development of Doctrine*. 2 vols. Chicago: University of Chicago Press, 1971–74.

———. *Christianity and Classical Culture: The Metamorphosis of Natural Theology in the Christian Encounter with Hellenism*. New Haven: Yale University Press, 1993.

Russell, Norman. *The Doctrine of Deification in the Greek Patristic Tradition*. Oxford: Oxford University Press, 2004.

Thomas, Aquinas, Saint. *Summa Theologica*. Translated by Fathers of the Dominican Province. Notre Dame, IN: Ave Maria, 1981.

Wilken, Robert Louis. "Augustine." In *The Sermon on the Mount through the Centuries*, edited by Jeffrey P. Greenman, Timothy Larsen, and Stephen R. Spencer, 43–57. Grand Rapids: Brazos, 2007.

Young, Frances M. *Biblical Exegesis and the Formation of Christian Culture*. Peabody, MA: Hendrickson, 2002.

2

Communion and Catholicity

Nyssa, Augustine, Aquinas

C. C. PECKNOLD

> Remember that you are catholic.
> —SAINT AUGUSTINE

THIS ESSAY EXAMINES HOW the Catholic tradition actually works on the question of the nature of the person as a subsistent reality, defined by intelligence and will, analogous to the Persons of the Most Holy Trinity. While this does not risk more abstract reflection on the category of tradition itself, this approach has the advantage of allowing us to see a tradition in action—living with a truth it has received and seeking to understand the faith. Thus, the majority of this essay will examine how the catholic tradition—through its greatest doctors, especially Augustine and Aquinas, but also Nyssa and others—develops an understanding of the person as an embodied rational and relational soul made for friendship with God. We will concretely demonstrate how the tradition develops distinctions that support a coherent understanding of the person as subsistent, rational, relational and embodied. The essay will conclude by turning to Joseph Ratzinger/Pope Benedict XVI as a contemporary articulation of how the catholic hermeneutic continually returns to the categories of substance and relation, precisely because it refuses to detach hermeneutics from metaphysics, and refuses to divorce metaphysics from theology. As Ratzinger notes, "the question of hermeneutics is, in the last analysis, the ontological one, the question of the oneness of truth in the multiplicity of its historical manifestations."[1] Any genuinely catholic hermeneutic of communion will thus attend to the nature of the person as the image of God, as a rational, embodied soul whose final good consists in the love the love of eternal truth, the unchangeable unity which is the Trinity.[2]

Let us first then examine the nature of the person in Augustine, Nyssa and Thomas Aquinas as a way of arriving at a catholic hermeneutic of communion that can help us to speak truly about the end to which the whole Christian tradition is ordered.

1. Persons in Communion: Augustine and Gregory of Nyssa

Tertullian is the first church father to develop the notion of the person in relation to the hermeneutic of communion, especially through his rejection of modalism and in favor of the tri-personal God of revelation who could not be reduced to "modes of relation" but must be understood as a communion of actual, subsistent Persons. Indeed, there is hardly a church father who did not find "the call to communion" everywhere in the scriptures, not only in the New Testament, but also in the Old. Not only are the Old Testament scriptures read figurally and typologically, in relation to Christ and his Church, but all history is read in the light of Christ who unites divinity and humanity in his very person. Church fathers often referred to this hermeneutic simply as the *regula fidei*—a rule for reading the scriptures, and all human history, that was to be passed on to children, carried by the hierarchy, liturgically celebrated and embodied by all Christians. Recently, Matthew Levering has spoken of this rule for reading as "participatory exegesis"—a hermeneutic for participation in the divine life.[3] Not accidently, this rule for reading later became associated with the Apostle's creed, and then the Nicene creed, the *symbolon*, precisely because that creed confessed the hope of the church that humanity may be raised up to participate in the divine nature—it ordered persons to deiform communion. The hermeneutic can

---

1. Ratzinger, *Principles of Catholic Theology*, 17.
2. Augustine, *De doctrina Christiana*, 2.20.
3. See Levering, *Participatory Biblical Exegesis*. On Scripture and Eucharist as interchangeable referents for the corpus mysticum in the early church, see de Lubac, *Corpus Mysticum*.

be observed in both the Latin and Greek traditions of the church as this first section will show.

Augustine

Augustine was well acquainted with the Nicene Creed as *regula fidei*. It had become for him the symbol of the faith, a rule for reading the scriptures in a way that truly led to communion with the triune God. That was particularly important for him because he had learned by painful experience that not just any reading of scripture would liberate the human being in truth. The nine years he spent as a Manichean reader of scripture (at the rank of "Hearer") taught him that multiple rules could be followed; different "lenses" or "angles of vision" for reading the scriptures produced conflicting accounts of reality, and conflicting accounts of the nature and ends of the person—accounts which were not easily squared with a hermeneutic ordered to participation in Christ's body. By the time he emerged from the Manichean sect, and beyond his restless Platonic wanderings, he was far from naïve. Upon reading a passage in Paul's Letter to the Romans concerning "putting on the body of Christ," Augustine recalls being flooded with light—as the psalmists says, "by God's light we shall see light" (Ps 36)—at this moment it is clear that Augustine receives a new hermeneutic for communion with God in the body of Christ Jesus.[4] Whether it was Manicheans reading an anti-materialism into Pauline definitions of "flesh," or Pelagians reading a strenuously moral Stoicism into the exemplarity of Jesus, it was his conversion to the Catholic faith in that Milanese garden that enabled Augustine to read the reality of the world in the light of the eternal and creative Word of God who made it. So how did how Augustine read the relationship between the Creator and creation after his conversion, and against this Manichean background?

Mani, who considered himself "an apostle of Jesus Christ," challenged the catholic view of the goodness of creation. Indeed, Manicheans, like the Arians, were arguing that they were the true catholics, the true exponents of authentic Christianity. Thus any genuinely orthodox catholic Christian committed to the rule of faith had to refute the Manichean view that the creation of matter was derived from a preexisting struggle between coeternal principles of light and darkness. When the Manicheans read Genesis, they saw Adam as a microcosm of this war between the enlightened soul and the "dark material" of the body. When they read the Gospels, Jesus was the revealer of the light principle. His suffering body was evidence of his

---

4. Augustine, *Confessions*, book 8.

battle against the dark principle. Manicheans considered Catholics heretics because they believed Jesus really had a physical body; they believed he was really born of Mary's flesh; they believed that he was really nailed to the cross. Those are all the things, Manicheans thought, from which Jesus came to release us. They rejected water baptism because it was too focused on the dark material of the body, preferring instead the "spiritual" baptism they thought Jesus himself commended. Augustine's catholic hermeneutic refutes the Manichean interpretation of Scripture, not only because he sees how they "seduce the faithful," but because he is mindful that they had once seduced him.[5] Indeed, with St. Paul he thinks that it is necessary for there to be such sects and heresies (*haireseis*) in order that "those who prove reliable may stand out among you."[6]

In the Nicene Creed, the council fathers teach that God is the creator of heaven and earth, and that this creation is the beginning of God's plan of salvation revealed in Christ. Augustine is aware, in his commentary on Genesis against the Manicheans, that this must mean that one cannot read Genesis 1 without also having read John 1 ("in the beginning was the Word and the Word was with God and the Word was God . . . and the Word became flesh and lived amongst us."). His commentary on the first chapter of Genesis is simultaneously a commentary on the first chapter of John's Gospel. In the light of Christ, "creation out of nothing" could not mean, as it did for Manicheans, that the material world was created out of preexisting "dark matter" (*nihil*), but creation was truly the effect of God's Word speaking creation into existence. "All things came into being through him, and without him not one thing came into being" (John 1:3). Rather than a battle between "two lights," eternally warring principles of light and darkness, Augustine follows John, for whom "the light shines in the darkness, and the darkness did not overcome it" (John 1:5). The "very goodness" of creation was caused by God, "the Giver of Life" (as Nicaea speaks of the Holy Spirit).

When Augustine turns to Genesis later in life, in *The City of God*, he is still exercised by the "two lights" which are discussed in Genesis 1. Augustine is particularly interested in the "lights" which precede the human creation because the Manicheans interpret them as the two principles at war. Augustine interprets the two lights as the creation of the angels, and "the fall" of part of their number.[7] This is a typical anti-Manichean interpretive move that is crucial for the way he understands the mystery of evil and its entry into the world, first through the angelic fall which makes it possible for there to be a tree of the knowledge of good and evil, and a serpent

---

5. Augustine, *Retractions*, 1.10
6. Augustine, *On Genesis*, 39, citing 1 Cor 11:19.
7. Augustine, *City of God*, 11.9.

to tempt God's "very good" creation: the human person, created male and female. In this way, Augustine consistently teaches that evil is not a divine principle, nor does it have a causative nature, as Manicheans thought (for whom the evil principle was what generated our bodies). Rather, Augustine insists that evil is only a privation of the good (*privatio boni*) which has no "causative nature." Evil is not a principle, it is a parasite! Far from there being a war between good and evil in God, Augustine argues that evil is not caused by God—and it is not eternal in the way that God is eternal. Evil enters the world, not through warring principles in God, but through the contingency of creatures created in freedom, the freedom to turn toward the Giver of Life or to turn human desire, irrationally, away from God's goodness. Evil is nothing but lack. It is not caused by God. It does not pre-exist creation. As he argues, God made the devil, but did not make him wicked.[8] This is an important point that Augustine learned to make over a very long period of time. In fact, Augustine made no fewer than five attempts at a commentary on Genesis, largely aimed at refuting the Manichean view of the body.

Augustine, like Paul, is a theologian teaching the world that the church is a new "Mystical Body," a participation in the new creation, the body of Christ. He is interested in how the members of this body may be cured or healed of those passions which enslave the soul because of the wounds of sin. It is not the body that imprisons the soul (as with Manicheans); rather it is sin that imprisons the soul. Augustine could embrace the goodness of the body, but it was the damage that sin did to the soul that concerned him. Everyone knows the famous story of Augustine stealing a pear in the second chapter of the *Confessions*. He notes how irrational the theft was, and notes that sin is a kind of flight from rationality precisely because it is a flight from communion with God—that is, Augustine seems to associate, *via negativa*, rationality and relationality right from the beginning. It would be wrong to say that his notion of the person created in God's image is simply reducible to rationality.

From the outset of the *Confessions* he tells us that even in the face of human sin, the fruit we really want to pluck, the true desire which we are restless for is God himself. He famously writes, "to praise you is the desire of man, a little piece of your creation. You stir man to take pleasure in praising you, because you have made us for yourself, and our heart is restless until it rests in you."[9] Far from an exclusively *rational* or *intellectual* understanding of the image of God, we might say with James K. A. Smith that Augustine's anthropology is even more deeply rooted in the desire to praise God (the

---

8. Augustine, *City of God*, 11.15.
9. Augustine, *Confessions*, 1.1.

human being is *homo liturgicus*).¹⁰ Put differently, the "desire to know" is indeed what sets human beings apart from the other creatures, but such a desire seems to lack an object—to know what? We might ask, rationality for what end? Augustine is convinced that the human "desire to know" derives from our having been originally constituted for communion with God—a decidedly relational end. Our desire to know is nothing other than the desire to know God. In fact, so great a desire in us was what made the serpent's offer to eat from the tree of the knowledge of good and evil so tempting. Original sin consists in the disordering of this desire, which alienates humanity from God, turns us away from the holiness of our original communion with the God who made us in his image and likeness. Sin is not only understood as the flight from rationality, but also as the flight from relationship with God. Augustine thus wants to know how we may return by way of the incarnate *logos* to true rationality, and also to communion with the triune God of love. Knowing and loving God in our present condition, however, means that we will, as the Apostle Paul says, have to look through a mirror darkly until that day when we see God face to face (1 Cor 13:12).

In *De Trinitate*, Augustine works through several created analogies in his quest to "seek understanding" of God, whose nature exceeds our rational capacities. Each are considered to be mirrors to help the pilgrim understand God's triune nature. All of them are inadequate—Augustine never fails to recognize the apophatic limits of analogy. Yet the analogy that seems to be given in scripture has by now been well established for him. He perfectly understands that the image of God is rational and it seems that he not reductively "rationalist" but "liturgical" in the limited sense that we are made with the desire to know God as cause of all that exists. What I want to suggest is that his analogy of the mind as "memory, intellect and will" cannot be reduced to a rationalist anthropology.¹¹ What becomes clear in *De Trin.* is that, rather than the "psychological" analogy helping us to understand the triune God, it is the Nicene definition of the Trinity which illumines how we understand the substantial unity of the soul as the tripartite image of God. Augustine provides his readers with the *regula fidei* of Nicaea

---

10. Smith, *Desiring the Kingdom*, 39ff. Smith rightly resists a "rationalist" anthropology in favor of a "liturgical" one, developing the notion of human beings as "liturgical animals" to complement Alasdair MacIntyre's view that we are "dependent rational animals" (MacIntyre, *Dependent Rational Animals*). Smith thinks that Augustine's own emphasis on the order of love justifies his view, but misses direct support for his view in the opening chapter of the Confessions: "to praise you is the desire of man." This essay will return to this theme in the conclusion.

11. Cf. my "How Augustine Used the Trinity," which argues that the whole structure of *De Trinitate* is anagogical; it is ordered to raising human reason to the praise of the triune God.

as illumination for the human person made for "face-to-face" communion with God.

Augustine tells us nothing "new" about God in *De Trinitate*, but integrates for us his biblical understanding of the *imago dei* with the church's Trinitarian creed for a highly complex yet essentially unified understanding of the human soul that should resist any intellectual reduction. As the analogy unfolds, it is clear that "memory, intellect and will" correspond to the Father, the Son, and the Holy Spirit. Even the *filioque* clause sheds light on anthropology, for he is keen to show that the human will "proceeds" from the relation of "memory and the intellect," *just as* the Holy Spirit proceeds from the Father *and the Son*. Do you see which way the analogy works? Moreover, shedding further Trinitarian light on the human person, Augustine is committed to showing how these distinct operations of the soul do not constitute a divided or fragmented image, but understands the mind as the essence of the soul. This does not mean that the human person is a mind, or that the analogy works to "disembody" the mind, though it might mean that a profound identity between the body and the rational soul is implicit in his analogy.[12] The Trinitarian rule ensures that his anthropology will have both a rational and relational depth and coherence. In maintaining the psychological analogy, the hermeneutical rule guides him to sustain the essential unity of the mind (the "essence" of the soul), while distinguishing distinct operations of the soul.

In this way, the light of the triune God is shed on the profoundly relational constitution of the human mind. Nicaea, once again, rules how the mature Augustine reads human nature. If we isolate passages in Augustine, we can certainly obtain anachronistic dualisms that seem to fit an exclusively rationalist anthropology (e.g., Descartes' thinking-reed). But so far we have suggested that only modern misreadings of Augustine could locate in him an essentially Cartesian, individualist and rationalist anthropology. The human person is created with a desire to know, and this desire is to know God—indeed, the triune God of love. But to strengthen further my patristic case for a "catholic hermeneutic of communion" that proceeds from a rational and relational account of the human soul, I also want us to consider another theologian guided by Nicaea: Gregory of Nyssa. Following Michel Barnes, Lewis Ayres, and others who have reversed the long-contested view of de Regnon that the Latin West focused on "essential unity" and the Greek

---

12. Rarely do theologians connect what Augustine is writing in *De Trinitate* with what he is writing, at basically the same time, in *De Civitate Dei*. Augustine's extremely strong, realist account of bodily resurrection in *DCD*, 22 is impossible to square with reading Augustine's anthropology as disembodied in the rational soul (which is always substantial for him).

East focused on "dynamic relations," we can also revise our understanding of the anthropological differences between Augustine and Nyssa—both of whom I want to affirm have a rational, embodied, relational understanding of the person.[13]

Gregory of Nyssa

Gregory of Nyssa (330–395), a Cappadocian father whose work may have been known to Augustine, also considers the "formation of man." He asks, "what is the meaning of the image?"[14] He wonders if there really is "resemblance to the original" after the fall. "If the imitation is perverted from its subject, then the thing is something else and not its image."[15] He asks, "How then is man, this mortal and passionate and shortlived being, and image of the unmixed and pure and ever-being nature?"[16] Surely this puts us in a quandary: if there is a resemblance, then this must mean either that God is passible or that man is impassible. Since neither of these are logical possibilities for Gregory, he momentarily considers that the resemblance has been wiped away—that sin and death have negated or removed God's image and likeness. While Augustine admits in his *Confessions* that the image of God is so securely written upon human nature that "not even iniquity itself can destroy it," Gregory weighs the possibility that our present misery and suffering is a sign that the image has been lost.[17] There is no analogy between God and humanity after the fall—we are "cut off" from communion with God. Yet Gregory returns to the second chapter of Genesis for a different kind of answer, one that goes deeper. He observes the two creation accounts and holds that they occurred simultaneously in time: "thus the making of our nature is in a sense twofold: one made similar to the divine [in the image of God]. The other divided according to that difference [sexual differentiation]."[18] He asks, "How was it that after the making of his image God contrived for his creature the difference according to male and female?"[19] In other words, he asks, if God has made humanity whole in

---

13. On the reversal of de Regnon's thesis in Trinitarian theology and its import for the *imago dei*, also see Pecknold, "How Augustine Used the Trinity."

14. Gregory of Nyssa, *De Hominis Opificio (On the Formation of Man)*, 16, cited in Ladner, "Philosophical Anthropology of Saint Gregory of Nyssa," 79.

15. Ibid., 64.

16. Ibid., 65.

17. Augustine, *Confessions* 2.8.

18. Gregory of Nyssa, *De Hominis Opificio (On the Formation of Man)*, 16, cited in Ladner, "Philosophical Anthropology of Saint Gregory of Nyssa," 72.

19. Ibid.

chapter one, why does God intend to do something "reproductive" through sexual differentiation in chapter two?

Gregory's answer to this question is fascinating, and initiates a patristic line of thinking that will be revisited in the thought of Thomas Aquinas. It also augments an important theme in Augustine's Trinitarian anthropology. Gregory suggests that the first account of being made in the image of God was the creation of an immutable, divine nature for humanity—and this image would have indeed been "eternally lost" after the fall *if* God had not in the second account made humanity with a mutable nature, which he links to our sexual differentiation. That is, Gregory understands divine providence to be at work in the two creation accounts, because in receiving this "changeable nature" we have the capacity to "make it back," that is, we have a capacity to return to the perfect, divine image—we have the capacity for deification precisely through our changeable, reproductive nature. Furthermore, the second chapter of Genesis makes it clear that God pre-ordained our changeable nature so that we could "return" to the pre-ordained divine fullness (*pleroma*) of our likeness to God. In other words, our sexual differentiation—our reproductive nature—is given by God as part of the process of healing the image, giving the soul a power, or capacity for healing and elevation. As Augustine would have it: *felix culpa!*

Perhaps surprisingly, given Gregory's stress on the changeable, reproductive nature of the human soul, our "carnality" does not come from being sexually differentiated bodies made for reproduction. Unlike Augustine, he does not identify sex with concupiscence or sin in the first instance. Rather "carnality"—the "lust of the flesh"—does not come into the picture until the third chapter of Genesis when Adam and Even put on animal garments, "tunics of skin." Carnality is the consequence of a more original sin marring our resemblance to God. It is our "animality" that weighs us down—a kind of proto-theory of devolution that echoes his point about whether our resemblance to God has been lost or not (if it has been lost, then we can only resemble other animals). But in this sense, he is like Augustine, for both believe that humanity can be made whole again by "putting on" the garments of Christ—through the sacraments of baptism and Eucharist in particular—which can now be worn in place of the "tunics of skin." Likewise, Christ's bodily resurrection reveals to us that all things will be restored to their original integrity, in the wholeness of humanity which he understands as Christ's humanity, which is the perfect image of God the Father.

The point of this excursus on Gregory of Nyssa is to demonstrate that in both the Greek and Latin fathers, there was a distinctive rule of faith that shaped how they read the nature of the human being in the book of Genesis. It most certainly is a "catholic hermeneutic of communion," universal to

Greek and Latin speaking Christians in the wake of Nicaea, but the hermeneutic was even then still in the process of unfolding. We can see that Augustine's rational soul is "made to know" but is "restless," and therefore reveals that what the rational soul is made to know is God—indeed, the triune God. The mind made to know God is also the image of God, and the analogy of the memory, understanding and will to the Father, Son and Holy Spirit already indicate that Augustine's reading of Genesis with a Nicene hermeneutic is similar to Gregory of Nyssa's. While Gregory certainly agrees with Augustine that the analogy between God and humanity can be located in reason (just as God is Mind and Word—*Nous* and *Logos*—so Gregory notes you can observe within yourself a word as well as an intellect), he takes the relational implications of the Trinitarian anthropology in a direction that does not occur to Augustine in his reading of Genesis, but certainly fits with it. The tensions between these two fathers do not suggest two different hermeneutics of communion, one Latin and one Greek, but a single hermeneutical vision with two different modes of signifying the same reality—modes of signifying that will be harmonized in the thought of Thomas Aquinas in a way that makes their agreement clear.[20]

2. Thomas Aquinas on the Embodied Nature of the Person: Elucidating the Catholic Hermeneutic for Communion

Earlier I suggested that the Aristotelian hermeneutical tradition was to be preferred partly because of the way it was absorbed and modified by the medieval Christian tradition. This can best be seen in the thought of Thomas Aquinas. Like Aristotle, Thomas is concerned with how we say (*predicatio*) things; or in his terms, our various modes of signifying the signified thing. Thus we can often find him making distinctions like: "necessity can be predicated in two ways." He is fully aware that there are multiple ways of reading and interpreting reality, but this does not deter him from seeking the distinctions that would enable him to follow the truth. Multiplicity is never a cause for doubt, but a call to make finer distinctions about the thing being signified. When he approaches the question of the image of God, it is crucial

---

20. This is not intended to elide the serious eschatological disagreements about the permanence of gender in human nature between the Greek and Latin theologians (Nyssa believes gender falls away in the resurrected body, Augustine does not)—but these disagreements about gender in the resurrected body should not distract from their implicit agreement concerning the relational, rational embodied soul created by God.

to see how he elucidates and unfolds the thought of St. Augustine, precisely through making finer distinctions. In this section of the essay I want to show how Thomas Aquinas remains faithful to how Augustine understands the nature of the person (a *substantial*, rational soul) and also show how he sheds light on its embodied, reproductive, relational, and thus communal nature (in ways that harmonize Greek fathers like Gregory of Nyssa and John Damascene with Augustine). In this way I hope to show that standing in a conversation with Augustine that has been extended over a very long period of time (Alasdair MacIntyre's rough definition of "tradition") bears fruit in the thought of Aquinas, and exemplifies a living tradition.

Losing the Mind for the Sake of the Soul?

Just as Augustine was keen to establish the essential unity of the soul in his Trinitarian anthropology, Thomas Aquinas resists any notion that our souls are composed of "parts." Some of his contemporaries, invested in debates about the "plurality of substantial forms," entertained distinct "substantial forms" for different parts and powers of the soul. Yet John P. O'Callaghan has persuasively argued that by the time Thomas Aquinas writes the *Summa*, he has largely ceased speaking of the image of God in terms of the mind as the essence of the soul.[21] This is not because Thomas rejects Augustine's substantial view of the soul, nor is it, as we have already said, because he is not interested in the unity of the soul. Thomas's turn from "mind" to "soul" in the *Summa* is in the service of Augustine's Trinitarian anthropology which had stressed the rational, substantial unity of the soul through the analogical attention to memory, understanding and will. This shift allows Thomas to make a new Aristotelian distinction between the powers of the soul (intellect and will) and the essence of the soul, which he takes to be known through its powers, which are in turn known through "acts," which are in turn known by their "objects."[22] This is a brilliant set of philosophical distinctions, but O'Callaghan seems to find only a philosophical point to it: "embodied engagement with the world."[23] While this is undoubtedly true, the theologian will see more clearly that what Thomas is doing here

---

21. O'Callaghan, "Imago Dei." While I largely agree with O'Callaghan's helpful discussion of Aquinas on this shift from mind to soul, his discussion of Augustine is often anachronistic in light of the thirteenth-century plural substantial forms debate (which also makes his Augustine curiously "Cartesian").

22. Ibid., 114.

23. Ibid.

is making more explicit the embodied (substantial) nature of Augustine's Trinitarian anthropology.

While Thomas largely refrains from using Augustine's language of mind, preferring instead the powers of intellect and will, he maintains the rational nature of the soul, but now in an explicitly embodied, "actualized" way. This enables Thomas to articulate an even more explicitly embodied anthropology than the mental analogy might suggest, thus bringing out Augustine's own striking commitment to the embodied nature of a properly Christian anthropology (recall Augustine commending the incarnation to disincarnated Platonists, and also the Pauline text about "putting on the body of Christ" that is central to his conversion account in the *Confessions*). O'Callaghan sees Thomas leaving Augustine's "mind" behind—allegedly because it cannot do justice to the simple unity of the soul, especially in light of the thirteenth-century debates raging about the plurality of substantial forms. However, it seems more fitting to see Thomas underscoring Augustine's own interest in reading the human person according to the Trinitarian rule of Nicaea. To be truly faithful to Augustine's analogy, we would have to understand the inner-outer relation, as well as the relation of the "parts," of the soul in a simple way. If we take Augustine's analogy seriously, then the soul must have an analogously simple unity to the unity of the triune God, just as it is analogous to the Persons. We do better then to speak of dynamic powers of the soul when we speak of the complexity of parts, but if God is Being Itself, as well as Pure Act, we need an analogous way of speaking of the human soul as substantial and united even in its complex operations. Staying with the Trinitarian analogy enables Thomas to stress with Augustine (*a*) the rational nature of the soul, (*b*) the parts of the soul as analogous to Trinitarian "persons," and (*c*) the essential unity of the soul in its interior essence and its exterior act.

We might ask, why does Thomas make these moves in anthropology? O'Callaghan is convinced that Thomas does so because he wants to defend Aristotle against some theologians (also seeking to be faithful to Augustine) who are defending a more Platonic line of thought regarding the plurality of substantial forms. I am certain there is some truth to this, but O'Callaghan's exclusive philosophical focus obscures what is theologically at stake: making the anthropology "fit" for communion with the triune God. If "our hearts are restless until they find their rest in God," it must be the case that we need to locate the true, real and actual nature of the human person. A philosophical anthropology can help us to say that we are open to God, but it cannot call us to communion with the triune God revealed in Christ. Thomas is certainly committed to an anthropology based on human reason alone (i.e., Aristotle's reason), but only if it fits with the Trinitarian anthropology that has been revealed to us in God's eternal Word in Christ. He makes this point explicit in his response to question 91, art. 6, "whether the image of God is in man as regards the mind only?"

> While in all creatures there is some kind of likeness to God, in the rational creature alone we find a likeness of "image" as we have explained above (1,2); whereas in other creatures we find a likeness by way of a "trace." Now the intellect or mind is that whereby the rational creature excels other creatures . . . the image of God is not found in the rational creature except in the mind; while in the other parts . . . we find the likeness of a "trace" . . . Therefore we may observe this difference between rational creatures and others, both as to the representation of the likeness of the Divine Nature in creatures, and as to the representation in them of the uncreated Trinity.[24]

In this response we see clearly that the Trinitarian analogy rules his predication about the *imago dei*. Thomas agrees with Augustine that image of God is the intellectual soul. But angels are intellectual souls as well, indeed, they are "pure intellect." Does that not suggest that angels are creatures who are more like God than we are?

In question 93, Thomas admits that angels *are* more perfectly like God if we are speaking only in terms of the intellectual nature. Indeed, if we take Augustine to mean that the image of God consists only in our rational nature, we will be able to say that no other earthly creatures bear this image, but we will not be able to say that angelic creatures do not. It is not enough simply to insist on the rational nature of the soul. It is our likeness to the *triune* God which remains the crucial theological background. Thomas seizes the opportunity to make a distinction that highlights how human persons are like God in a way that angels cannot: "man proceeds from man, as God [proceeds] from God."[25] The Trinitarian language of processions is pronounced, and profoundly elucidates Augustine's Trinitarian anthropology. As O'Callaghan notes, "the reference to the generation of God from God calls to mind the Nicene Creed, and pertains to the unity of nature, that is, to the anti-Arian creedal affirmation of unity, while in man it pertains to reproduction."[26] In this way, Thomas comes to the stunning conclusion that the image of God is not reducible to our rational nature, but also pertains to the *reproductive* capacity of humanity. After all, God did not say "be fruitful and multiply" to the angels.

24. Aquinas, *Summa Theologica*, I.91, art. 6
25. Aquinas, *Summa Theologica*, I.93, art. 3, resp.
26. O'Callaghan, "Image of God," 141.

At this point of the essay, I simply want to point out that coming to such a conclusion harmonizes Augustine with a trajectory among Greek speaking fathers, well-represented by Gregory of Nyssa. Thomas follows Augustine in locating the image in the substantial rational soul, but follows the incarnational and trinitarian implications of what it means *for that rational soul to be the form of the body*. In this we can say that Thomas refines and deepens Augustine's "substantialist" account of the soul, by fitting Aristotelian categories to the higher reason of the revelation of the triune God. If we are the image of the "generative" processions of the triune God, then we are not merely "rational souls" created "a little lower than the angels," but we are embodied persons, male and female, marked by a generative relational capacity.

So far I have argued that the "catholic hermeneutic of communion" is demonstrated in a common way of describing the creation of the human person in the opening chapters of Genesis. I have also argued that the councils of the church tradition have played the decisive role in shaping the very catholic nature of the hermeneutic, and that the hermeneutic is consistently directed toward the object of communion with God. In doing so, we have frequently called upon the Council of Nicaea. In concluding the patristic and medieval sections of this chapter, it is important to recall that Council of Nicaea was an anti-Arian council, and Augustine's battle with Pelagius was an extension of the orthodox, "catholic hermeneutical" resistance to Arianism. In Thomas, we can also see the same hermeneutic at work. Context matters. The wariness of Christians toward Aristotle was partly due to the philosopher's association with Muslim theology—and we must not forget that Muslims were not thought of as some other "religion" (in the constructed way we use that term today) but were seen as a branch of Arianism. In other words, there was a palpable sense in the thirteenth century that Aristotle could lead to the heresy of Arianism rather than to orthodox, Trinitarian theology. Thomas shows why this is emphatically not the case. He remains faithful to Augustine's anti-Arian image of the divine nature of the unity of the soul, and utilizes Aristotle not only to make this point, but also to elucidate the relational aspect of Augustine's Trinitarian anthropology. This has the effect of heightening his "Augustinian" substantialist account of the soul in an embodied way, and at the same time, it allows him to incorporate the importance of the changeable, reproductive account of the soul in Gregory of Nyssa in a remarkable theological synthesis that bears witness to the very catholicity of the tradition on the nature of the image of God.

In the remaining part of this essay, we will examine how the integration of the rational and the reproductive come together in modern modes of describing the image of God. This can be seen first and foremost in the Catechism of the Catholic Church which consistently describes the capacity of the human person to know God (rational) and to love God (relational) in a way that highlights the catholic nature of this hermeneutic carried across time. It is a hermeneutic that was articulated in the twentieth century in dynamic terms that were both new and old, just as Thomas Aquinas sought to be faithful to Augustine (and Gregory) as he engaged a new context.

3. The Ecclesial Person: From Henri de Lubac to Pope Benedict XVI

Henri de Lubac has often been called an "Augustinian-Thomist," though others have located him in an "Augustinian-Scotistic" line.[27] That he is read so differently within the catholic communion is often a neuralgic point in contemporary theology. Much hinges on how to read Thomas Aquinas on the nature of the person, and what exactly the Augustinian "restlessness" of nature means. Are we creatures whose nature is so infinitely distant from God's nature that we can only say that this "restlessness" is something which only God elicits in us, or can we say that the restlessness comes from something innate in us? Does our desire for God come from God alone, or does it have any ontological roots in our nature? Such questions that have raged around the nature-grace controversy that is so associated with the name of Henri de Lubac.

I do not wish to rehearse those debates, nor make claims for de Lubac as an interpreter of Augustine or Thomas Aquinas. Whatever help he may or may not provide for readers of St. Thomas, it is clear that he paved a profoundly Augustinian way for us to understand human nature in light of God's call to communion with himself. In short, de Lubac offers the world a catholic hermeneutic for communion that refreshes and renews from the deepest wells of the tradition. De Lubac's influence is probably most powerfully seen today in the theology of Joseph Ratzinger/Pope Benedict XVI. His frequent use of the phrase "called to communion" has penetrated the *Catechism of the Catholic Church* and countless magisterial documents, both before his elevation to the papacy and after. It is a lucid and elegant crystallization of what the catholic hermeneutic has always aimed at.

Ratzinger's work as an academic theologian can be taken separately from what he teaches us in the office of St. Peter. So let us examine how

---

27. See Lawrence Feingold's important, detailed critique of Henri de Lubac along these lines in *The Natural Desire to See God according to Saint Thomas and His Interpreters*.

he looks at the traditional hermeneutic, with a sampling from his teaching prior to his elevation, and then briefly compare this with both the *Catechism* and what he writes in his encyclicals *Deus Caritas Est* and *Caritas in Veritate*. Let us first look to an essay that he published over twenty years ago in the international journal *Communio* on "the notion of person in theology."[28] It is often cited as representative of his Trinitarian anthropology and it is also invested in the same argument for a catholic hermeneutic that we have been reviewing here in these pages. In this essay, Ratzinger argues that

> in God there are three persons which implies, according to the interpretation offered by theology, that persons are relations, pure relatedness. Although, this is in the first place only a statement about the Trinity, it is at the same time the fundamental statement about what is at stake in the concept of person.[29]

The notion of "pure relatedness" could seem to privilege the divine *prosopon*, only to undercut the divine *ousia*, and thus analogically to deny the integrity of individuated natures. I do not think this is Ratzinger's intention, or if it was then, I hope to show that by participating in this living tradition, he was able to correct any imbalance between the categories of substance and relation. Ratzinger's original concern is not to privilege relation over substance but rather to overcome, or resist, a philosophical and theological hermeneutic that authorizes modern (post-Kantian) individualism. To this end, Ratzinger is even willing to indict Augustine in his desire to resist any theological support for an individualistic anthropology. He identifies an "incompleteness" in Augustine's analogy and argues that the Doctor of Grace does not follow his Trinitarian anthropology toward its proper theo-logical conclusion:

> Augustine explicitly transposed this theological affirmation into anthropology by attempting to understand the human person as an image of the Trinity in terms of this idea of God. Unfortunately, however, he committed a decisive mistake here . . . In his interpretation, he projected the divine persons into the interior life of the human person and affirmed that intra-psychic processes correspond to these persons. The person as a whole, by contrast, corresponds to the divine substance. As a result, the trinitarian concept of person was no longer transferred to the human person in all its immediate impact.[30]

---

28. Ratzinger, "Retrieving the Tradition."
29. Ibid., 447.
30. Ibid.

This is partly true, *prima facie*, but as we have already seen, for Augustine it is the mind which analogically corresponds to the divine substance, and the operations of the mind analogically correspond to persons. That is not exactly the same thing as saying that the person as a whole corresponds to the divine substance. In fact, Augustine would most certainly not want to say that, as it would predicate corruptible materiality to the divine substance! Augustine intends no such analogy, and does not even intend the analogy to work in this way. Indeed, the analogy works to show that the human person is a substantial rational soul whose nature is relationally constituted for communion with the triune God. While we can certainly admit that Augustine's analogy has limitations—indeed, Augustine thinks his analogies fail miserably (a point frequently missed by his readers)—it is not entirely fair to expect his own analogy to take into consideration all the developments that were to come after him.

In this middle period of his theological development, Cardinal Ratzinger argues on both philosophical and theological grounds that the concept of the person is not simply rooted in the category of substance (which he finds operative in both Augustine and Thomas), but also in the category of relation (which he finds operative in the Victorines). It is difficult to assent to his conclusion that the "anthropological turn" in Augustine's doctrine of the Trinity is causally related to later attempts to narrow anthropology into an "I/Thou relation" which further narrows into the individualist "I."[31] However, it is certainly the case that Augustine could have further developed his Trinitarian anthropology in a way which could have forestalled any possible "bracketing" of the reality of the relationally-constituted "we" of the triune God (rather than the inscrutable "I" of the God of nominalism), and thus forestall any possible Lutheran or Cartesian turn toward the isolated nature of the self before God. But at times it can seem like Ratzinger forgets that the human person is only analogously like the Trinitarian persons, who are indeed relationally constituted; in Thomas, the divine persons simply are subsistent relations. Human persons, though, are not "subsistent relations." Only in God does a relation subsist. We are constituted by our bodies. Our relation to God is always already implied in being the creatures that we are, but our relation to God follows on the *being of the* creature, relationality is the flowering of our nature. We could not even be "restless," nor could we hope for a bodily resurrection in the beatific vision unless we were substantially constituted to begin with.

In addition to Ratzinger's challenging account of Trinitarian anthropology, one that contributes to emerging discussions of a relational ontology,

---

31. Ibid., 454.

we can also see his attentiveness to the theme of reproduction, which seems to require total integration of the categories of relation and substance. We see Ratzinger as a theologian on the move in the tradition. We can see him work this out in a pastoral way in a series of homilies he delivered on Genesis: *In the Beginning: A Catholic Understanding of the Story of Creation and Fall*. Aware of his task as shepherd, we see an even more fecund account of the hermeneutic of communion. As we saw with Augustine, his reading of Genesis is also inseparable from his reading of John 1. As he understands it, this is because the catholic hermeneutic has no interest in reading anthropology merely "off the page" of Genesis. "As Christians," he writes, "we read Holy Scripture with Christ. He is our guide all the way through it." He writes that Christology must be our criterion for anthropology, and thus must guide how we understand the *imago dei*, the union of the material and spiritual, the reproductive nature of being created male-female, and even the "we" structure of our being made at all ("Let *us* make man in our image"). Ratzinger goes so far as to say that not only salvation history should be read in the light of Christ, but also that the whole of creation, including "the body of history," be read through the catholic hermeneutic of communion.[32] This is because it is only "in Jesus Christ [that] we can discern what the human being, God's project, is, and thereby also our own status."[33]

It is precisely in his christological criterion that Ratzinger also points us to a profound integration of the catholic hermeneutic of communion, especially through the christological and Trinitarian notion of the person in theology. In these homilies he is not at all concerned to dismantle the traditional thesis concerning the substantial nature of the rational soul. "Rationality" remains crucial to his understanding of the person, but he implicitly asks us, "rationality for what purpose?" Scripture and perennial philosophy alike can agree that human beings have a desire to know. We are rational animals. Yet this tells us too little. What, or whom, are we made to know? For biblical faith, Ratzinger thinks the answer is obvious: God creates us with a desire to know in relation. We are made to know God, which is also to say that we are made for friendship with God. To become the creatures that we have been made to be is to become persons whom God has raised to friendship with himself. For in Ratzinger, the "rationality" of the traditional notion of the *imago dei* already implies "relationality." We have seen how this was implicit in both patristic and medieval theology, that is, we have seen this as an unfolding of the traditional Trinitarian hermeneutic which I earlier referred to as the "rule of faith." Ratzinger does not avoid

---

32. Ratzinger, *In the Beginning*, 34.
33. Ibid., 57.

the intellectual understanding of the image, but he thinks that "relationality" penetrates deeper into the God's intellect and will, goes to the heart of creation in relation to the Creator by seeing the person of Christ as our true humanity, the pinnacle of this relation, and also our participation in being the persons we were created to be.

This is also evident in the *Catechism of the Catholic Church*, which stresses four things about the human person: that man is in the image of God, that his nature unites material and spiritual worlds, that he is "male and female," and that he is made for friendship with God, made to share in God's life.[34] And it is for this reason that the Catechism almost always refers to the *knowledge and love of God* in a single breath, as if knowledge and love, rationality and relationality, were inseparable.

As Pope Benedict XVI, his first encyclical *Deus Caritas Est* gives us a magisterial teaching that reaches even deeper into the heart of the catholic hermeneutic. Here we can see how the tradition has operated upon the theologian, for now there is no suggestion that we are "relationally constituted," but now as Pope Benedict, the thrust of his arguments concern the priority of substance, the priority of nature, of a truth which precedes us, that is not made by us. In *Caritas in Veritate*, he writes that "*nature expresses a design of love and truth. It is prior to us, and it has been given to us by God as the setting for our life. Nature speaks to us of the Creator (cf. Rom 1:20) and his love for humanity.*"[35] Yet not only is "nature" (metaphysics) prior to our making of the world, but so is God. It is not really the priority of substance, and the need to rethink the category of relation that drives him, though these are distinctions that matter to him as a supreme exemplar participant in the great tradition of the church. What most drives him is in the proclamation of the Trinitarian faith:

> The Trinity is absolute unity insofar as the three divine Persons are pure relationality. The reciprocal transparency among the divine Persons is total and the bond between each of them complete, since they constitute a unique and absolute unity. God desires to incorporate us into this reality of communion as well: "that they may be one even as we are one" (John 17:22). The Church is a sign and instrument of this unity. Relationships between human beings throughout history cannot but be enriched by reference to this divine model.[36]

---

34. *Catechism of the Catholic Church*, 355–84.
35. *Caritas in Veritate*, 48.
36. Ibid., 54.

Pope Benedict sees clearly that there is an analogical relationship between human persons and divine persons. He manages to affirm the metaphysical priority of nature, as the substantial ground for the flowering of human relations, without ever diminishing the truth that our rational subsistent natures would not be natures at all without the love and truth of God who has called us into being for communion with himself. The Church as the sign and instrument of this unity depends on a hermeneutic of communion which is deeply wed to the categories of substance and relation, but is above all wed to the ancient Trinitarian faith, the rule for reading Scripture, tradition, the nature of persons and the nature of communion itself.

An Ecumenical Epilogue for a Catholic Hermeneutic of Communion

By focusing on Augustine, Gregory of Nyssa, Thomas Aquinas, and Joseph Ratzinger, I do not mean to suggest that the "catholic hermeneutic" belongs only to Roman Catholics (quite the opposite!). Augustine remains a beloved touchstone of orthodoxy for Protestant Christians, just as Gregory of Nyssa does for Orthodox Christians. Ratzinger himself was formed under the tutelage of Gottlieb Söhngen, whose work paralleled the dialogue between Hans Urs von Balthasar and Karl Barth (especially on the topic of the *analogia entis*), which has always been charged with such ecumenical hopefulness. Furthermore, one could point to Alan Torrance's *Persons in Communion*, as an example of a contemporary Protestant theologian whose work seems to follow the same Trinitarian rule of faith that we saw was crucial to the catholic hermeneutic.[37] The work of the Orthodox theologian John Zizioulas has been enormously fecund in this regard, evidenced by the dialogical fruit it bears in relation to both Protestant (like Alan Torrance) and Catholic theologians (like Paul McPartlan).[38] Without a doubt, it is reasonable to say that each of these theologians demonstrates a catholic hermeneutic of communion. But we might, then, ask, why not actually be in communion with one another? All Christians can rationally assent to the marks of the church as "one, holy, catholic and apostolic" but the ecumenical challenge is to develop our "ecclesial theologies" in ways which demonstrate that this catholic hermeneutic is not a disincarnate idea, but must be substantial, relational, embodied and visible.

---

37. Torrance, *Persons in Communion*.
38. McPartlan, *Eucharist Makes the Church*.

For Augustine, that catholic hermeneutic was embodied in the act of receiving Christ in the Eucharist. Augustine tells his flock that it is by "putting on Christ's body" that they become the persons that God has made them to be. He tells them that through the bread and wine they are about to receive mysteriously in the sacrament of the altar the substance of who they are most truly—persons in communion with the triune God of love—Christ's body, the church. As Augustine tells them, "Be what you can see, and receive what you are."[39] Here we see the substance of things hoped for—in the Eucharist we become one, holy, and catholic in Christ.

Bibliography

Augustine. *Confessions*. Translated by Henry Chadwick. Oxford: Oxford University Press, 1998.

———. *On Genesis: A Refutation of the Manichees; Unfinished Literal Commentary on Genesis; The Literal Meaning of Genesis*. Translated by Edmund Hill. The Works of Saint Augustine: A Translation for the 21st Century I/13, edited by John E. Rotelle. Hyde Park, NY: New City, 2002.

———. *Sermons 230-272*. Translated by Edmund Hill. The Works of Saint Augustine: A Translation for the 21st Century III/7, edited by John E. Rotelle. Hyde Park, NY: New City, 1993.

Benedict XVI, Pope. *Caritas in Veritate*. San Francisco: Ignatius, 2009.

Dauphinais, Michael, Barry David, and Matthew Levering, eds. *Aquinas the Augustinian*. Washington, DC: Catholic University of America Press, 2007.

Feingold, Lawrence. *The Natural Desire to See God according to Saint Thomas and His Interpreters*. 2nd ed. Ave Maria, FL: Sapientia Press of Ave Maria University, 2010.

Ladner, Gerhart B. "The Philosophical Anthropology of Saint Gregory of Nyssa." *Dumbarton Oaks Papers* 12 (1958) 59–94.

Levering, Matthew. *Participatory Biblical Exegesis: A Theology of Biblical Interpretation*. Notre Dame: University of Notre Dame Press, 2008.

Lubac, Henri de. *Corpus Mysticum: The Eucharist and the Church in the Middle Ages*. Translated by Gemma Simmonds. Notre Dame: University of Notre Dame Press, 2007.

MacIntyre, Alasdair. *Dependent Rational Animals: Why Human Beings Need the Virtues*. Chicago: Open Court, 1999.

McPartlan, Paul. *The Eucharist Makes the Church: Henri de Lubac and John Zizioulas in Dialogue*. London: T. & T. Clark, 1996.

O'Callaghan, John P. "Imago Dei: A Test Case for St. Thomas's Augustinianism." In *Aquinas the Augustinian*, edited by Michael Dauphinais, Barry David, and Matthew Levering, 100–144. Washington, DC: Catholic University of America Press, 2007.

Pecknold, C. C. "How Augustine Used the Trinity." *Anglican Theological Review* 85 (2003) 127–41.

---

39. Augustine, Sermon 272.

Ratzinger, Joseph. *In the Beginning: A Catholic Understanding of the Story of Creation and the Fall.* Translated by Boniface Ramsey. Grand Rapids: Eerdmans, 1995.

———. *Principles of Catholic Theology: Building Stones for a Fundamental Theology.* San Francisco: Ignatius, 1987.

———. "Retrieving the Tradition: Concerning the Notion of Person in Theology." *Communio* 17 (1990) 439–54.

Smith, James K. A. *Desiring the Kingdom: Worship, Worldview and Cultural Formation.* Grand Rapids: Baker, 2009.

Thomas Aquinas. *Summa Theologica.* Translated by Fathers of the English Dominican Province. Allen, TX: Christian Classics, 1981.

Torrance, Alan J. *Persons in Communion: Trinitarian Description and Human Participation.* London: T. & T. Clark, 1996.

3

The Hermeneutics of Schism and the Question of "Sister Churches"

WILL T. COHEN

1. Introduction: The Great Schism as Question or as Answer

TRUTH TAKES TIME. INASMUCH as this may serve as a statement of the Incarnation itself, it would seem that Christians, of all people, should be least prone to lose sight of the relationship between truth and temporality. The basic Christian notion of discernment certainly attests to truth's temporality, too: if truth were always immediately manifest there would be no need to discern it. At least, there would be no struggle in this, no period of unknowing prior to the moment of clarity.

Interpretation—hermeneutics—takes place in the period of unknowing. Hermeneutics is purely a function of the temporal character of truth. At the heart of hermeneutics is what one of its foremost theoreticians has called the priority of the question.[1] To acknowledge that one is engaging in an act of interpretation of a text or of an historical development is already to understand that its true meaning remains to be brought out. The matter is not settled; there is a question.

In what follows, I will seek to show how the expression "sister churches," as used in the modern period across the division between Catholic and Orthodox Christianity, is, in its authentic sense, best understood as a means by which the East-West schism came to be seen in the latter part of the

---

1. Gadamer, *Truth and Method*, 363. See section 2 below.

twentieth century as a question: an historical development the meaning of which is not just self-evident but requires the struggle of an interpretation, and therefore an initial acknowledgment—a full, humble, all-important acknowledgment—that one does not know what it means. I will argue that the most formidable impediment to Orthodox-Catholic rapprochement is not the challenge of coming to agree on this or that issue of doctrine, church structure, or liturgical or devotional practice, but rather this difficulty of simply coming to see the schism as an ongoing question, rather than an answer.

For in fact, to many people's minds, if there ever was a question of the relationship between the Catholic Church and the Orthodox Church, it has long since been answered with sufficient clarity by the fact of the schism itself. Where long ago there had been one church, there came in the course of time to be two. Insofar as Christians believe in precisely *one* holy, catholic, and apostolic church, the break between them could only mean that one of the two is the continuation of the true church while the other has fallen away from it. Until relatively recent times, this view of the schism as a *fait accompli*, as providing its own definitive answer to any question that might arise in our minds about how each of the traditions relates to the other, was the view held by virtually everyone on either side of the divide. Catholics identified the one true church as the Catholic Church; Orthodox identified it as the Orthodox Church. From as early as the sixteenth century and certainly by the middle of the eighteenth, this idea had come to be very entrenched on both sides, namely, that one's being the church excluded the other's being the church if the two were not in communion with each other.[2]

Then the expression "sister churches" emerged in exchanges between Orthodox and Catholic Christianity in the latter half of the twentieth century.[3] It did not emerge in a vacuum, of course; it was one element in a larger matrix of developments leading to new forms of ecumenical engagement and to a certain reappraisal of each side's tradition from within. But the term "sister churches" seemed to go especially far in forcing such a reappraisal,

---

2. The comment of Pascal is representative: "All virtues, martyrdom, austerities, and good works, out of the pale of the Church, and of communion with the head of the Church, the Pope, are useless" (*Pensées*, 139). Although Eastern Christianity persisted longer in maintaining a certain openness in regard to the schism and the ecclesial status of the Latin West, examples of ecclesiological exclusivism in the East are also not hard to find from the eighteenth century on. See, for example, the 1755 decree of Patriarch Cyril V of Constantinople, titled, *A Definition of the Holy Church of Christ defending the Holy Baptism given from God, and spitting upon the baptisms of the heretics which are otherwise administered*, discussed at length in Timothy (now Metropolitan Kallistos) Ware, *Eustratios Argenti*.

3. For a detailed study of the term, see Cohen, *Concept of Sister Churches*.

for there was no obvious sense in which it could be used without directly challenging understandings of the division that, on either side, went back centuries.

An observation by the Orthodox historian and theologian Fr. John Meyendorff may serve to bring the point into focus. Reflecting on the origins and nature of the East-West division, Meyendorff suggested that it had by no means been understood as a "definitive schism" in the initial decades and even centuries following 1054, and that it was only after the failure of the Council of Florence (1438–42) that "the separation reached a stable state."[4] In light of this significant idea of *a stable state of separation*, it may be said that an overarching significance of the remarkable emergence of the language of "sister churches" between Catholics and Orthodox five hundred years later was to render their separation *unstable* again. The expression's emergence presented, in this respect, a conundrum, a difficulty or ambiguity (in very much the sense in which Maximus the Confessor included certain theological problems under these categories[5]). Specifically, what the expression "sister churches" rendered ambiguous was the schism itself. Use of the phrase really meant that the schism went from having the character of an answer to having the character of a question once again.

The hermeneutics of tradition becomes pivotal at just this point. Just as in theology there is a certain type of liberal for whom all is open to reappraisal since there really are no answers (at least none that can be considered definitive), so too there is a kind of conservative for whom there are no more questions; he regards tradition as infallibly offering up a supply of ready-made answers and as requiring nothing of us who live today apart from our submission to its clear dictates. He is suspicious of subjecting tradition to something as capricious and as all-too-human as the activity of *hermeneutics* would seem to him to have the propensity to be. He has the idea that to be "traditional" is somehow a straightforward matter of just looking at what the tradition says and sticking to that. Tradition is of God; interpretation is of man. Certainly anything that would have the complexion of a *re*interpretation—for example, presuming to revisit and reconsider a question of which the tradition seemed to have given an interpretation in the past—is viewed with the greatest suspicion.

4. Meyendorff, "Eglises-soeurs," 38.

5. In Louth, *Maximus the Confessor*, the title given to these types of treatises by Maximus is "Difficulty," while in Blowers and Wilken, *On the Cosmic Mystery of Jesus Christ*, it is rendered in Latin as "Ambiguum." Later in the essay I will invoke another term, *aporía*, which has been applied to ecumenical problems by the contemporary theologian Waclaw Hryniewicz ("Ecumenism and Kenotic Dimensions of Ecclesiology," 145–46).

An example of such "traditionalism" in theology is found in a letter of 1994 written by a North American Orthodox archbishop to his Metropolitan, explaining why he is opposed to the language of sister churches to describe relations with the Catholic Church:

> What are we to do with the Fathers and the councils which indeed considered the things that Christ entrusted to His Church the exclusive property of the One Holy Catholic Apostolic Orthodox Church? Will we simply ignore them, declare that they were mistaken, or boast that we at the end of the twentieth century have some better understanding of the issues involved?[6]

For the present discussion, we may leave aside the matter of what texts of the Fathers and the Councils the Archbishop might specifically have had in mind (for in fact, on important ecclesiological questions such as the nature of the sacraments of schismatics or heretics, they present us with substantial complexity and variety[7]). Of more pressing interest is the Archbishop's overall presupposition that what has come down to us from tradition is fixed entirely, and that to take up aspects of one's tradition as still open to interpretation is really a betrayal of tradition. Who are we to boast that we could have some better understanding of the issues?

This anti-hermeneutical stance in theology turns out to be a variant of Romanticism's reaction against the Enlightenment. The Enlightenment and Romanticism alike posited much the same antithesis between the authority of the present and that of the past, a past conceived as self-contained, as entirely crystallized, impervious to current developments. Romanticism with its longing to escape the cold rationalism of modernity longed for this past (of whatever epoch) and invested it with ultimate authority, while the Enlightenment instead simply put all its faith in the present age and meanwhile applied its "hermeneutic of suspicion" to the past. In his unsurpassed analysis of these dynamics in European intellectual history the German philosopher Hans-Georg Gadamer portrays the Enlightenment outlook in the following terms:

> It is not tradition but reason that constitutes the ultimate source of all authority. What is written down is not necessarily true. We can know better: this is the maxim with which the modern Enlightenment approaches tradition and which ultimately leads

---

6. Archbishop Dmitri of Dallas and the South, Letter of September 23, 1994, 2. Mention of Archbishop Dmitri's letter and a substantial quotation from it appeared in *Sourozh: A Journal of Orthodox Life and Thought* 63 (1996) 52.

7. See Erickson, "On the Cusp of Modernity," 45–66. Cf. also Cohen, "Sacraments and the Visible Unity of the Church," 68–87.

it to undertake historical research. It takes tradition as an object of critique, just as the natural sciences do with the evidence of the senses.[8]

As the source of all authority, reason is ascribed (tacitly) a quasi-divine status; Enlightenment hermeneutics, in the mode of the historical-critical method, considered itself an endeavor of pure objectivity. It sought to expose tradition's foundations as mythical, merely human constructs. Gadamer calls this the Enlightenment's "schema of the conquest of mythos by logos."[9] In effect, interpretation is of God; tradition is of man.

The ensuing reflections draw on the work of Gadamer and that of another twentieth-century writer of very different background and sensibility, the Russian émigré theologian Vladimir Lossky, to provide an account of hermeneutics and tradition in which neither is vaunted at the expense of the other, but in which they integrally and naturally belong together. The concern will be to demonstrate the importance of this account for the hermeneutical task of understanding the meaning of the East-West schism of the past thousand years and the language of "sister churches" in more recent Catholic-Orthodox relations. The actual specifics of that task will not be delved into here, or not very far. It will be the more limited concern of this essay to demonstrate that *there is a real task to be carried out*, that the tradition is open for interpretation on the issue of the schism.

As will be seen, to say that tradition is open to interpretation is insufficient without adding that it is within the stream of tradition that interpretation is always done. Tradition is in no way a frozen stream, sealed off from the currents of time and history; it is always continuing to unfold. Yet simply to know oneself to be somewhere in this stream, without also knowing its source and goal, cannot guarantee that the direction in which further interpretation of tradition will move will be along truthful lines. Knowledge of the source and the goal of tradition—the alpha and omega—is what makes it possible to discern true from false directions in the movements of tradition. All of this implies a certain closure, or boundedness, to tradition. Although Gadamer's reflections on tradition do not exclude this element of closure, and at times point to it indirectly, they do not concern themselves very much with the way in which true interpretation may be distinguished from false. For this aspect of our account of tradition we will draw on Lossky's work with its stress on the church's fullness of knowledge. What Lossky brings to the table is a robust pneumatology—and hermeneutics without the eternal Spirit of truth can only be, in the end, and in the

8. Gadamer, *Truth and Method*, 272.
9. Ibid., 273.

worst sense, endless. At the same time, even while Lossky's vision fills in a lacuna that from the perspective of Christian theology is left by Gadamer's approach to hermeneutics, Lossky's approach itself has a certain potential to be misleading. This is due to Lossky's less than adequate appreciation of the temporal in his pneumatology. We will do well, then, to seek to hold the respective visions of these two thinkers together, Gadamer with his emphasis on the need for us to recognize where and when we do not know the answer to what confronts us in tradition, and Lossky with his emphasis on the fullness of knowledge available to us in the tradition of the church. We turn first to Gadamer and the emphasis on not knowing.

2. Tradition and Openness

If there is to be real apprehension of the truth that tradition bears, engagement with tradition must be interrogative. This is the thesis of Hans-Georg Gadamer in his well-known work *Truth and Method* in which genuine experience of being human is understood as a matter of "being aware of our finitude and limitedness," which itself comes from the "learned ignorance" that Socrates famously attained and preached, the "knowledge of not knowing."[10] It is from Plato's account of Socrates that Gadamer derives the principle of what he calls "*the priority of the question* in all knowledge and discourse."[11] He asserts that "the path of all knowledge leads through the question," and elaborates thus:

> To ask a question means to bring into the open. The openness of what is in question consists in the fact that the answer is not settled. It must still be undetermined, awaiting a decisive answer. The significance of questioning consists in revealing the questionability of what is questioned. It has to be brought to this state of indeterminacy, so that there is an equilibrium between pro and contra. The sense of every question is realized in passing through this state of indeterminacy, in which it becomes an open question.[12]

Although Gadamer's use of the word "indeterminacy" might set off alarms, it should be emphasized that unlike postmodern Deconstruction, which also lays great stress on the indeterminacy of meaning, Gadamer does so in a qualified way. He does not see it as an end, but speaks of it in the passage

10. Ibid., 362.
11. Ibid., 363.
12. Ibid.

above as a state that must be passed *through*. Implicitly he affirms the integral link between true questions and the real potential of their satisfactory resolution; this is evident in his allusion to the "decisive answer" that is awaited whenever a question is truly posed. When Gadamer writes, further on, "This is the real and fundamental nature of a question: namely to make things indeterminate,"[13] it is clear that he wishes not to make an ontological pronouncement on some fundamental indeterminacy of reality but only to underscore the way in which things must become indeterminate *to us* if we are to come to a true understanding of them. Our coming to recognize that we do not know is a preparatory knowledge, enabling us to be ready to receive—from outside ourselves, from the other with whom we are in dialogue—something that we can then recognize as true in contrast to what we had thought we had known to be true before.

For Gadamer, then, it is not as though there are questions and not answers. The priority of the question serves precisely to make it possible to *arrive* at an answer that is real and authentic rather than false and premature. Nonetheless in Gadamer's work overall the aspect of openness is emphasized and elaborated much more strongly than that of closure in his thinking about hermeneutics and tradition.

Why this is so is not difficult to grasp given Gadamer's purpose of exploding the Enlightenment's understanding of tradition as a closed and irrational world from which the present observer stands free, at an objectifying distance. One of the central insights of Gadamer's work is that there is no perch outside the flow of history from which to make detached judgments. "Every historian and philologist must reckon with the non-definitiveness of the horizon in which his understanding moves. . . . Historical tradition can be understood only as something always in the process of being defined by the course of events."[14] The openness of tradition in Gadamer's presentation has to do with our participation in it in the present. This participation is hermeneutical in its essence, since tradition responds to questions that must be ours. As Gadamer puts it, "questions concerning tradition that we are interested in pursuing are motivated in a special way by the present and its interests."[15] In a more comprehensive way he observes, "Tradition is not simply a permanent precondition; rather, we produce it ourselves inasmuch as we understand, participate in the evolution of tradition, and hence

---

13. Ibid., 375.

14. Ibid., 373. Gadamer continues in the same vein: "it is the course of events that brings out new aspects of meaning in historical material."

15. Ibid., 284.

further determine it ourselves."[16] Tradition's meaning is not enclosed within tradition as something inert; it comes to clarity ever anew only through our participation in an act of understanding. "For tradition is a genuine partner in dialogue, and we belong to it, as does the I with a Thou."[17]

In an important passage on tradition and openness, Gadamer sheds further light on this notion of mutuality in the hermeneutical task of understanding.

> To be situated within a tradition does not limit the freedom of knowledge but makes it possible. . . . Knowing and recognizing this constitutes the . . . highest type of hermeneutical experience: the openness to tradition characteristic of historically effected consciousness. It too has a real analogue in the I's experience of the Thou. In human relations the important thing is, as we have seen, to experience the Thou truly as a Thou—i.e., not to overlook his claim but to let him really say something to us. Here is where openness belongs. But ultimately this openness does not exist only for the person who speaks; rather, anyone who listens is fundamentally open. Without such openness to one another there is no genuine human bond. Belonging together always also means being able to listen to one another. When two people understand each other, this does not mean that one person "understands" the other. Similarly, "to hear and obey someone" (auf jemanden hören) does not mean simply that we do blindly what the other desires. We call such a person slavish (hörig). Openness to the other, then, involves recognizing that I myself must accept some things that are against me, even though no one else forces me to do so. . . . This is the parallel to the hermeneutical experience.[18]

The epistemological grounds on which "I myself must accept some things that are against me" are not laid out by Gadamer. What is certainly implied, however, is that *it is because they are true* that I must accept such things I would not otherwise have wished to accept. Also implied is that I have the means to recognize them as true, and to submit myself to them in a free act of obedience. Gadamer argues that none of this is possible in our relationship to tradition without our first passing through the *not knowing* associated with the question.

Interestingly, then, there is one level on which Gadamer shares, with the Orthodox archbishop quoted earlier, a critical view of the modern

16. Ibid., 293.
17. Ibid., 358.
18. Ibid., 361.

person's presumption to be able to "know better" than his or her forebears. The other, the "Thou" that in Gadamer's reflections is identified as tradition, has something to say to me that has its own claim and to which therefore I must listen and be open. I cannot simply make it say whatever I want, for that would be to deny the otherness of tradition, its status as a "thou." But Gadamer (unlike the Orthodox Archbishop quoted earlier) has a critique also of the kind of slavish, blind obedience to tradition that would effectively deny my own status as an "I." In other words, tradition does not simply supply the answers, to which I submit. I must engage in a genuine dialogue with it, for it is open. The *not knowing* with which I enter into this dialogue is not to be misunderstood as a matter simply of *my not knowing* as much or as well as the *tradition knows*, as though the latter were an open book, ripe for immediate application to my present set of questions. Rather, it is a more complex matter of my not knowing what the tradition itself means to say to my questions.

This is where Gadamer's sense of tradition parts ways with the Orthodox Archbishop's conception. According to Gadamer, just what tradition meant by expressing a certain thing is itself a hermeneutical question. Every statement, every word that comes to us from within tradition is understandable only as an answer to a question. So the process of coming to understand a text is that of coming to understand the question to which it is an answer.[19] Catholic ecclesiologists such as Francis Sullivan and Avery Cardinal Dulles have perceived this and have done much to draw out its implications in relation to the meaning of magisterial texts in Catholic tradition; they have sought to dispel the notion that such texts can be apprehended without coming to understand the questions to which they were answers at the time they were written. So, for example, the meaning of the bull *Unam sanctam* (1302) of Pope Boniface VIII, which contains the words, "Furthermore we declare, state and define that for every human creature it is necessary for salvation to be subject to the Roman pontiff," can be grasped only in the context of Boniface's conflict with Philip the Fair of France, which led Boniface to develop his "medieval theory about the supremacy of the spiritual power over the temporal power, giving the pope as head of Christendom the authority to 'institute and to judge' temporal rulers."[20] It would therefore be a gross distortion of the statement's significance were it to be applied to today's world in accordance with what would seem to be its plain sense (which would mean that Protestant or Orthodox Christians cannot be saved). As Sullivan explains, "[Boniface's] theory is obviously dependent on

19. Ibid., 370, quoting R. G. Collingwood's *Autobiography*.
20. Sullivan, *Creative Fidelity*, 87–88.

the cultural situation of Europe in the middle ages, when kings and emperors were crowned by popes, and as Christians were subject to their spiritual authority."[21] It can be seen from this example that the act of *interpreting*, rather than just accepting at face value, the fourteenth-century pontiff's statement, far from being a matter of presuming to know better than he knew, actually arises out of a humble recognition of not having immediate access to the meaning of his statement in the first place.

Gadamer also insisted on another step beyond this. It is not enough, he said, to revisit the historical circumstances in order to get back into focus the question that a given text or dogmatic ruling answered initially. Gadamer asserts that the hermeneutical task of understanding must be more than "a kind of reconstruction which in effect repeats the process whereby the text came into being."[22] Understanding in a real and authentic sense is impossible without its being preceded or prompted by a question that is current, open for oneself. As Gadamer writes, "To understand a question means to ask it." What was once a question for others but is no longer one for us cannot produce understanding of the kind that Gadamer has in mind.

> Only in an inauthentic sense can we talk about understanding questions that one does not pose oneself—e.g., questions that are outdated or empty. We understand how certain questions came to be asked in particular historical circumstances. Understanding such questions means, then, understanding the particular presuppositions whose demise makes such questions "dead." An example is perpetual motion. The horizon of meaning of such questions is only apparently still open. They are no longer understood as questions. For what we understand, in such cases, is precisely that there is no question.[23]

3. Tradition and Closure

Any comprehensive approach to tradition in which "there is no question" is inadequate. Gadamer's reflections on the subject make this much clear. Tradition without the indeterminacy of which Gadamer speaks would be simply annihilating of the humanity of those who inhabit it. Where it brooks no question, tradition becomes merely the haven of those unwilling to endure the struggle to come to clarity, to live in the tension of *docta ignorantia*.

---

21. Ibid., 88.
22. Gadamer, *Truth and Method*, 373.
23. Ibid., 375.

However, it has also become apparent, if not as much emphasized by Gadamer explicitly, that what is really at issue is the tension not just of knowing that one does not know, but the incomparably more fruitful tension of knowing that one does not know *what may yet be known*, to oneself and to others.

For from the point of view of Christian anthropology, simply to know is impossible and unreal; it is to deny one's finitude and creatureliness. (This is the standard and apt critique of positivism.) Yet simply to know that one does not know is also inadequate and unreal, in a different way; for this is to deny the reality of God's communion with us. (Here lies the problem with skepticism.) To know that one does not know what may yet be known: this is the complete expression of what it is to live in the genuine tension of Christian faith. Moreover, it is not only at the end of history that what one knows one does not yet know may become known. There is always the potential for it to become known before the end of history—by the turn of the century, by decade's end, before next year expires. In what Gregory of Nyssa wrote in reference to the beauty of God, that "it is constantly being discovered anew," one finds both the principle of not knowing and that of coming to know. Nyssa adds that God's beauty "is always seen as something new and strange in comparison with what the mind has always understood. And as God continues to reveal himself, man continues to wonder. . ."[24]

For Vladimir Lossky, Tradition is the mode by which we come to know what is true. It is "the unique mode of receiving Revelation."[25] Although Lossky will lay stress positively on knowledge and our capacity to receive and transmit it in the bosom of the church, at least two elements distinguish his thought from epistemological positivism in the usual sense. First, Lossky explicitly rejects the view that the content of tradition is always able to be grasped straightforwardly by those who merely wish to adhere to it. Like Gadamer he is clear in saying that critical discernment on the part of those living in the present is essential for the faithful carrying on of tradition. Lossky writes that "the Tradition is in no way automatic," and explains,

> it is the condition of the Church having an infallible consciousness, but it is not a mechanism which will infallibly make known the Truth outside and above the consciousness of individuals, outside all deliberation and all judgment. In fact, if Tradition is a faculty of judging in the Light of the Holy Spirit, it obliges those who wish to know the Truth in the Tradition to make incessant efforts: one does not remain in the Tradition by a certain

---

24. Gregory of Nyssa, *Homilies on the Song of Songs*, 11 (246).
25. Lossky, "Tradition and Traditions," 155.

historical inertia, by keeping as a "tradition received from the Fathers" all that which, by force of habit, flatters a certain devout sensibility. On the contrary, it is by substituting this sort of "traditions" for the Tradition of the Holy Spirit living in the Church that one runs the most risk of finding oneself finally outside the Body of Christ. It must not be thought that the conservative attitude alone is salutary, nor that heretics are always "innovators."[26]

To say that there is no possibility of remaining in the Tradition except by making "incessant efforts" to know the Truth is to acknowledge that one does not and cannot immediately or automatically know already what the Tradition authentically says. Interpretation is necessary. Lossky in a subsequent passage goes as far as to say that "Tradition represents the critical spirit of the Church."[27] Although Lossky makes plain, as Gadamer does not, that the principle of critical discernment is none other than the Holy Spirit, there is, in both thinkers, a shared perception that only by means of an effortful discernment is the true meaning of tradition disclosed. Lossky, then, would not be likely to disagree with Gadamer's central contention that *the condition of knowing that one does not know* is an essential state of mind with which one must embark upon the hermeneutical task of understanding, if one's encounter with tradition is to be a real and dynamic encounter. The encounter is implicitly dialogic for Lossky, as well; for it is the encounter with the Holy Spirit, whose presence in the task of interpretative judgment *and* in the content being interpreted is simultaneous: *in thy light shall we see light*. Interpretation and tradition are one. Both are of God—and both are participated in by man.

In a second respect, Lossky makes clear his departure from any form of epistemological positivism when he draws a connection between Tradition and silence. Lossky introduces this idea with the help of a quotation of St. Ignatius of Antioch: "He who possesses in truth the word of Jesus can hear even its silence."[28] The notion that there is always something more to hear than words themselves is indicated by Jesus, Lossky reminds us, in His oft-repeated appeal: "He who has ears to hear, let him hear." Lossky observes about this, "The words of Revelation have then a margin of silence which cannot be picked up by the ears of those who are outside."[29] It is this

26. Ibid., 155–56.

27. Ibid., 156.

28. St. Ignatius, *Letter to the Ephesians*, 15:2, quoted by Lossky, "Tradition and Traditions," 150.

29. Lossky, "Tradition and Traditions," 150–51.

margin of silence surrounding the Word and belonging to it that makes of it a living Word. So Lossky is able to draw the conclusion, full of implications for hermeneutics, "Tradition is Silence."[30] He quotes St. Basil on the theme: "There is also a form of silence, namely the obscurity used by the Scripture, which is intended in order to make it difficult to gain understanding of the teachings, for the profit of readers."[31]

We may notice again that within the silence of which Basil speaks, identified by Lossky *as* Tradition, understanding is gained not at once or automatically but only with difficulty. Lossky writes,

> This silence of the Scriptures could not be detached from them: it is transmitted by the Church with the words of Revelation as the very condition of their reception. If it could be opposed to words (always on the horizontal plane, where they express the revealed Truth), this silence which accompanies words implies no kind of insufficiency or lack of fulness of Revelation, nor the necessity of adding to it anything whatever. It signifies that the revealed mystery, to be truly received as fullness, demands a conversion towards the vertical plane, in order that one may be able to "comprehend with all saints" not only what is the "breadth and length" of Revelation, but also its "depth and its "height" (Eph 3:18).[32]

In this conception of Tradition as silence, a silence "transmitted by the Church with the words of Revelation as the very condition of their reception," Lossky contributes the crucial idea that the fullness of the meaning of Revelation is always something more than any of tradition's transmitted words can ever convey alone. The "silence" that is transmitted along with the words is the vehicle of this "something more." The silence might also be considered as a space, a distance—what Lossky calls a "margin." We may say that it is the arena in which the struggle occurs (of which Basil speaks in the quotation above), the struggle to gain understanding: at once a hermeneutical struggle and, as Lossky suggests when he mentions conversion, a spiritual struggle.

Lossky is correct to say that there is no contradiction between the margin of silence and the fullness of Revelation. To the latter there is no need of adding anything. Revelation would not somehow be *more* full were the space of silence to be filled in; rather, the silence is itself constitutive of the

---

30. Ibid., 151.
31. Basil the Great, *De Spiritu Sancto*, 27 (pg. 32, col. 189 BC), quoted in ibid., 150.
32. Ibid.

Revelation, which is complete. God has indeed revealed Himself fully in Jesus Christ.

In one sense, certainly, this is so: there is no further word to add to this definitive Word of God. Yet in another and equally certain sense this one Word of God must be continually spoken anew, into the world of sinning human beings and their circumstances, particular circumstances misshapen in such particular ways, in such new combinations, that it will always be inadequate simply to apply an old word to them. By and large the old word in the new circumstance will mean something different from what it meant before. At each stage of the life of the church it is necessary to speak the complete and self-subsistent Word of God by means of a fresh transposition. On the simplest but also undoubtedly the most essential level of the church's life this occurs in the homily, which is a midrash on the Gospel. The homily steps into the silence that Lossky identifies as Tradition. But also, of course, the homily must bring forth from out of that margin of silence something that is not strictly confined to it, namely words—words adequate to the shape of the mystery that only the silence can measure. Lossky writes, "it is in the light of the fullness that one knows 'in part,' and it is always through this fullness that the Church judges whether or not the partial knowledge expressed in this or that doctrine belongs to Tradition."[33]

Here and elsewhere in Lossky's exposition, we find a pair of correlations: first, a correlation between the "fullness of knowledge" and *silence*; second, a correlation between "knowledge in part" and *speech*. Doctrinal formulations belong to the realm of partial knowledge, yet they retain a correspondence to the realm of the fullness of knowledge. It is by the fullness of knowledge (surpassing speech) that the church judges whether or not the partial knowledge (articulated as speech) "belongs." Lossky writes that when in the world to come we come to know in full, the knowledge in part, *ek merous*, "will not be suppressed because it was false, but because its role was merely to make us adhere to the fullness which surpasses every human faculty of knowledge."[34]

In the background of these reflections are, of course, fundamental assertions of St. Paul, above all the passage in 1 Corinthians 13: "Love never ends; as for prophecies, they will pass away; as for tongues, they will cease; as for knowledge, it will pass away. For our knowledge is imperfect and our prophecy is imperfect; but when the perfect comes, the imperfect will pass away. . . . Now I know in part; then I shall understand fully, even as I have been fully understood." Also pertinent is the statement Paul makes in

33. Ibid., 161.
34. Ibid.

2 Cor 12:4, speaking of himself in the third person: "and he heard things that cannot be told, which man may not utter." All of this certainly points to a kind of inadequacy of human speech to express the fullness of the transcendent mystery of God. Like the luminous darkness of the mystic's experience of God's presence, so there is an eloquent silence that may be more transparent to the divine reality than any word or words could be. Lossky's way of identifying tradition as silence is well warranted on these grounds.

At the same time, Lossky's association of fullness of knowledge with silence and his association of partial knowledge with speech may also have its limits and pitfalls. The biggest danger is that of a theology of speech and silence that would separate the one from the other, or would so privilege silence over speech that the latter would be relegated to something only instrumental. Lossky acknowledges, as we have seen, that the partial knowledge that speech imparts is not false, and this is important, but there is still a sense in which Lossky's presentation seems to locate speech / partial knowledge in the realm of the human, and silence / fullness of knowledge in the realm of the divine. But of course in the Incarnation, not only did the invisible become visible, but the ineffable became audible. Together with the passages of St. Paul adduced above, others of no less importance include the saying of Jesus in John 12:49–50, "All that I speak, I speak just as the Father told me," and Paul's words in 1 Thess 2:13: "And we also thank God constantly for this, that when you received the word of God which you heard from us, you accepted it not as the word of men but as what it really is, the word of God, which is at work in you believers." Not only within Scripture but in the ongoing life of God's people, there do exist words in the here and now that are perfectly adequate to the circumstances into which they are spoken. Since they are always embedded within the particulars of history, they can never render unnecessary for the future all effort to come to understand them, to interpret them anew, within the horizon of another context. But they are, nevertheless, just the right words for the occasion; nothing about them is inadequate to the fullness of truth as this comes to be embodied at a given moment and in reference to a particular question that has required response.

If Christian tradition means anything it is this: that God provides through His Holy Spirit, alive in those who subordinate themselves to Him in love, adequate words with which to speak God's will into circumstances in which that will has been in question on one point or another. God provides words with which to make His will known. "Do not be anxious how or what you are to answer or what you are to say; for the Holy Spirit will teach you in that very hour what you ought to say" (Luke 12:11b-12).[35] For human subjectivity this implies, again, an initial disposition of not knowing, in this case not knowing what to say. In order to be taught by the Holy Spirit how to speak truthfully one must first know that one does not already possess the knowledge; but one must also, of course, trust that that knowledge can be given and received in an adequate way. Something comes indeed to be said, and to be said adequately. Indeterminacy gives way to an authentic moment of closure. Where there had been a question, now there is not.

It should be said, in bringing our reflections on Lossky's perspective to a close, that Lossky does not always seem to give sufficient attention to the moment of perplexity prior to the moment of clarity. "At every moment of its history," Lossky writes, "the Church gives to its members the faculty of knowing the Truth in a fulness that the world cannot contain." But at every moment, does the church, comprised of her members, discern the Truth in its fullness? To say that the church is the "pillar and ground of the truth" (2 Tim 3:15) should not be taken to exclude the idea that the communication of the truth imparted by the Holy Spirit within and through the living communion of the church is a process that unfolds, that takes time. The working out of what the truth means and how it is to be lived can take decades or even centuries, during which, as the history of the church shows, God allows the church to go some time visibly doing and more or less thinking what it will come to see was wrong. Peter openly refused to have table fellowship with those who were not circumcised. This was after Pentecost. Peter and James and their entourage did not cease to be the church, even the very ones through whom decisions in the church must pass in order for them to be binding. There was really no question here of Paul's excommunicating Peter. It was necessary for him to convince Peter of the error of his, Peter's, ways, and Paul knew this was possible; but in any case while the dispute raged, and even in the moments before it sprang fully into the open and while something wrong in the church was being done, the church did not cease to be the church, the pillar and the ground of the truth—not even while it lived momentarily in error in its way of interpreting its own tradition and embodying that interpretation in the present.

It is noteworthy that what ensued between those who had the mind of Christ in the circumstances, Paul being the leading figure among them, and those like Peter who did not, was precisely a conversation, a dialogue, in which in the end Peter was forced—not by anything but his own aptitude for the truth—to admit what was against him. In some significant degree, he

---

35. Cf. also Exod 4:12, where God reassures Moses, "I will help you speak and will teach you what to say."

was convinced by the force of Paul's argument, made with all the gifts of human rhetoric and reason of which Paul was amply endowed. Lossky's ruminations sometimes give too little value to human dialogue on the horizontal plane. "The pure notion of Tradition can then be defined," Lossky writes, "by saying that it is the life of the Holy Spirit in the Church, communicating to each member of the Body of Christ the faculty of hearing, of receiving, of knowing the Truth in the Light which belongs to it, and not according to the natural light of human reason."[36] Is it necessary to set the two in opposition to each other? When Lossky writes in another place, "[Tradition] is not the content of Revelation, but the light that reveals it; it is not the word, but the living breath which makes the words heard at the same time as the silence from which it came,"[37] we are led at once to wonder why there must be an either-or between the content and the light, between the word and the breath (it would seem better at each turn to say "not only" rather than "not"). If the words can easily be misunderstood apart from the silence that is "the condition of their reception," it must also be said that it is possible for the silence that surrounds them to be sensed *from the words*. If this were not so, then it is hard to see what need there would be for anything *but* the silence. Why should there be words at all? We must say with all insistence that the silence of tradition does not swallow the world of speech up into itself but gives words their true weight and meaning.

4. "Sister Churches" and the Meaning of the Schism

By and large, those who object to the language of "sister churches" in recent Catholic-Orthodox relations view the Great Schism as something that *happened*. Those who support the expression, meanwhile, generally view the schism as something in the process of happening. In the first way of thinking, a completed event of the past is disclosive of the fullness of truth available in Tradition and dictates what is to be permitted in the present. In the second, an ambiguous event of the past awaits an interpretation in the present which will disclose the truth about that event more fully than has yet been wrought. In this second approach is contained the idea of the possibility that earlier interpretations of the ambiguous event were prematurely conclusive.

The unfolding life of the church is full of such moments of premature resolution: occasions when something seemed to be settled, only to be

---

36. Lossky, "Tradition and Traditions," 152.
37. Ibid., 151.

64   Part One—Tradition: Evangelical, Catholic, and Orthodox

recognized later on as something in need of being reopened and reexamined.[38] It would be possible to compile a long list of reversals, but perhaps no moment in Church history more memorably dramatizes the staunch refusal of the contemporary people of God to have their hands tied by decisions made in the past than does the event by which the Arsenite schism was brought to an end in the Byzantine Church of the early fourteenth century. Patriarch Arsenius had excommunicated the emperor, Michael VIII Palaiologos, for having blinded the preceding emperor, the young John IV Doukas Laskaris, of whom Michael had been the joint guardian together with Arsenius. In response to Arsenius' excommunication of him, emperor Michael VIII in 1265 deposed Arsenius, whose followers then for the next forty-five years rejected the Paleologan dynasty and all its patriarchal appointees, until the year 1310 (September 14 to be precise, the Feast of the Eevation of the Cross) when the two sides were reconciled. How their reconciliation occurred was by means of a ceremony held at Hagia Sophia in Constantinople at which, by the agreement of both parties, a document absolving all whom Arsenius had once anathametized was placed in the skeletal hand of Arsenius' exhumed corpse, freshly dressed for the occasion in his patriarchal vestments.

This episode amply demonstrates a profound conviction of the Byzantine churchmen of the period that tradition was not irrevocably fixed by previous generations but was still in some sense unfolding in the present. It might be tempting to view the episode cynically and suppose that the figure of Arsenius was being mocked or even somehow desecrated by being suited up in fanciful clothing and made to hold an envelope containing words that had never been his, but it would be more appropriate to view it as an utterly concrete enactment of the "I-Thou" character of the hermeneutics of tradition that Gadamer goes to such lengths to bring out. What Auden wrote in his elegy for W. B. Yeats, "The words of a dead man are modified in the guts of the living," might also be considered as a relevant statement of the same basic point: the dead could not possibly know in their own lifetime all of what they would effectively turn out to say to those who live after them. Like a chemical reaction, their words must come into contact with us, with our world of ideas and concerns, before their meaning for us can emerge, a meaning we must articulate with words of our own, new words to interpret the old. Whenever responsible scholars today proceed—as they must—to

---

38. According to Augustine (*De Trinitate*, Book II, prologue, para. 1), "there are two things which are very hard to tolerate in the mistakes people make: presumption, before the truth is clear, and defense of the false presumption when it has become so." On this view, the church should perhaps be willing to put more emphasis on its own track record of having gotten some things wrong on the way to getting them right.

"modify the words of a dead man," they are usually careful to note that they are not saying that the author actually *said* this or that, but only suggesting that the trajectory of the author's thought might open up avenues that may be reasonably understood to lead in this or that direction—we have become masters of the art of the tentative, imagining that our high standards of scholarship demand it. Of course the ancient practice was considerably less fussy: Second Isaiah, whoever he was (or she was, or they were), went right ahead and attributed to Isaiah himself brand new words that Second Isaiah was inspired to put forward in Isaiah's name. It is doubtful that the people of Israel of the sixth century BC when Second Isaiah composed his text were "fooled" that these were literally Isaiah's words, any more than the Byzantine Christians of 1310 were fooled into thinking that Arsenius had been literally the one to originate the words contained in the envelope held in his skeletal hand. Rather they understood instinctively what is also understood as a given in the field of hermeneutics: namely, that to think again, to add on, to re-state in new terms for new circumstances, has always been and will always be a necessity in the unfolding of any living tradition.

This is also why the doctrine of infallibility as it was initially put forward by the Franciscans in the thirteenth century was consistently opposed by all the popes of that time, who feared that its primary consequence would be to *limit* their sovereignty by tying their hands with the decisions of their predecessors (which was just what the Franciscans aimed to accomplish by it).[39] Even when Augustine made the famous remark, in the context of the controversy with the Pelagians, "Rome's reply has come: the case is closed," it is doubtful that he had in mind any idea that it would be inconceivable for future bishops of Rome to reconsider this or other matters which prior Roman bishops had decided; the point was rather that the "court of final appeal" had issued its verdict and that there could be no present response to it, other than obedience, that would be consistent with the order and unity of the church.

What neither the concept of Tradition nor that of the infallibility of the church or of its extraordinary magisterium can possibly mean is that there is no possibility for the body of the faithful, including their shepherds, to arrive any longer at any condition of not knowing. On the contrary, both concepts, those of tradition and of infallibility, presuppose, in their proper meaning, that the church *will* pass again and again through periods of not knowing what the true and orthodox position will turn out to have been

39. See Tierney, "Origins of Papal Infallibility." In its modern form, the dogma of infallibility had quite different underpinnings, which can be understood only within the framework of the rise of modern nationalism and the nineteenth-century Roman Catholic battle against Gallicanism.

on a given matter of doctrine with which the church is confronted in a new way. This includes matters that had seemed to be, in previous circumstances, "closed cases."

It seemed strange and incredible to some observers that nothing prevented Pope Paul VI and Patriarch Athenagoras I from revoking in 1965 the anathemas of 1054 between Rome and Constantinople. (Can you just do that?) Had the actual corpses of Michael Cerularius and Humbert of Candida been able to be located and exhumed, it is unlikely that enough of them would have been left for an envelope to be placed in anything still sufficiently intact to be recognized as a hand, and of course no such method of reinterpretation of the events of the past was going to be attempted in this case, as it had been in the circumstance of the fourteenth-century Arsenite schism. Yet with no less clarity of purpose, the pope and patriarch undertook to put an event of earlier history—centuries earlier in this case, rather than decades—in a new and different light by their action in the present. Paul VI and Athenagoras I together recognized that what the earlier historical event *meant* was still subject to history's further unfolding. In Gadamer's words, "Historical tradition can be understood only as something always in the process of being defined by the course of events."[40] Schism itself, in this perspective, is best understood as a question still in process of being answered: whether it will have turned out to be a permanent break, or an only partial and temporary fissure that never developed so far as to be a total rupture, cannot be determined without reference to where things go from here.

St. Basil of Caesarea recognized this aspect of schism as a question with reference to the future when he wrote of the "old authorities" that "they used the names of heresies, of schisms, and of unlawful congregations. By *heresies* they mean men who were altogether broken off and alienated in matters relating to the actual faith; by *schisms* men who had separated for some ecclesiastical reasons and questions capable of mutual solutions; by *unlawful congregations* gatherings held by disorderly presbyters or bishops or by uninstructed laymen."[41] Basil's point in making these distinctions was to say that only in the case of heresies[42] were baptisms not accepted. As he put it in the same letter, "it seemed good to the ancient authorities to reject the baptism of heretics altogether, but to admit that of schismatics, on the

---

40. Gadamer, *Truth and Method*, 373. See above in the present essay.

41. Basil of Caesarea, *Ep. clxxxviii*, I, 223–24, original emphasis.

42. It may be noted, incidentally, that numerous heterodoxies that are commonly described today as heresies would not have qualified for that designation in Basil's judgment. As he used the term, not even Arians qualified as heretics, but were counted as schismatics.

ground that they still belonged to the Church."[43] Obviously, the sense in which the schismatic did still belong to the church was more ambiguous than in the case of others who were not separated. Indeed, Basil also envisioned circumstances where the act of schism brought upon the schismatics a loss of "the grace of the Holy Spirit, for it ceased to be imparted when the continuity was broken."[44] On the whole, what comes through from Basil's reflections on the topic is the basic insight that each Christian division requires discernment and interpretation.

Lacking from Basil's discussion, however, is anything but the utmost confidence that the "old authorities" were all in perfect agreement. Basil may have recognized the need to discern and interpret each schism in its own right, but at least in this text he does not conceive of the possibility that the relevant passages from the "old authorities" might have conflicted in such a way that presented more questions than answers. Basil does not make explicit, at least, any moment of "not knowing" what to make of the texts he was consulting from tradition. In the scholarship of modern theologians, it is quite different; here admissions of perplexity are common. Indeed on the specific topic of ecclesial division, Fr. Georges Florovsky felt free to admit a certain perplexity as characteristic of the Eastern Orthodox tradition as a whole. Writing of what he called "the problem of the nature and meaning of schisms and divisions in the Church," he observed that "in the East, for centuries, this problem has never been faced as a genuinely theological issue."[45] Waclaw Hryniewicz, a Polish Catholic theologian active in Catholic-Orthodox dialogue, hints at a similar kind of collective, ecclesial perplexity when he speaks of "ecumenical aporetics," the word *aporía* in its Christian context deriving, as Hryniewicz notes, from the passage in St. Paul's Second Letter to the Corinthians when the apostle exclaims that "we are perplexed, but not driven to despair" (ἀπορούμενοι ἀλλ' οὐκ ἐξαπορούμενοι [2 Cor 4:8]). Hryniewicz observes, "*Aporía* means an apparently insurmountable difficulty or contradiction.... To put it more descriptively: we do not know what to do, the situation seems to be desperate, we worry, there is no solution to our difficulties, but nevertheless we do not give up."[46] Hryniewicz does not interpret the specific issue of "sister churches" in these terms himself, but his notion of aporetics has an important application in this context. Churches that have long identified themselves by their division from one another now identify themselves *with* one another across

---

43. Basil, *Ep. clxxxviii*.
44. Ibid.
45. Florovsky, "St. Cyprian and St. Augustine on Schism," 48.
46. Hryniewicz, *Challenge of Our Hope*, 45.

that division, prior to and in anticipation of bridging it. As used by Catholics and Orthodox in the twentieth century, the term "sister churches" has a significance it did not bear in previous epochs: namely, the significance of surprised discovery, which can only be understood against the background of the centuries-old schism. Because, until recently, each tradition had perceived the schism as an irreversible fact of history, taking the step of calling one another sister churches really has meant that each institution has put itself at odds with *itself*. The expression implies a self-critique by each tradition of its own standard account of the division. It makes the ongoing circumstance of the division appear, suddenly, nonsensical. That is, either the phrase itself is nonsensical—unable to withstand the reality and the logic of the schism—or the schism is what is nonsensical, as the phrase serves to illuminate. Whichever of the two shall turn out to be the case, in the meantime there is certainly a contradiction, an *aporía* or impasse in which the two traditions together may be able to say (so long as the schism persists, together with the new mutual recognition as sister churches) "we do not know what to do," thereby entering into the condition of *docta ignorantia* that Gadamer rightly describes as necessary for hermeneutics.

Would not such a moment of true and blessed ignorance, of not knowing what to do, have to have preceded the hermeneutical act of those fourteenth-century Christians in Constantinople whose unexpected way out of their impasse involved exhuming the body of the former patriarch Arsenius? Theirs was not the "what are we to do" of the North American Orthodox archbishop quoted earlier who based his opposition to "sister churches" on just this question, "*What are we to do* with the Fathers and the Councils . . . ?"—as though there were no option between an unthinking obedience to the plain sense of their words and an annihilation of their authority. The important element in the Archbishop's manner of posing the question is that it was rhetorical rather than sincere; in other words, for him *there was no question*, no real question as to what to do, at all; all had been already decided, for him and for us, by "the Fathers," whose perspective on the schism in their own day he claimed to be able to grasp fully and *to extract meaning from simply and directly* for an understanding of the schism today. But if, as I am arguing, the fourteenth-century Christians who exhumed Patriarch Arsenius' corpse also said to themselves, prior to doing so, "What are we to do?" their question would obviously have been much more desperate and real, and their answer was different: it was to dig up their Father in the faith and make him speak new words—which is what happens whenever we participate in the hermeneutics of tradition.

5. Conclusion

Christian tradition entails a continual process of discerning whether evidently resolved questions have really been resolved, not only for their own time but for the present as well. Not every challenge to old answers will prove to be warranted or will bring about different answers for today. Nor is there anything wrong with a tradition in which many old answers still hold. Gadamer, we saw at the end of section II, described questions that once were open but no longer are so as questions that have come to be "dead," and it might be a short step from saying this to saying that any tradition in which questions are too surely or too regularly resolved is itself a dead or a deadening tradition. In other words, it might easily be imagined that where tradition is concerned, questions are enlivening and answers stultifying. But of course it is not to this conclusion that the argument in this essay has led. Instead, the argument has led to the conclusion that where something that is actually still a question is denied the status of a question this is stultifying of tradition, and that where something that is no longer a question continues to be pursued as one, this, too, is stultifying of tradition. Openness and closure are both proper to tradition, and the important thing is not to prefer one over the other but to know where and when each is in order.

In the New Testament, a strong caution against applying the principle of openness in a general or indiscriminate way is clearly offered by Paul in his complaint about those who are "always learning, and never arrive at the knowledge of the truth" (2 Tim 3:7). On the other hand, the idea that the members of the church possess the truth in such a way as to leave no aspect or implication of it obscure to them is also precluded by the statement of Jesus that the Spirit will "guide you into all the truth" (John 16:13). If in Gadamer's philosophy of hermeneutics, with its emphasis on the "priority of the question," there is a danger of never arriving at the knowledge of the truth, or, perhaps worse, of conceiving of such arrival at knowledge as a sort of death, in Lossky's theology of tradition with its attention to the "fullness of knowledge" available to the church there is a danger of imagining that the truth that the church apprehends is immediate and atemporal, transcending the time-bound processes of speech and dialogue.

To be able to perceive and avoid closure that is premature and yet always to be, as it were, open to closure that is authentic—this, one could say, is the essence of theology, and it is what is really at issue in the hermeneutics of tradition. Where the question of the schism between Catholic and Orthodox Christianity is concerned, each tradition has had its own settled answer unsettled in the past half-century or so, not least by the expression "sister churches" which gained currency in bilateral relations from the 1960s to the end of the twentieth century. Although theologians in these decades have addressed and discussed numerous issues of real theological and ecclesiological importance that have long been associated with the division, an overarching challenge that remains, and perhaps will remain for members of both traditions is the broader issue of how one's own tradition could go from excluding to embracing the other without losing continuity with itself. Up to this point, Catholic ecclesiologists have perhaps done more than their Orthodox counterparts to prepare the ground for an appreciation of how tradition's flexibility and openness are to be properly acknowledged and even celebrated, as not mere arbitrariness. In any case, further theological reflection is needed to give Christians of both traditions the compass by which to steer a course between positivism and skepticism. Is it not a struggle for every Christian, today, neither to be puffed up with the zealot's confidence of already possessing the whole truth on every key issue of our time, nor to be shot through with a kind of exhaustion and scorn for the very notion that there could be any use in trying to resolve such issues, since it is all so much vain groping in the dark? The bifurcation between theological arrogance and indifference seems to be a product of a deep crisis in the hermeneutics of tradition—a crisis that may be encapsulated by the false alternatives: (1) my tradition knows and can tell me everything; (2) it knows and can tell me nothing. As an antidote to this false either-or, it might be helpful if our pastors were to lead us in collective prayer not only to address—as must always be done—the needs of the hungry and the poor but also to receive from God the wisdom to come to clarity about the open questions of our time, and even before that to perceive, together, what these questions are. Surely, one of them is the question of the Schism: the question of whether and in what way the long-separated Christian East and Christian West will turn out to have been, and to be, one, or two. To bring this question into focus as a question and to pray, together, from our perplexity even in the face of all that we have thought we have known: "Lord, we do not know what to do," and then to ask God to show us: perhaps then and only then, in the context of the full, public and liturgical acknowledgment of our ecclesial *docta ignorantia*, will the answer(s) come. Theology must better and more broadly articulate how this ecclesial *docta ignorantia* is consistent with the church's identity as the pillar and the ground of the truth. By doing so, it will offer a service of preparing the whole people of God to share more consciously in the holy task of "passing through the questions" that continually arise in the life of the church.

Bibliography

Archbishop Dmitri of Dallas and the South. Letter of September 23, 1994 to His Beatitude, Theodosius, Archbishop of Washington and Metropolitan of All America and Canada. Obtained through the archives of the Chancery of the Orthodox Church in America, Syosset, NY.

Augustine. *De Trinitate (The Trinity)*. Translated by Edmund Hill. The Works of Saint Augustine: A Translation for the 21st Century I/5, edited by John E. Rotelle. Hyde Park, NY: New City, 1991.

Basil of Caesarea. *Ep. clxxxviii*. In vol. 8 of *The Nicene and Post-Nicene Fathers*, Series 2. Edited by Philip Schaff. 1886–1889. 14 vols. Reprint, New York: Cosimo Classics, 2007.

Blowers, Paul M., and Robert Louis Wilken. *On the Cosmic Mystery of Jesus Christ: Selected Writings of St. Maximus the Confessor*. Crestwood, NY: St. Vladimir's Seminary Press, 2003.

Cohen, Will T. "The Concept of Sister Churches in Catholic-Orthodox Relations since Vatican II." PhD diss., The Catholic University of America, 2010.

———. "Sacraments and the Visible Unity of the Church." *Ecclesiology* 4 (2007) 68–87.

Collingwood, R. G. *An Autobiography*. Oxford: Oxford University Press, 1982.

Erickson, John. "On the Cusp of Modernity: The Canonical Hermeneutics of St. Nikodemus the Haghiorite (1748–1809)." *St. Vladimir's Theological Quarterly* 42 (1998) 45–66.

Florovsky, Georges. "St. Cyprian and St. Augustine on Schism." In *Ecumenism II: A Historical Approach*. Collected Works of Georges Florovsky 14. Belmont, MA: Norland, 1972.

Gadamer, Hans-Georg. *Truth and Method*. 2nd rev. ed. New York: Continuum, 1989.

Gregory of Nyssa. *Homilies on the Song of Songs*. In *From Glory to Glory: Texts from Gregory of Nyssa's Mystical Writings*, edited and translated by Herbert Musurillo, selected and introduced by Jean Daniélou. Crestwood, NY: St. Vladimir's Seminary Press, 2001.

Hryniewicz, Waclaw. *The Challenge of Our Hope: Christian Faith in Dialogue*. Washington, DC: Council for Research in Values and Philosophy, 2007.

———. "Ecumenism and Kenotic Dimensions of Ecclesiology." In *The Challenge of Our Hope: Christian Faith in Dialogue*. Washington, DC: Council for Research in Values and Philosophy, 2007.

Lossky, Vladimir. "Tradition and Traditions." In *In the Image and Likeness of God*, 141–68. Crestwood, NY: St. Vladimir's Seminary Press, 1985.

Louth, Andrew. *Maximus the Confessor*. Early Church Fathers. London: Routledge, 1996.

Meyendorff, John. "Eglises-soeurs: Implications ecclésiologiques du Tomos Agapis." *Istina* 20 (1975) 35–46.

Pascal. *Pensées*. London: Fount, 1995.

Sullivan, Francis. *Creative Fidelity: Weighing and Interpreting Documents of the Magisterium*. 1996. Reprint, Eugene, OR: Wipf and Stock, 2003.

Tierney, B. "Origins of Papal Infallibility." *Journal of Ecumenical Studies* 8 (1971) 852–62.

Ware, Timothy. *Eustratios Argenti: A Study of the Greek Church under Turkish Rule*. Oxford: Clarendon, 1964.

Part Two

Tradition: Ancient, Late-Medieval, and Modern Analyses

4

The Holiness of the Church in North African Theology

J. Patout Burns Jr.

This essay traces the interpretative changes in the explanation of the holiness of the church and its power to sanctify in Christian North Africa from the late second century through the middle of the fifth century. During this period, a closely related set of issues was addressed, using an overlapping set of scriptural texts. As circumstances and even techniques of interpretation changed, scriptural texts were used in different ways and combinations to develop theologies which would justify practices of admitting, retaining, or excluding sinners from the communion and clergy of the church. Since second- and third-century justifications were generally known to the fourth- and fifth-century writers, these later theologians were both interpreting the scripture texts to develop explanations and criticizing the interpretations (and explanations) offered by their predecessors. In this sense, then, this essay attempts to track the interpretation of a theological tradition.[1]

1. Tertullian's Protest

The second-century Carthaginian Christian, Tertullian, raised issues with his church's practices of baptism and repentance for sins committed after baptism. In the first instance, he insisted that baptism could be effective in

---

1. For a fuller discussion of the issues, see Burns, "The Holiness of the Church in North African Theology."

purifying a candidate from sin only when it was performed within the unity of the true church. Communities that professed a false belief, and thus failed to relate to the true God, were incapable of sanctifying their initiants. The second issue was the bishop's claim to the power to forgive already baptized sinners whose illicit sexual practices violated the Christian body as a temple of God and to readmit them to the eucharistic communion. His explanations of the sources and proper exercise of the church's power to forgive sins were developed in a series of treatises.

The dispute over baptism arose because a female minister preached a false doctrine and practiced a false ritual of Christian initiation, one that did not use washing with water.[2] Tertullian argued that baptism could be given and received only by those who properly professed God and Christ, and who performed the traditional Christian ritual.[3] These restrictions were not the policy of the African church at that time, though they were adopted in the decades following Tertullian's death. He further argued that any person who had received baptism or participated in the eucharist could perform those rituals for others. For the sake of good order and to prevent competition within the church, the bishop had the primary responsibility for presiding at baptism and the eucharist. In the absence of the bishop and in case of emergency, any Christian could and should perform baptism; in private celebration where the clergy were not present, anyone could preside at the eucharist. He restricted the exercise of these powers to the male members of the community, however, on the grounds that women were forbidden to exercise a leadership role in the church.[4]

The second dispute was more acrimonious because it involved members of the community rather than an outsider. Adapting the apostolic decision reported in Acts 15:29, which forbade uncleanness, idolatry, and blood, church leaders had refused reconciliation and readmission to communion to baptized Christians who were guilty of adultery, apostasy, or murder. The conflict in Carthage focused on the first of these sins: sexual relations with a person to whom the Christian was not married. Tertullian himself argued that the list should be expanded to include all sins forbidden by the Decalogue.[5] Persons guilty of the three sins were excluded from communion, urged to undertake penance, and promised the community's intercession as they sought forgiveness from God.[6] Faced with a lifetime of repentance and an uncertain judgment by Christ, these sinners sought alternate means

2. *Bapt.* 1–2.
3. *Bapt.* 12.3,15; *Pud.* 19.5
4. *Bapt.* 1–2, 17.4–5.
5. *Pud.* 12,18–19; *Marc.* 4.9.6; *Idol.* 1.
6. *Pud.* 3.

to regain the relative security of the church's eucharistic communion. They appealed for help to Christians who had "confessed" Christ before imperial authorities and as a consequence were imprisoned in anticipation of judicial review or already serving sentences of hard labor in the mines. Their confession of Christ had itself indicated the presence and operation of the Holy Spirit (Matt 10:16–20). Moreover, Christ was suffering in them and could be petitioned by them.[7] They were, therefore, judged to have intercessory power which could gain from God the forgiveness of sins normally considered beyond the power and authority of the church. Not to be outdone by these confessors, the bishop of Carthage apparently claimed the power to forgive at least one such sin, adultery, on the basis of his episcopal office. The Carthaginian bishop evidently regarded himself and each of his colleagues as successors of Peter, inheriting his power of binding and loosing, and exercising it in their individual churches. This claim was different from the one later made by the bishop of Rome to be chief among his fellow bishops. That Petrine office had not yet been plausibly claimed for the Roman bishop alone.

Tertullian denied the claims made for both the confessors and the bishop. The confessors, he observed, were still struggling to secure their own salvation and must not presume to promise God's favor to another. They should be content with achieving the forgiveness of their own sins through their witness to Christ. The authority given to Peter, he argued, was personal rather than official; it was not passed to anyone else. He had exercised that power in the establishment of the church: receiving Gentiles, limiting the authority of the Mosaic Law, and punishing severely those who lied to God. Bishops must regard themselves as servants of the divine power to forgive, without authority to extend its exercise beyond the limits set by the apostles (Acts 15:29) or more recently announced through Christian prophets by the Holy Spirit.[8]

In his treatise *On Modesty* responding to the claims of the bishop of Carthage, Tertullian added a new interpretation of the church's power to forgive. He established a relationship between the gift of the Holy Spirit and the power of forgiveness, asserting that the Spirit did bestow this power on the church, as a whole, rather than on the bishops alone. That power was to be exercised only by persons who were actually endowed with the Spirit, which was manifest by their following the rigorous discipline of the New Prophecy movement that itself required the withholding of forgiveness of all serious post-baptismal sin. This restriction was ordered by the Spirit, he

---

7. *Pud.* 22; *Mart.* 1.6; *Fug.* 14.3.
8. *Pud.* 21.

explained, so that the granting of mercy for past sins did not itself encourage future sinning.[9] The proper practice was that any who had sinned seriously could undertake penance and then appeal to the mercy of Christ at the judgment. The church could encourage and intercede for them but could neither grant forgiveness nor readmit them to its communion.[10]

Tension between two foundations for the church's power to forgive sins was already evident in Tertullian's time. The bishops claimed the power as belonging to the office established in Peter. That power was more generally assigned to the confessors, and by Tertullian to ascetic followers of the New Prophecy. The church's power to sanctify by forgiving sins would be more clearly identified with the operation of the Holy Spirit and its exercise regularly restricted to the clergy. The link between the clergy and the Spirit became the focus of debate.

2. Episcopal Decisions

During the four decades separating Tertullian's controversies from the episcopacy of Cyprian, the bishops of Africa changed their practice on the two issues Tertullian had raised. They formally approved the forgiveness of adultery and allowed these sinners to return to the communion of the church after appropriate public penance. No surviving record details the specific arguments that were used to justify this new policy. Cyprian later claimed that the change had not resulted in a significant increase in sinning or decrease in ascetic practice.[11] In the same or a different synod, the bishops adopted the policy Tertullian had advocated about heretical baptism. They agreed to require converts from communities professing a false faith to submit to a new baptism upon entering their church. Subsequent debate about converts from schismatic communions who shared the orthodox faith and creed indicates that this decision was focused on baptism performed by heretics who did not profess the same faith as these bishops and their congregations.[12]

---

9. *Pud.* 21–22.
10. Tert. *Paen.* 7.10; *Pud.* 3.3–5, 6.1, 9.20, 18.18, 19.6.
11. *Ep.* 55.20.2, 21.1.
12. *Ep.* 71.4.1; 73.3.1.

3. Cyprian's Theology of Church Holiness

The experience of the Decian persecution in the middle of the third century forced the Christian bishops to revisit the decisions on baptism and post-baptismal sins; they had to adapt and justify their practices anew. The crisis and response to the challenges of the persecution developed over nearly a decade. Many Christians failed to confess Christ during the enforcement of the imperial edict, and some willingly performed the required idolatrous ritual. Conflicts over the church's power to forgive and reconcile apostates—willing, reluctant, or coerced—resulted in a division of the African church into three competing communions. This in turn brought new questions about the efficacy of baptism performed in a community that shared faith in the same God and Christ but broke communion over the disciplining of sinners. Cyprian of Carthage extended the earlier condemnation of heretics to schismatics. He claimed that only a church which maintained historical continuity with the apostles and communion with the rest of the Christian world actually held and exercised the power to sanctify and forgive.

The initial conflict arose over the church's power to forgive the sin of apostasy, committed by either failing to confess or actually denying Christ when confronted by the Roman authorities. The bishops were not confident that they had the power to forgive a sin that had been committed against Christ himself and to admit to communion a sinner whom Christ had threatened to condemn in heaven, according to Matt 10:32–33. Their prior decision to offer reconciliation to adulterers did not provide a precedent for this case.[13] During and immediately after the persecution, Cyprian recommended the public reversal of the apostasy by confession of Christ before imperial authorities as the only sure way to repent of the sin and secure salvation. The anticipated consequences of such a course of action—certain suffering and possible death—limited its use.[14]

Some of the lapsed attempted that earlier practice to which Tertullian had objected. They solicited letters of recommendation from confessors in prison attesting to their repentance and urging that they be allowed to return to the communion of the church. Tertullian's warning that the confessors themselves were still being tested may have brought a change in the earlier practice. These confessors were thought to become effective intercessors only after they had completed their own witness by actually dying for Christ, not while they were struggling to remain faithful.[15]

---

13. Cyprian made the case clearly in *Lap.* 17.

14. *Ep.* 19.2.1; *Lap.* 36. Some of the fallen did reverse their failure in a second trial during the persecution, *Lap.* 13.

15. *Ep.* 14–17, esp. 15.3.1. The high status of the "confessors" was however reflected in their subsequent flaunting of some moral norms, *Ep.* 13.5.1.

A group of the "standing"—those who had not failed—in Africa followed the policy of the rigorist party in Rome. They insisted that any Christian who had denied Christ during the persecution must be permanently excluded from the eucharistic communion. The church, they claimed, had no power to forgive such a sin and must avoid any appearance of condoning it. The faithful could assist the penitents only by praying that God would forgive their sin at the time of the judgment.[16] They espoused the position Tertullian had upheld.

Cyprian began consulting with his episcopal colleagues in Africa and received advice from the presbyters who were governing the Roman church after the martyrdom of its bishop. He allowed the letters of the confessors and martyrs to function as evaluations of the sincere repentance of the apostates and thus recommendations to the bishop but not as evidence that they had actually been granted forgiveness by God.[17] He required that all the lapsed undertake public penance at once and, following the policy of the Roman presbyters, promised to admit such penitents to communion in anticipation of their imminent death.[18] The penitents could thereby face the judgment of Christ as members of the church. This policy acknowledged the intercessory power of the martyrs (as well as that of the bishops and the faithful) but limited its efficacy to the judgment of Christ, which was to be passed immediately after death. In response to this decision, a group of Cyprian's own clergy initiated a schism in Carthage. They immediately readmitted to communion all who held letters from the martyrs, without requiring that they undertake penance under the clergy's supervision.[19]

After the persecution, the bishops of Africa met in a series of councils to decide how to adjust to changing imperial policy. At their first meeting in Spring 251, they reviewed the scriptures for guidance but could not identify a solution on the basis of the scriptures alone.[20] At that point, they agreed to continue the practice of admitting to communion all who had already undertaken penance for their sins of apostasy and were in immanent danger of death. A problem arose, however, because some of the penitents survived their brush with death and had to be allowed to continue within the communion of the church.[21] Two years later, under continued pressure from

16. *Ep.* 30–31.

17. *Ep.* 15–17.

18. *Ep.* 16.2.2–3; 17.2.1–3.2; 18.1.2,2.1; 19.2.1–3; 20.3.2. For the influence of the Roman church, *Ep.* 8.2.3–3; 30.8.

19. *Ep.* 16.2.3, 33; 41.2.1–2; 42; 43.1.2.

20. *Ep.* 55.6.1.

21. *Ep.* 55.13.1, 17.3.

advocates for the penitents and under a threat of renewed persecution by the empire, the bishops agreed to admit to communion immediately all the apostates who had voluntarily undertaken formal penance within the unity of the church. They argued that sharing the eucharist would strengthen the fallen for the approaching battle and empower them to reverse their failure by confessing Christ.[22]

Even in making this concession, the African bishops rejected the claims of both the laxist and rigorist schismatics by insisting that the church, and the bishops in particular, had an essential role in the restoration of apostates. They accepted the intercessory role of the martyrs but not the efficacy the laxists assigned to it. They recognized that the decision of Christ was final but insisted, against the rigorists, that the bishops had been assigned a preliminary judgment. To support their position, Cyprian and his supporters insisted that only the college of legitimate and faithful bishops unified throughout the world had access to the power both to sanctify and to forgive through baptism and the ritual of repentance after baptism.[23] As a result, they rejected not only heretical baptisms but even those performed in schismatic communions by and for persons who affirmed the orthodox creed. They also asserted that anyone who died—even as a martyr—outside the communion of the one true church would be lost. Only those baptized in and sharing the communion of the united church might be sanctified and saved.[24] This decision, ironically, brought the Africans into a divisive conflict with the church in Rome, which continued to accept baptism performed in both heresy and schism.[25]

Although the development of policy within the African church was driven by challenges posed by the defections during the Decian persecution and the division of the communion these provoked, the bishops had to justify their decisions to the lapsed—both in schism and within the unity of the church—and their supporters. They also had to explain their policy to the leaders of overseas churches, with whom they both agreed and disagreed. The Roman church, for example, supported the Africans' decision to reconcile penitent apostates but rejected their stance on baptism performed in schism, although it was supported by the bishops of Asia. Cyprian's surviving correspondence with his colleagues in Africa, Rome, and Asia provides an adequate record of the scriptural justifications upon which he and his episcopal colleagues relied.

22. *Ep.* 57.1.1; 68.5.1.
23. *Ep.* 45.1.2,4.1; 59.10.1; 65.1.1.
24. *Ep.* 70; 72.1.1–3.
25. *Ep.* 74.1–3.

Cyprian argued that Christ had conferred the power to forgive sins upon the bishops, as represented by the apostles. He gave it first to Peter alone (Matt 16:19), in order to demonstrate that it was one and indivisible, and then to the whole body of apostles (John 20:21–23), to show that they all held it in common. The second conferral also clearly associated the power to forgive with the gift and presence of the Holy Spirit. By identifying the group of apostles as the foundational episcopal college, he explained that individual bishops participated in the commonly held power through incorporation into the worldwide communion of bishops. They could exercise that power for the benefit of their local churches only by maintaining their own participation in the unity of the episcopal college. Individual bishops also had to remain pure and fit dwellings for the Holy Spirit. If they left the college by joining a schism or proved unworthy through apostasy or any other significant sin, they would lose access to the gift of the Spirit and thereby the power to forgive sins. Their episcopal colleagues and local churches must then remove them from office and replace them. A sinful bishop could deprive a local church of access to the power of sanctification and would threaten the episcopal college with contamination by his sin. To tolerate a sinful bishop was, then, to participate in his failure.[26] Cyprian insisted that the episcopal college received its power directly from Christ and that Peter served as a symbol, both of the college as a whole and of each bishop as an individual; he was neither the head of the college nor an intermediary between Christ and his fellow bishops.[27] Although Cyprian asserted that the power to forgive had been conferred upon the bishops, he recognized that Christ himself would review their judgments and himself reject anyone who had deceived a bishop by feigning repentance for sin. A bishop who callously withheld mercy from a penitent would himself be judged by Christ for his harshness.[28]

Cyprian made no explicit provision for the bishop's delegation of the sanctifying power to anyone else. In practice, he did recognize that the presbyters and deacons acted as agents of their bishop, but he seems to have made

---

26. Cyprian attempted to enforce this policy in Africa and overseas; see *Ep.* 59.10.1–11.3; 67.6.1–3.

27. Cyprian's theory developed gradually and was explained in different settings. He first set it forth during the persecution in *Ep.* 33.1.1–2; 43.5.2. Immediately upon his return to Carthage, he articulated it in *Unit.* 4–5, which was subsequently revised and clarified. In subsequent letters associated with the controversies over reconciling the lapsed and rejecting schismatic baptism, he further elaborated it; see *Ep.* 57.1.1,4.1–5.3; 59.10.2; 65.1.1–5.2; 67.2.1–3.2.

28. *Ep.* 55.18.1; 57.1.1, 3.3, 4.3–5.2.

no provision for even emergency sacramental ministry by the laity.[29] Unlike Tertullian in his early writings, Cyprian did not recognize a sanctifying or priestly power shared by all, or at least all male, Christians. This omission may have been a consequence of his denial of such power to the confessors and martyrs. In addition, Cyprian insisted that the power to sanctify had been permanently communicated to the church, in and through the college of bishops. In his final writings, Tertullian had contended that the church's power was held and exercised by spiritual persons individually endowed with the gift of the Holy Spirit and following the discipline announced by the New Prophecy.

4. The Treatise on Rebaptism

A treatise, *On Rebaptism*, whose author has not been identified and which cannot be securely dated in relation to the writings of Cyprian, engages the issues at play in the controversy over the efficacy of schismatic baptism, and it challenges Cyprian's conclusions. The baptismal ritual of washing and invocation of Christ or the Trinity must be distinguished from the Spirit baptism, which is usually linked to the bishop's imposition of hands following them.[30] The first two may be conferred outside the unity of the church but are not salvific unless the convert also receives Spirit baptism.[31] A holy bishop acting within the unity of the church is the normal minister of that Spirit baptism. Some situations, however, require that God confer the Spirit baptism directly, without using a human minister. When a bishop is unworthy of his office, he does not have the gift of the Spirit to confer; when the bishop is absent, the baptism must be performed by a presbyter, deacon, or some other person who does not share the episcopal power of giving the Spirit; when a catechumen confesses Christ in the power of the Spirit and is martyred before being ritually baptized by a bishop. All these instances show that Spirit baptism can be given directly by God when the normal human mediation is unavailable or inadequate.[32]

By attending to these practical considerations, *On Rebaptism* clearly identified the problems inherent in Cyprian's insistence that the ministry

---

29. *Ep.* 18.1.2; 34.1; 41.1.1–2.2; 42. Indeed, Cyprian's explanation makes no provision for the interim between the death of a bishop and the ordination of his successor, such as the one in Rome which lasted more than a year during the Decian persecution when the church was guided by presbyters; see *Ep.* 8.

30. *Rebapt.* 3,7.

31. *Rebapt.* 6,8–9.

32. *Rebapt.* 3,10–12.

of a worthy bishop was essential to the efficacy of baptism, especially in the case of a martyr or other sincere convert. Yet the treatise shares Cyprian's assumption that only a bishop—not even presbyters or deacons—could serve as minister of the ritual through which Spirit baptism was given. Thus, it notices the problem in the Carthaginian practice that was overlooked during Cyprian's exile. The same problem also occurred at Rome during the interval between the martyrdom of Fabian and the election of Cornelius. The treatise focuses on that practice to point out the vulnerability of Cyprian's theory because of the essential role he assigned to the holiness of the episcopal minister of the ritual. The problem of unworthy bishops would arise again half a century later during the Diocletian persecution; it would force a reconsideration of Cyprian's theology and a reinterpretation of the scriptural texts on which it was based.

5. The Diocletian Persecution and Donatist Schism

The Diocletian persecution at the beginning of the fourth century resulted in failures by bishops which revealed a limited commitment to and inconsistent application of the policies that had been worked out a half-century earlier. Episcopal actions at Cirta in Numidia, at Carthage, and in Gaul challenged those decisions.

As the persecution lifted in Numidia, bishops convened at Cirta to supervise the election and ordination of a new bishop for that city. The primate of the province, Secundus of Tigisis, challenged the qualifications of some bishops who arrived to participate in the ordination. They had somehow emerged unscathed from visitations by imperial or municipal officials demanding that they turn over the scriptures and sacred vessels for destruction. They were asked to explain how they had faithfully refused that demand and yet escaped punishment. One of the bishops freely admitted his failure and warned the primate not to pursue the matter. The assembled bishops then agreed to leave the status of each to divine judgment and proceeded to the ordination. They then approved the election to episcopal office of a deacon to whom members of the congregation objected on the grounds that he too was guilty of the crime of handing over the sacred vessels.[33] The election of such a candidate and his ordination by such colleagues were direct violations of the policy adopted and enforced in Cyprian's time.

A few years later, members of this same group of Numidian bishops participated in a challenge to the ordination of the deacon Caecilian, who

---

33. For the records of the episcopal meeting, see Aug. *Cresc.* 3.27.30. The charges against Silvanus were recorded in an imperial inquiry some years later, *Act. Zeno.* 13.

was elected to succeed Mensurius as bishop of Carthage. They charged that one of Caecilian's consecrators, Felix of Abthugni, had himself been guilty of handing over the scriptures. This crime would not only have made Felix incapable of communicating the Holy Spirit to Caecilian but, according to Cyprian's theology, would have made Caecilian himself guilty of the apostasy he tolerated by entering into communion with this consecrator. The Numidian bishops proceeded to declare Caecilian disqualified; they elected, ordained and attempted to impose a certain Majorinus as the rightful bishop of Carthage. Caecilian refused to concede the position and the local church was divided. Supporters of the rival bishops of Carthage formed competing parties and divided the African church.[34]

Attempts to resolve the dispute between Caecilian and Majorinus—who soon died and was succeeded by Donatus—engaged both the bishop of Rome and the Emperor Constantine. Bishop Miltiades ruled in favor of Caecilian and attempted to heal the division by offering to receive into communion any bishop who had joined the schism or been ordained in it. He agreed, moreover, that the schismatics should be allowed to retain their offices if they entered into unity. He did, however, require that all apostate bishops be removed from office whenever they were discovered, though their baptisms and ordinations were to be accepted as effective.[35] When the schismatics refused this decision and offer, Constantine assembled bishops from the western part of the empire at Arles in 314 CE to hear their appeal. That council also decided in favor of Caecilian and set down a general principle for settling such questions: bishops who could be proven to be apostates were to be removed from office, but any baptisms and ordinations they had performed, either in unity or in schism, were to be recognized as effective.[36]

These attempts to deal with alleged failures of clerics during the Diocletian persecution demonstrated the tensions within Cyprian's explanation of the holiness of the church and the efficacy of its ministry. Secundus of Tigisisis and his colleagues meeting in Cirta might be credited with

34. The events are reported in Optat. *Parm.* 1.18–19. The charges against Felix were later established by an imperial investigation as baseless; see *Act. pur. Fel.* 8. The surviving evidence may be found assembled and explained in Maier, *Le Dossier du donatisme*, 1:128–35.

35. This action is reported in Aug. *Ep.* 43.5.16. The Council of Nicaea, in canon 8, specified that schismatics who called themselves Cathars were to be allowed to remain in the clerical order if they joined the unity of the Catholic church. The council specified the imposition of hands as the ritual for their reception. The African version of this canon specified the meaning of the ritual as reconciliation. Turner, *Ecclesiae occidentalis monumenta iuris antiquissima*, 1.2.122–24.

36. Canons 9,14.

attempting to preserve unity by tolerating colleagues whom an investigation would prove unworthy and thus require that they be removed from office. In Carthage, however, these same bishops upheld episcopal purity even at the cost of disrupting unity. These events demonstrated the difficulty of applying Cyprian's test for a bishop's access to the sanctifying power of the Holy Spirit. Charges of apostasy were easy to make but difficult to adjudicate and then enforce. In its attempt to settle the controversy, the council of Arles applied the evidentiary standards of the imperial judiciary to the bishops: only apostates proven guilty by public process rather than private accusation were to be removed from office.[37] Furthermore, although the bishops gathered at Arles had upheld the standard of apostasy, they refused to enforce the crime of schism as a disqualification for episcopal office. They insisted, moreover, that sacramental acts of baptism and ordination performed by both apostate and schismatic bishops were to be accepted as effective. They did not pollute or disqualify an otherwise worthy candidate. In Africa, the Caecilianist party was forced to choose between its standing in the communion of the worldwide church and upholding Cyprian's teaching that apostasy and schism were equally disqualifications for episcopal office and effective ministry. The Caecilianists preferred the former and had to revise Cyprian's theology to defend a practice of recognizing the baptism or orders of converts from schism. The Donatist party, having been denied the unity of the church, staked its claim to being the true church on the purity of its bishops. It, too, would have to develop Cyprian's theory to justify this decision and to apply that standard of holiness.

6. Parmenian and Optatus of Milevis

Constantine and his sons made sporadic attempts to bring the Christian church in Africa into unity and the universal communion. Donatus died in exile under Constans but his partisans were allowed to return to Africa during the reign of Julian. Parmenian was chosen bishop of Carthage and served that church for thirty years. Parmenian was not a native African and had been won over to the Donatist cause by the exiles.[38] In taking up the leadership of the Donatist community in Africa, Parmenian was faced with a challenge to their traditional understanding of the church as a pure body by new techniques of biblical exegesis developed by Tyconius, a lay member of his own party. Early in his tenure, he also composed an attack on the

---

37. Canon 14.
38. *Parm.* 2.7.

Caecilianists which was then answered by Optatus, the bishop of Milevis in Numidia.[39]

Episcopal failure, even within the true church, had been shown by Tyconius to be scripturally witnessed; it should no longer be ignored or denied. According to Optatus, Parmenian anchored the holiness of the church in the endowments which it enjoyed as the bride of Christ: the episcopal authority (*cathedra*), the bishop (*angelus*), the Spirit of God, the baptismal font, the creed (*sigillum*), and the altar (*umbilicum*). These gifts identified the true church.[40] Optatus also claimed that Parmenian had used these endowments to guarantee the efficacy of the ministry of a bishop who had proven himself unworthy of office.[41]

The first of the endowments of the true church listed by Parmenian was the *cathedra* or throne of the bishop. Cyprian had referred regularly to the chair as the symbol of the bishop's authority within the church.[42] In the struggle with the schismatics who had set up a second chair in rebellion, he also stressed episcopal authority as the foundation of the church's unity.[43] In two instances, he identified the throne with the *primatus*, the bishop's authority to govern the church.[44] Cyprian also referred not only to the local bishop but more specifically to the Petrine throne (*cathedra Petri*) in Rome as the touchstone of the authority of the episcopate for the whole church.[45]

Second on Parmenian's list of endowments, the bishop stands at the heart of Cyprian's understanding of the holiness and unity of the church. In his letters and treatises he never referred to the bishop himself as *angelus* but as *sacerdos*. Such a reference can be found, however, in the collection of scriptural testimonies grouped into themes which he addressed to Fortunatus. In the set of scriptural texts focused on martyrdom, Cyprian expanded on the symbolism of seven brothers in Maccabees 7 by referring to the seven lamp stands and the seven stars held in the right hand of the splendid standing figure in Rev 1:12–20. These represented the seven churches and their bishops.[46] This connection between martyrs and bishops might well have

39. This sequence is drawn from Congar's note, "Parménien et Tyconius."

40. *Parm.* 2.2–8,13.

41. *Parm.* 22.9–10, 5.3. In *Reg.* 2, Tyconius had specifically asserted the unworthiness of some bishops but did not draw the conclusion that their ministry was ineffective.

42. Cypr. *Ep.* 3.1.1; 17.2.1; 55.8.4, 9.1; 73.2.3.

43. Cypr. *Ep.* 43.5.2; 52.1.2; 68.2.1.

44. Cypr. *Unit.* 4 (primacy version); *Ep.* 69.8.3.

45. Cypr. *Unit.* 4 (primacy version) and *Ep.* 59.14.1. In two other instances, the reference to Peter indicates the local bishop, though one of these is in Rome, *Ep.* 43.5.2; 55.8.4

46. *Parm.* 2.6. Cypr. *Fort.* 11. The text is Rev 1:12–20.

inspired Parmenian to claim the holiness of its bishop as a support for the efficacy of the church's ministry.

The altar, to which Cyprian never referred as a navel (*umbilicus*), played a major role, somewhat like that of the *cathedra*, in his description of the truth and holiness of the church. The holiness of the altar of God required that all who served at it should themselves be holy.[47] Being rejoined to this altar of God would provide strength to the penitents to defend their faith.[48] Schismatics were rebels against the altar of God found in the true church; they set up their own profane altar in opposition,[49] which Cyprian identified as the altar of the devil.[50]

Similarly, Cyprian asserted that the font was found only within the true church and signified its exclusive access to the holiness given in baptism.[51] He used the text of Song 4:12–15 to characterize the church as a walled garden in which the sealed fountain was to be found. Only those within the church had access to its saving waters.[52] The term *sigillum* appeared only in this context, as the sign with which the font was sealed.[53]

Optatus, however, accepted only five of these endowments, excluding the claim that only the true church held the Spirit of God. The divine Spirit, he asserted, acted with a sovereign freedom which could not be limited to or by any human institution.[54] Optatus also disputed Parmenian's claim that the Donatist church held episcopal authority (*cathedra*), because its episcopate did not derive from or maintain unity with the historic college of bishops founded upon the apostles and, in particular, with the *cathedra* of the chief of the apostles, Peter, established in Rome. Peter's successors in that chair had maintained ties with the Caecilianists but had rejected the Donatists.[55] In what might have been a reference to the creed or *sigillum*, Optatus also faulted Parmenian's neglect of the faith of the recipient of baptism and insistence on the holiness of the bishop who served as its minister.

Both Parmenian and Optatus seem to have used the theology of Cyprian in naming and claiming endowments for their churches, especially

47. Cypr. *Ep.* 65.1.2,2.1,3.2–3; 67.1.2,4.4; 72.2.2; 73.8.2
48. Cypr. *Ep.* 61.2.3; 66.5.2.
49. Cypr. *Unit.* 17; *Ep.* 3.3.2; 43.5.2; 69.1.4; 72.2.1; 73.2.3.
50. Cypr. *Ep.* 55.14.1; 59.12.2; 65.1.2.
51. Cypr. *Unit.* 11; *Ep.*70.1.2; 73.10.3–11.2.
52. Cypr. *Ep.* 69.2.1; 74.11.2.

53. This appears only in the response of Firmilian of Caesarea in Cappadocia *Ep.* 75.15.1, which presumably repeated Cyprian's own language in this instance, as it did in some others.

54. *Parm.* 2.7.
55. *Parm.* 2.2–4.

in the dispute over the bishop's throne as the source of power and unity within the true church. Optatus developed Cyprian's two references to the *cathedra Petri* as the foundation of the authority and unity of the church. Clearly, he was attempting to make a special claim for the Caecilianist party, which was in communion with that chair, while the Donatists had not only been refused recognition but failed in their attempt to establish a significant community in Rome.[56]

Parmenian may thus be understood as having used the church's objective endowments—episcopal authority, bishop, font, creed, altar, and Holy Spirit—primarily to identify his own communion as the true and holy church. He did not neglect the traditional reliance on the bishop's personal possession of the gift of the Holy Spirit as a requirement for the efficacy of its ministry. Any Donatist clergy who had joined the Caecilianist communion during the exile of their leaders, for example, were forced to do penance and were removed from office.[57] Yet Parmenian may have recognized that some bishops in the Donatist communion might not be holy and might have argued that in those cases, the holiness of the church itself supplied for the defect of a particular bishop.

Optatus also objected to the emphasis which Parmenian placed on the role of the minster in accounting for the efficacy of the ritual of baptism. As has already been noted in the discussion of the endowments of the church, he refused to recognize that the sovereign freedom of the Holy Spirit could be limited by or to human institutions. He also insisted that the power to forgive sins belonged to God alone and thus could not be appropriated by any human officeholder. Two elements, Optatus explained, were unvarying and thus constitutive of the ritual of baptism: the operation of the Trinity and the faith of the recipient. The minister of the sacrament was varying and as a consequence his qualifications made no essential contribution to the efficacy of the ritual. The stable and unvarying human contribution came from the whole body of Christ into which the baptized were received.[58] In this explanation, Optatus aligned himself with the author of *On Rebaptism* in objecting to the role that Cyprian had assigned to the episcopal office and the personal holiness of the minister. He, however, introduced a consideration of the body of Christ that Cyprian had overlooked but Augustine would exploit.

---

56. *Parm.* 2.2–4.

57. The clergy, congregations, and even basilicas were ostentatiously purified when the Donatist exiles returned. Optat. *Parm.* 2.21–26, 6.1–8.

58. *Parm.* 5.1–5.

The writings of Parmenian and Optatus provide the first surviving reconsideration of the holiness of the church and its power to forgive in more than a century. Each engaged the explanation and arguments that had been presented by Cyprian and by *On Rebaptism* but their debate also shows the influence of new considerations arising from the sustained conflict in Africa.

7. Parmenian, Tyconius, and Augustine

During his second decade as bishop, Parmenian was challenged by the work of Tyconius, whose exegetical methods yielded conclusions about the unity and purity of the church significantly different from those traditionally affirmed by Donatists. Parmenian secured an episcopal condemnation of Tyconius and followed with his own letter against him. Portions of that letter survive in Augustine's refutation, written perhaps two decades later.[59]

Tyconius, a Carthaginian layman working in the second half of the fourth century, developed a set of seven rules for the interpretation of the entire scripture as referring to Christ and the church. In order to carry out his program, he had to distinguish the different ways that a biblical text might refer to Christ. The same text, he contended, sometimes addresses Christ both as an individual and as a group or body. Even the tempter, for example, recognized that Ps 91:11–12, "he will give his angels charge of you to guard you in all your ways," referred to the Savior himself. What followed, "With long life I will satisfy him, and show him my salvation," however, could not be applied to Christ as an individual but only in his identification with the social body of the church.[60] The application of these principles of christological interpretation led Tyconius to two judgments which contradicted the Donatist understanding of the church: the body of Christ on earth was not a pure body but one in which good and evil people were mixed together; it was, moreover, spread all over the world rather than surviving only as a faithful remnant in Africa. Daniel 2:34–35, he explained, clearly referred to Christ himself as "a stone cut from the mountain," but then shifted to the visible body of the church in saying that this same stone, "became a great mountain and filled the whole world."[61] In a similar way, Song 1:5, "I am black and beautiful," shows that the same bride of Christ was both holy and unholy. More specifically, the angels of the seven churches are presented in

---

59. Again, this chronology is derived from Congar's note, "Parménien et Tyconius."
60. Tyc. *Reg.* 1; Burkitt, 3.12–24.
61. Tyc. *Reg.* 1; Burkitt, 2.15–3.11. He rejected the explanation that Christ was everywhere in power. A stone, he insisted, can only be the symbol of a visible body.

Rev 2:3 as both blessed and wicked.⁶² The *Book of Rules*, in which Tyconius explained and established his methods of interpretation, would be used by Augustine to demonstrate that the claims made for the Donatist church were incompatible with the scriptures themselves. Augustine would also use these methods for the purposes that Tyconius originally developed them: to elaborate his understanding of both Christ and the church.

Augustine, in his own analysis of Parmenian's letter, did not attend to the endowments of the church but focused on the claims for the holiness of the bishop. He reviewed a series of scriptural texts the Donatist primate had used to demonstrate that the holiness of the bishop was essential to the church and its ministry. Sirach 10:2 asserts that the character of a city is determined by that of its ruler. Isaiah 66:3, Sir 34:23, and Prov 21:27 warn that the sacrifices of the impious are rejected by God. Exodus 19:22 and 30:20–21, along with Lev 22:21, threaten any unworthy priest who approaches the altar. Finally, in John 20:21–23, Christ gave the apostles the Holy Spirit and the power to baptize only after he had excluded the traitor, Judas, from the group.⁶³ Augustine focused in particular on Parmenian's assertion that because the bishop functions as mediator between God and his people, his own good standing before God was essential to the success of his ministry.⁶⁴

Augustine's *Against the Letter of Parmenian* provided his first evaluation of the bishop's role as mediator. Parmenian had asserted that, according to John 9:31, God does not hear the prayers of sinners but only of those who do God's will. Augustine countered with 1 John 2:1–2, which names Jesus Christ the just one who advocates for sinners before the Father and himself serves as the propitiation for sin. He continued with the assertion of 1 Tim 2:5 that the one mediator between God and humans is the man Jesus Christ. He then reminded his readers that the text cited by Parmenian was attributed to the man born blind who had, at that point in the Gospel of John (9:31), recognized Christ only as a prophet. Christ's own statement on this question was to be found in the story in Luke 18:10–14 that contrasts the prayer of the sinful publican to that of the bragging Pharisee. Next, he developed the argument by distinguishing between the intercession of Christ, prefigured by that of the high priest who went alone into the sanctuary, and the prayer of Christians for one another, prefigured by the people standing together

---

62. Tyconius opposed blackness and beauty within the church as a whole; see *Reg.* 2, Burkitt, 10.13–11.1. He then showed that scripture proves that the bishops and leaders were also sinful, Burkitt, 11:1–11.

63. Aug. *Parm.* 2.4.8–2.7.12.

64. *Parm.* 2.4.8–2.7.12.

outside the sanctuary. The prayer of an unfit bishop could, he concluded, be heard because of the devotion of his people.[65]

In a long sermon preached about the same time, Augustine contrasted the false mediation of the devil to the true mediation of Christ. Parmenian's letter came to mind and he gave voice to his outrage at the audacity of the claim made there. This Donatist bishop had asserted, he recalled, that the bishop was the mediator between the people and God. The people in question was the church of Christ. While Christ alone was the mediator and priest, every Christian was anointed and the whole church was the body of the priest. A bishop was given the title of priest, Augustine explained, because he was set in charge of this priestly body; he, however, was really a priest in the same way as any other Christian, as a member of the body of the one priest. To drive home the point, Augustine recalled the discussion of Christ's priesthood in the Letter to the Hebrews. The one priest went ahead into the sanctuary to make the offering: on earth in the figure of the high priest; in heaven in the reality of his own person. Where, Augustine asked his congregation, was their bishop during the offering? Was he inside an earthly sanctuary repeating the symbolic role of the Israelite high priest or was he standing with the rest of Christ's people? He was indeed right where the people were, hoping to be admitted as one of them into the heavenly sanctuary where they would all be forever with Christ. Any bishop who dared to claim Christ's mediating role, he concluded, was a false mediator like the devil.[66]

Tyconius' influence is clearly evident in Augustine's explanation of the sharing of Christ's priesthood with the church as his body. This element would be expanded and developed as he attempted to engage and assimilate Cyprian's theology. In the conflict with Parmenian, however, his intention was to deprive the bishop of a priestly role that would require his own holiness to insure the efficacy of his sacramental ministry.

8. The Revolt against Primian

Primian became Donatist bishop of Carthage upon the death of Parmenian but did not enjoy the same success as leader of that party. In 393, his local congregation revolted and, with the assistance of bishops from the neighboring province, deposed him and elected the deacon Maximian as his replacement.[67] The numerical strength of the Donatist party was not in

---

65. *Parm.* 2.8.15–17.
66. *Serm. Dolb.* 26.49–52.
67. Acts of the Council of Cebarsussi are in Aug. *Psal.* 36.2.20.

Proconsular Africa and Byzacena but in Numidia; there Primian sought the support of the most powerful of his colleagues, Optatus of Timgad. More than three hundred Donatist bishops met at Bagai in Numidia in 394 CE to condemn the rebels. The bishops at this council set a deadline before which the Maximianist bishops might return to Primian's communion and retain their episcopal status. They also agreed to recognize the baptisms and other sacred actions the rebels might have performed while in schism.[68] By a combination of legal maneuvers and Optatus' exercise of force, Primian recovered his position.[69]

In accepting the rebel bishops back into communion in their offices and recognizing the baptisms they had performed while in separation, the Donatist bishops who met at Bagai violated the principles of Cyprian's theology that made an attack on the unity of the church equivalent to apostasy and thus a disqualifying crime.[70] They explicitly violated the judgment of Cyprian's councils, which both prohibited schismatic bishops from returning to office in unity and rejected the efficacy of their sacramental actions.[71] The Caecilianist bishops did not hesitate to call attention to these discrepancies.[72] The Roman bishop Miltiades had made a similar concession, it will be recalled, in his attempt to heal the division between Donatus and Caecilian.

The Donatists seem to have made a clear distinction between the crimes of apostasy and schism. The supporters of Maximian had been guilty of the second by rejecting Primian; had they gone over to the Caecilianist side, however, they would have been infected with the apostasy contaminating that entire party. In that case, they would immediately have been deprived of the power of sanctify and could never have been allowed to return to their offices in the Donatist communion. The Donatists bishops at Bagai, like Secundus of Tigisisis some ninety years earlier, might have justified their concession as necessary to restore the unity of the church.

---

68. See the fragments of the Council of Bagai preserved in various writings of Augustine, *Cresc.* 3.53.59, 4.10.12, 4.28.35; *Petil.* 1.10.11. These are assembled in CSEL 53:276–8. A fuller account, with all relevant documents, is found in Maier, *Le Dossier du donatisme*, 2:73–91. For a brief account of the events, see Lancel, *St. Augustine*, 169–70, and Bonner, *St. Augustine of Hippo*, 246–49.

69. See Aug. *Psal.* 21.2.31 for a citation of the record. Optatus may have had an irregular militia at his disposal.

70. For example, the Donatists invoked the rebellion of Kore, Dathan and Abiron (Num 16:32) *Cresc.* 3.21.24, which had been a favorite of Cyprian, *Unit.* 18, *Ep.* 67.3.2; 75.16.2.

71. Cypr. *Ep.* 72; *Sent.* 1,2,5,7,9, etc.

72. *Reg. Carth.* 69.

9. Petilian, Cresconius, and Augustine

Petilian was a successful rhetor and a catechumen in the Caecilianist communion. He was prevailed upon by the Donatists (Augustine claimed that force had been used) to accept baptism and then ordination as their bishop at Constantina in Numidia.[73] As bishop, he wrote a letter to his clergy defending the Donatist cause against Caecilianist charges. Intermediaries provided first a partial and then a full copy of that letter to Augustine, who wrote a response to each version. Petilian himself responded to Augustine's consideration of the partial copy and Augustine immediately replied.[74] The Donatist layman, Cresconius, also undertook a response to Augustine's first attack on Petilian, to which Augustine then replied. Because Augustine transcribed the initial letter of Petilian in his responses and quoted liberally from Petilian's response to him, the surviving documents of this exchange provide an unusual opportunity for understanding a fifth-century Donatist position.

Petilian asserted that the efficacy of baptism depended on the holiness of the bishop administering the ritual. He was willing to be quite specific. The faithfulness of the minister was the source of the fidelity of the baptized; he served as root and spring for the initiant.[75] Thus, a bishop who was faithful and pure in conscience could cleanse from sin and make the person he baptized a faithful Christian.[76] In contrast, being washed by a minister who was spiritually dead (i.e., a Caecilianist bishop) did the recipient no good at all.[77] An unfaithful minister would share his infidelity and pollute the baptized with his sin.[78] The good effects, he concluded, followed baptism in the Donatist church and the evil ones in the Caecilianist.

Petilian's original letter to his clergy focused on the crime of betrayal of the scriptures, of which Caecilian had been charged because of his ordination by an alleged apostate, Felix of Abthugni. He would have infected all the bishops who entered into communion with him—as well as all they had subsequently ordained. These betrayers of Christ neither gave nor received

---

73. Aug. *Serm. Caes. eccl.* 8. Petilian became bishop about 395.

74. Thus the first two books of Augustine's *Contra litteras Petiliani* deal with the two versions of Petilian's original letter and the third book addresses Petilian's *Littera ad Augustinum*, in response to Augustine's first book. No record has survived of a further response by Petilian.

75. *Petil.* 1.2.3, 1.4.5.

76. *Petil.* 2.3.6, 2.35.61, 2.53.121.

77. *Petil.* 1.9.10.

78. *Petil.* 2.4.8, 2.7.14, 2.36.83.

the gift of the Holy Spirit; as a result, none of them could baptize.[79] Having themselves violated what is holy and sacred, they could not pray for others effectively.[80] To strengthen the case against Caecilianist bishops of his own time, Petilian argued that they had been deprived of the Holy Spirit not only by their episcopal lineage but had forfeited it by actively participating in the crime of persecuting the true (Donatist) church and their use of the coercive force provided by imperial law to promote conversions to their own church.[81]

The sacramental efficacy of secretly unworthy bishops within the Donatist church was not considered by Petilian until Augustine forced it upon him in his initial review of the letter to Donatist clergy. In portions of his responding *Letter to Augustine*, Petilian displays his difficulty understanding the question itself. He claimed that Augustine had misrepresented his statement by leaving out a word. He had actually written, "The conscience of the minister who baptizes in a holy way (*sancte*) cleanses the conscience of the recipient but whoever knowingly receives faith from an unfaithful minister receives not faith but guilt."[82] Moreover, Petilian replied, the situation that Augustine himself had posed was fanciful and unrealistic. How could anyone fail to know the status of a minister? All a person had to do was make the obvious inquiries.[83] In reply, Augustine insisted that the question addressed a real situation. Even a diligent catechumen could be quite legitimately ignorant of the religious standing of the bishop to whom he was about to submit for baptism.[84] The disciplinary records of both Donatist and Caecilianist churches provided ample evidence that bishops were often secretly sinful and later were discovered and removed from office.[85] In his own rejoinder to Augustine, Cresconius followed much the same line as Petilian. A catechumen could, he claimed, rely on the good reputation of his bishop.[86] He later added what may be more useful evidence for Donatist belief: not every kind of sin would disqualify a bishop.[87] Both Petilian and

---

79. *Petil.* 2.33.77.

80. *Petil.* 2.105.240.

81. *Petil.* 2.11.25, 2.75.167–2.97.223. He conveniently ignored, Augustine rejoined, the coercion that Optatus of Timgad had exercised against the supporters of Maximian, *Petil.* 1.10.11, 2.11.26.

82. Conscientia sancte dantis attenditur, quae abluat accipientis. *Petil.* 3.8.9, CSEL 52:171.9–10. The quotation is reproduced at *Petil.* 3.15.18, 3.20.23

83. *Petil.* 3.21.24–22.26, 3.27.32.

84. *Petil.* 3.19.22, 3.20.23; the point is repeated in 3.22.26–23.27

85. *Petil.* 3.29.34–32.37, 3.34.40

86. *Cresc.* 2.17.21–18.22. Augustine cited this response again at *Cresc.* 4.12.14.

87. *Cresc.* 2.28.36–29.37. The context is a discussion of being baptized by the dead.

Cresconius must have held that only certain kinds of sin were relevant to the fidelity of a bishop and, thus, his power to forgive sins and communicate both faith and the gift of the Holy Spirit. The disqualifying sins must have been easily discoverable by a person of ordinary prudence.

Augustine's attack on the Donatist theology was based on the supposition that it did or at least should teach that the full range of serious sins, against God and fellow human beings, would deprive a bishop of the Holy Spirit and thereby render his sacramental ministry ineffective. This seems not to have been the position his opponents were actually upholding. They had apparently narrowed the criteria to violations involving idolatry. Yet the only contemporary occasion for such a crime that Petilian could identify was cooperating in the imperial suppression of Donatism. Otherwise, the disqualifying sin had to be inherited from Caecilian[88] or his consecrator Felix through episcopal succession and communion. By such a limited standard, holding episcopal office in the Donatist church might have been regarded a plausible indicator of a pure conscience and, thus, a guarantee of effective sacramental ministry.

10. The Program of the Caecilianist Party

Under the leadership of Aurelius of Carthage, the African bishops in the Catholic communion adopted a program that would enable and encourage their Donatist counterparts to enter into union with them. As Emperor Theodosius and his sons gradually withdrew state support from the traditional Roman cult, idolatry among Christians became an insignificant issue—at least in its historically troublesome form.[89] In resolving the revolt against Primian, moreover, the Donatist bishops had shown themselves willing to tolerate former schismatics within their own ranks.

Cresconius intended to assert that idolatry was not the only disqualifying sin but apparently overstated his case, realized the error, and narrowed his assertion, *Cresc.* 2.27.33.

88. The Donatist version of *The Acts of the Abitinian Martyrs* is translated into English, with an introduction, in Tilley, *Donatist Martyr Stories*, 25–49. For the consideration on which she judges the document contemporary to the events, rather than late fourth-century propaganda, see 26 n. 4. The most recent edition is that of Franchi Pio d'Cavalieri, which is reproduced in Maier, *Le Dossier du donatisme*, 1:57–92.

89. The legislation restricting traditional practice began with the outlawing of sacrifice in 392; it continued with the closing of temples in 395 and the abolishing of the privileges of the civil priests in 396. See *C.Th.* 16.10.12–14. The shutting down of the traditional practices in Carthage is reported by Augustine in *civ.* 18.54. Augustine identified other forms of idolatry which still flourished: fortune-telling, cures for illness, and good-luck charms. See *Serm.* 286.7; 318.3; 328.8; *Serm. Dolb.* 26(198*).58; 18(306E).7–8; *Serm. Guelf.* 18(260D).2; *Serm. Lamb.* 6(335D).3,5.

Seizing the initiative, the Caecilianists bishops agreed to explore a proposal that would allow Donatist bishops to retain their episcopal offices upon entering the Catholic communion. One of two conditions had to be met: the Donatist bishop must never have rebaptized any convert from the Caecilianist side or he must be able to bring his congregation along into unity. The Caecilianist bishops justified their proposal by arguing that the prayers of the two congregations, finally united in peace, could be expected to win divine forgiveness for any failings of the bishops who united and presided over them.[90] After an unsuccessful attempt to win the support of the bishops of Rome and Milan for this program, the Africans decided to act on their own authority. At the Council in Carthage in September 401, the bishops voted to allow Donatist clergy to exercise their offices in a Caecilianist congregation. The bishops governing the Caecilianist churches in the affected region were required to judge that this dispensation promised to promote unity among Christians.[91] They forbade the application of the provision to any Donatist cleric who had earlier abandoned the Caecilianist for the Donatist communion.[92] This offer was renewed by the Caecilianist bishops in advance of the imperially sponsored meeting between the two parties in Carthage in June 411. The imperial judge made provision for the implementation of this program in his decision at the end of the meeting.[93]

The policy adopted by the Caecilianist bishops could be justified by a compromise between the positions of Cyprian of Carthage and Miltiades of Rome. A council of 71 bishops meeting in Carthage in the spring of 256 CE under Cyprian's presidency had decided that anyone who had left the Catholic communion or who had been ordained in schism could be received into communion only among the laity and would not be allowed to exercise clerical office. The bishops offered two reasons: first, that such persons had attacked the unity of the church and were thus unworthy of office; second, that they were responsible for the loss of anyone who had died in schism

---

90. The proposal is recorded in *Bru. Hipp.* 37. This is attributed to the Council of Hippo in 393 but it may actually have been adopted at the Council of Carthage in August 398.

91. *Reg. Carth.* 68. A council of bishops from Proconsular Africa, meeting in June of the same year, had agreed to send legates seeking the approval of the overseas bishops, *Reg. Carth.* 57.

92. Aug. *Cresc.* 2.11.31–12.14, 2.16.19.

93. Augustine proposed this scheme in *Ep.* 128.2–3 before the conference and reported it in his summary of the proceedings, *Coll.* 1.5. Years later, he recalled it in trying to win over Emeritus, who had been his counterpart as representative of the Donatist bishops at Carthage, *Emer.* 5. Augustine also made public reference to the proposal in *Serm.* 358.4 and *Serm.* 359.5, which are dated immediately before and after the conference. Marcellinus' judgment is found in *Edictum cognitoris*, CCL 149A:178.65–179.79.

after being led astray by them.[94] Taking an opposed position, Miltiades had attempted to restore unity in the initial stages of the Donatist schism by allowing returning schismatics to regain their offices in his communion.[95] Both the Council of Hippo in 393 CE and the Council of Carthage in 401CE justified the revival of Miltiades' program by appealing to Cyprian's appreciation of the efficacy of the unity of the church. This rationale was most fully developed by Augustine, who also argued that Cyprian had tolerated unworthy bishops as ministers of the sacraments for the sake of unity.[96]

11. Augustine and Cyprian

In his effort to unify the African church, however, Augustine had to demonstrate that the Caecilianists were the true heirs of Cyprian and that they, rather than the Donatists, were developing the most fundamental principles of his theology. The Diocletian persecution had revealed the tension between unity and purity within Cyprian's theory. Cyprianic standards of purity proved unenforceable in the ecclesial disciplinary procedures following the persecution, even with the aid of the imperial judiciary's investigative powers, which Constantine brought to bear.[97] The challenge that Roman traditional religion had posed to Christian purity had been subsequently dissipated through Constantine's patronage of the church and Theodosius' suppression of its polytheist rivals. Competition within the Christian movement now presented the greatest threat to the purity of the church and its effective mediation of the salvation offered by Christ.

Cyprian, Augustine asserted, had in practice preferred unity to purity. He had tolerated sinful bishops within the unity of the church and recognized that their celebration of the sacraments was actually being treated as effective. When a bishop within the unity of the church was discovered to have been deceitful and therefore bereft of the Holy Spirit, neither Cyprian nor his Donatist disciples repeated the baptisms and ordinations the

---

94. Cypr. *Ep.* 72.2.1–3.

95. Aug. *Ep.* 43.5.16.

96. Augustine's interpretation of Cyprian position is most fully presented in his *De baptismo*. The argument that unity was more important than purity begins at *Bapt.* 1.18.27 and continues through 2.8.13. His evidence for Cyprian tolerating unworthy colleagues is found at *Bapt.* 4.9.12, 10.16, 12.18–19, where he cited Cyprian's *Ep.* 11.1, 55.25.1–2, and *Lap.* 6.

97. Even in his own lifetime, Cyprian had discovered that the church could not actually remove and replace deviant bishops in Spain and Gaul; see *Ep.* 67, 68.

sinner had performed.[98] Cyprian and his colleagues had even agreed that each bishop within their communion could refuse to rebaptize a convert originally baptized in heresy or schism. When questioned, they agreed that participation in the unity of the eucharistic fellowship would itself cleanse and sanctify the convert who had not received proper baptism as a result of misjudgment rather than obstinancy.[99]

The problem of secretly unworthy bishops, which had originally been raised against Cyprian's theology in *On Rebaptism*, had remained unresolved despite the efforts of Parmenian and Petilian. Augustine and Optatus of Milevis insisted that the personal holiness of the bishops could not be essential to the efficacy of the church's sacramental ministry.[100] That, Augustine charged, would incur the curse of Ps 117:8 by placing trust in another human being rather than in God.[101]

Yet Augustine refused to accept the solution offered by *On Rebaptism* and Optatus, a solution that relied upon a direct divine action, unmediated by the church, to confer the gift of the Spirit upon the baptized. He upheld Cyprian's fundamental theses that Christ had indeed conferred upon the church the power and responsibility of forgiving sins, that this power was identified with the gift of the Holy Spirit, and thus that it could be held and exercised only by Christians who were actually holy. Unlike Cyprian, he identified the recipients of the power of sanctifying not as the college of bishops but as the body of faithful Christians, those who were joined together in the love of God and neighbor within the communion of the church. The power to sanctify he identified as the gift of the Holy Spirit given in baptism to all Christians rather than in ordination to the clergy alone.[102] In their sacramental ministry, the clergy functioned as agents for the union of those faithful who constituted the true church, and thereby for Christ himself.

The argument for this reinterpretation of Cyprian was based upon the penitential practice of the church and was then extended to its baptismal ministry. The formal ritual of penance over which the clergy presided had always been an exceptional and unusual means of seeking and receiving the forgiveness of sins. It was used for only the most serious, and notorious,

---

98. *Bapt.* 4.9.12, 10.16, 12.18–19, 7.49.97.

99. *Bapt.* 2.15.20, 5.2.2. Cyprian made this concession to past practice; see *Ep.* 73.23.1–2.

100. *Bapt.* 4.10.15, 4.12.18, 4.13.19, 5.12.14.

101. *Petil.* 1.3.4, 2.97.223, 3.50.62.

102. *Serm.* 264.5, 354.2; *Psal.* 25.2.5–6, 85.4, 119.9, 126.8, 127.11, 146.9.

sins.[103] The mutual forgiveness that Christ authorized and required in Matt 18:18 was the normal and regular practice through which forgiveness was offered, sought, and received. In the Lord's Prayer, Christians promised to offer one another that forgiveness which they each sought from God.[104] Their forgiveness of one another on earth, Christ assured them, mediated the divine forgiveness: it was effective in heaven.[105] Refusing to forgive others, however, would bind Christians in their own sins, even those which had earlier been forgiven, as was illustrated in the parable of the debtor servants which follows immediately in the Gospel of Matthew.[106] The gift that empowered Christians to exercise God's own forgiveness toward one another and thus to receive it for themselves, Augustine explained, was the charity inspired in their hearts by the Holy Spirit.[107] This he confirmed by citing 1 Pet 4:8: "charity covers a multitude of sins."[108]

Having established this foundation upon scriptural texts that Cyprian had neglected, Matt 18:18 and 1 Pet 4:8, Augustine then advanced his own interpretations of those texts to which Cyprian had appealed. Reversing Tertullian's position, Cyprian had insisted that in receiving the power to bind and loose (Matt 16:19), Peter had represented not the spiritual persons in the church but individual bishops and the episcopate as a college or group.[109] Augustine revised Cyprian's interpretation and asserted that Christ had conferred that power upon Peter in response to his confession of faith and thereby upon Christians who followed him in acclaiming Jesus as Son of God.[110] He then noted that Cyprian had misread the text of John 20:19–23 in which Jesus confers the gift of the Holy Spirit and the power of binding and loosening upon the "disciples." Cyprian had restricted this

---

103. When the sin was well known, it was publicly confessed: *Con. Carth.* a. 390, 7; *Bru. Hipp.* 30c; *Serm.* 232.8. When, however, it was secret, the bishop was not allowed to expose the sinner: *Con. Carth.* 30 May 419, 132–33. Reaffirmed: *Con. Hipp.* a. 427, 8. Instead, he conducted the penance in private: *Serm.* 82.8.11–9.12, 232.8.

104. *Serm.* 58.6.7, 206.2, 210.10.12, 211.5, 259.4, 278.6.6, 10.10–11.11; *Psal.* 131.2, 147.13.

105. *Serm.* 82.4.7.

106. *Serm.* 57.11.11–12.12, 59.4.7, 211.5.

107. *Bapt.* 1.11.12–16, 1.12.19, 3.14.19, 4.13.20.

108. *Bapt.* 1.18.27, 3.16.21, 6.24.45; *Unic. Bapt.* 13.22, 15.26.

109. Cyprian, *Unit.* 4–5. Tertullian's opponent had claimed the power for every bishop, *Pud.* 21–22.

110. For the confession of faith, see *Serm.* 270.2, 295.3.3. The conferral of power is in *Serm.* 67.3, 76.1, 149.6.7–7.8, 232.3–4, 295.2.2; *Serm. Mai.* 16(23A).2; *Serm. Guelf.* 16(229N).2; *Serm. Lamb.* 3(229P).1,4; *Psal.* 54.5,101.2.3, 108.1; *Eu. Io.* 50.12; *Ep. Io.* 10.1,10.

reference to the apostles as the first bishops, and thus to their successors.[111] These "disciples," however, were all those gathered behind locked doors on the evening of the resurrection of Jesus, Augustine pointed out, and thus represented the whole community of the faithful. They symbolized the saints who make up the body of the true church.[112]

Thus, Augustine reached the conclusion that the power of sanctifying had been conferred upon and was exercised by those faithful Christians who cooperated with the gift of love that the Holy Spirit had poured into their hearts (Rom 5:5). This same gift established and maintained, through the saints, the unity visible in the worldwide communion of the church.[113] Both charity and the forgiveness of sins could be received and maintained only by adhering to the communion of saints.[114] In Augustine's graphic image, the church sanctifies by chewing, swallowing, and digesting sinners, by assimilating them and sharing life as Christ's Body.[115]

Using the Pauline understanding of the church as the body whose head is Christ, Augustine elaborated an explanation of the church's access to the divine power of sanctifying. The power to forgive was properly divine but it was exercised by Christ in his humanity, both as an individual and through the ecclesial body whose head he had become.[116] Christ sanctified and shared his own power with his body; he exercised that power with and through all faithful Christians.[117]

Thus the communion of saints within the church, as the body of Christ, acted in unity with its head as the subject of the power to forgive sins. The power and operation of sanctifying was shared by all the saints. Those of the clergy who were not among the saints did not participate in the sanctifying power. They, however, were agents designated through their ordination, to act for Christ and his saints.

---

111. The *Vetus Latina* database has nine instances of "apostoli" instead of "discipuli" in verse 19 and two instances in verse 20. Cyprian might have had a different version of the text.

112. *Bapt.* 3.18.23, 5.21.29, 6.1.1,3.5,14.23; *Eu. Io.*121.4.

113. *Serm.* 99.9; 295.2. The parallel explanation can be found in *Bapt.* 1.11.15, 3.18.23, 5.21.29, 6.3.5, 6.14.23, but not elsewhere in the writings of the Donatist controversy.

114. *Bapt.* 6.4.6,14.23.

115. *Serm. Denis* 15(313B).3; *Psal.* 34.2.15, 88.1.24, 94.11, 103.3.2, 123.5.

116. *Serm.* 99.9; 149.7; 295.2; *Serm. Guelf.* 16(229N).2; *Serm. Dolb.* 26.49–53; *Ep. Io.* 1.8.

117. *Serm.* 341.1–3,11; *Serm. Dolb.* 22(341*).20; *Psal.* 85.4; *Eu. Io.* 108.5.

12. Conclusion

Many observations could be made about the relationships of the authors and their systems of accounting for the sacramental efficacy of their church and the futility of their opponents' ministry. For purposes of this study, however, the more important factors are those that drove the development of the systems, that prevented the repetition of earlier explanations, and that built a tradition of interpretation.

The first surviving indication of the question of church holiness dates to the beginning of the third century, in a debate recorded (and perhaps forced) by Tertullian. At that point, the focus was on the purity of the church and its rejection of sinners who fell into sexual irregularities. Tertullian refused to accept an institutional or bureaucratic account of the holiness and sanctifying power of the church, one which would locate these in the episcopal office. He insisted that the Christians who held and exercised the power to sanctify had to be holy; he defined that holiness according to the standards of the Decalogue and the revelations of the New Prophecy.

The Decian persecution in the middle of the third century gave rise to new conflicts and questions. Dealing with sinners guilty of apostasy by denying or failing to confess Christ under imperial pressure resulted in divisions within the community in Carthage. The problem of purity gave rise to the question of unity. Cyprian won the support of his episcopal colleagues for a program that focused the purity of the church and its power to sanctify on the episcopal college. This justified the toleration of repentant apostates among the laity. At the same time, it deprived those outside the unity defined by the episcopal college of access to the power of sanctifying. Although Cyprian's theology relied on the unity and holiness of the episcopal college, it did require that individual bishops meet a standard of moral practice and religious fidelity in order to guarantee their continued possession of the gifts of the Holy Spirit received in baptism and ordination. Cyprian's theory focused on the college of bishops within the church for mediation of the salvation provided by Christ.

Questions soon arose about the capacity of individual bishops to maintain the standards of purity and fidelity required by Cyprian's theory. The author of *On Rebaptism* argued that in certain cases, God had to act immediately to forgive sins because of the inadequacy or absence of a bishop serving as minister of the ritual of baptism. This limitation on the mediating role of the church and its ministers would play a role in church practice and theory for more than a century in Africa, and much longer in Europe. The Numidian bishops meeting in Cirta in the aftermath of the Diocletian persecution were unwilling to enforce the purity standards of Cyprian's theology on their own colleagues. They referred the judgment of individual conscience to Christ and relied on God to act directly when the episcopal ministers of baptism and ordination were inadequate. A decade later, the Roman bishop intervened to heal the division within the African church; Miltiades must have assumed that the sacramental ministry of schismatic and even apostate bishops was guaranteed by divine intervention. After a little more than fifty years, Cyprian's explanation of the holiness of the church and its power to sanctify was being overwhelmed by the failures of bishops.

In the late fourth and early fifth centuries, the Donatist writers attempted to justify their church and condemn the Caecilianists by adapting the requirements of Cyprian's theology to the realities of episcopal performance. In general, they upheld the necessity of episcopal holiness but modified the standards so that they could be applied more easily. Parmenian of Carthage affirmed the role of the bishop as mediator between God and his congregation. He appealed to the permanent endowments of the church itself to guarantee the efficacy of sacramental ministry rather than to episodic divine interventions. He rejected Tyconius' argument that Cyprian's standards of episcopal fidelity were contrary to the scriptures themselves. Primian, the next Donatist leader, effectively eliminated schism as a crime that would permanently disqualify a bishop. Petilian of Constantina also attempted to institutionalize the purity standard. Any minister could be trusted on the basis of his holding office in a church that claimed its bishops had never betrayed the gospel or collaborated in the persecution of Christians.

Optatus of Milevis challenged the theory of Parmenian for the Caecilianist side. He, however, adapted the solution of *On Rebaptism* by arguing that the personal holiness of the minister was irrelevant to the efficacy of the sacramental rituals. God always responded directly to the faith and repentance of the recipient. The bishop was responsible only for performing the ritual.

Augustine demonstrated some familiarity with the entire range of solutions that had been offered. He introduced an understanding of the relationship between Christ and the church to displace Cyprian's reliance on bishops. Through the union of divine and human in the incarnation, he argued, the power of sanctification was given human mediation. The Savior himself exercised that power during his earthly life; after his ascension to heaven, he continued to exercise it with and through the saints upon whom he conferred the Holy Spirit to form his ecclesial body. The saints exercised Christ's power to forgive for one another, acting both individually and corporately. The clergy were ordained to serve as agents of the union of saints within the church, of the members of the body of Christ and, thus, of their head. Using Tyconius' principles of scriptural interpretation, Augustine modified the explanations of Tertullian and Cyprian to identify the saints within the church as the human mediators whose holiness guaranteed the efficacy of the sacramental ministry of the clergy.

This African tradition of interpretation was modified as it was subsumed by the Roman church and later by the medieval scholastics. The history or "afterlife" of this interpretative tradition is longer, more complex, and not so well documented. The African insistence on the human mediation of divine grace and its preference for holy mediators survived in the laity's preference for monastic clergy, the cult of the saints, and the honorific titles conferred upon ministers.

Bibliography

Bonner, Gerald. *St Augustine of Hippo: Life and Controversies.* Norwich: Canterbury, 1996.
Burns, J. Patout, Jr. "The Holiness of the Church in North African Theology." *Studia Patristica* 49 (2010) 85–100.
Congar, Yves. "Parménien et Tyconius." In *Traités anti-Donatistes*, 718–20. Oeuvres de saint Augustin 28. Bibliothèque augustinienne. Paris: Desclée de Brouwer, 1963.
Franchi de' Cavalieri, Pio. "La *Passio* dei Martiri Abitinensi." In *Note Agiografiche* 8, 65:3–46. Studi e Testi/Biblioteca Apostolica Vaticana. Città del Vaticano: 1935.
Lancel, Serge. *Saint Augustine.* Translated by Antonia Neville. London: SCM, 2002.
Maier, Jean-Louis. *Le Dossier du donatisme.* 2 vols. Texte und Untersuchungen zur Geschichte der altchristlichen Literatur 134–35. Berlin: Akademie-Verlag, 1987.
Ticonius. *The Book of Rules of Tyconius.* Edited by Francis Crawford Burkitt. Vol. 1. Texts and Studies 3. Cambridge: Cambridge University Press, 1894.
Tilley, Maureen A., ed. and trans. *Donatist Martyr Stories: The Church in Conflict in Roman North Africa.* Texts for Historians 24. Liverpool: Liverpool University Press, 1996.
Turner, C. H. *Ecclesiae Occidentalis Monumenta Iuris Antiquissima.* 2 in 7 vols. Oxonii: E Typographeo Clarendoniano, 1899.

5

Martin Luther's Hermeneutics of Christ's Deified Flesh

ADAM G. COOPER

IN A BOOK ADDRESSING the topic of the hermeneutics of tradition, and in which the goal of many chapters is largely to affirm the crucial logic of continuity for Catholic Christianity, it may well be wondered whether any positive appraisal of the theology of Martin Luther and the Reformation associated with his name is at all possible. Whatever that Reformation was, whatever its own logic, history attests to its deeply schismatic character and results. For centuries scholars have been tempted to account for this schism by reducing its irreducibly complex elements to a single criteriological principle: faith alone, scripture alone, conscience alone—and so the list of "solas" goes on. This chapter represents an attempt to enter a little way into certain aspects of Luther's theology with a view to destabilizing this simplistic picture and to suggesting instead that a far more complex logic was at work, a logic within which the hermeneutics of tradition or continuity were not entirely absent, either in principle or in fact. It comes from someone who, having been raised in a deeply sacramental and liturgical strand of the Lutheran tradition, has come to discern its strengths and shortcomings from within, and for whom the decisive move out of that tradition into fellowship with the Catholic Church required a concentrated act of abstraction.

As far as I can tell, Thomas Cajetan was the first person to discern and name in the theology of the young Luther a hermeneutics of rupture. In 1518 Cajetan had been Master General of the Dominican Order for a decade. Appointed to serve as papal legate, he had been sent by Pope Leo X to Augsburg for the Imperial Diet convened there by Emperor Charles V—

primarily to discuss ways of consolidating the dissolving unity of the Empire in the face of an impending Turkish invasion. On hearing that Luther's teaching had been causing no small stir in Saxony, Pope Leo requested Cajetan while in Augsburg to meet with the controversial Wittenberg theologian with a view to shocking him back into line. It had thus fallen to Cajetan to study Luther's *Ninety-five Theses,* by then a year old, and his subsequent *Explanations* of the same, and to offer a considered rebuttal of points suspected of error for immediate clarification or retraction. But for a whole host of reasons, the meeting was a failure. It was not Luther's anti-papalism that proved the issue, for on this score the Dominican himself was no servile monarchialist. Rather Cajetan reacted sharply to Luther's claim that in addition to contrition, a person approaching the sacrament of penance should have personal faith or confidence in the actual efficacy of absolution in his case. To Cajetan this amounted to little short of a person's presumptuous adumbration of a judgment solely the prerogative of God. Luther's teaching on this matter appeared to him as "a novel idea," a "fanciful notion," an "alien" teaching pitted against "the ordinary understanding of the Church."[1] The German's attempt to incorporate into the traditional definition of the sacrament of penance a necessary reference to personal faith was finally "to construct a new Church!"[2]

Since that precipitous occasion, to which the whole unfolding "ecclesiological dualism"[3] of subsequent decades may be traced, reasons for interpreting Luther's theology as epitomizing a hermeneutic of rupture have multiplied. From Johann Cochlaeus in the sixteenth century to Heinrich Denifle in the nineteenth, Luther has been portrayed as a bitter protagonist of the subjectivistic and individualistic religion of private conscience over against the stable sacramental and social forms of traditional Catholicism, and identified as the arch-catalyst for the modern wave of spiritual individualism with its rejection of dogma, ritual, community, institution and authority. Luther may be credited with having begun with a legitimate attack on the presumptuous exaltation of reason over revelation, but he is equally blamed for modernism's triumph of private judgment and individual feeling, not to mention the social chaos that goes with them. Thus the true Lutheran, alleged Etienne Gilson, is not drawn to seek God in external realities; "he feels God at work within his soul, and that is enough for him."[4] Or as Joseph Ratzinger has argued, by making the experiential concepts of fear

---

1. Wicks, *Cajetan Responds,* 49–50.
2. Ibid., 55.
3. Yeago, "'Christian, Holy People,'" 105.
4. Gilson, *Spirit of Medieval Philosophy,* 244.

and consolation the determinative keys by which to measure and judge the ontological statements of the church and the effects of her liturgy, Luther's theology automatically resulted in a "changed view of ecclesial ministry" and thus a changed doctrine of the church.[5]

This disjunctive image of Luther and the Lutheran ecclesial movement is further compounded by a tradition of Protestant interpretation that hails the rupture which Luther brought about. In his *Philosophy of History*, Georg Hegel (1770–1831) paved the way for a portrait of Luther that discounted any continuity between the Reformer and traditional Catholic sacramentalism. Hegel's disgust with early and medieval Christianity, both Byzantine and Occidental, lay precisely in its overt externality, its interest in the sensuous embodiment of God. Against this "vitiating element of externality," Hegel pitted none other than Luther as the champion of "free spirit." "Luther's simple doctrine is that the specific embodiment of deity . . . is in no way present and actual in an outward form. . . . This abrogation of externality imports the reconstruction of all the doctrines." In their place Hegel has Luther exalting "subjective assurance" and "absolute inwardness of soul."[6]

Two quite different modern interpreters paint a similar picture. In the 1930s Swedish Lutheran Anders Nygren dramatized the basic opposition between Catholicism and Lutheranism in terms of a far-reaching antithesis between two kinds of love: *eros* and *agape*.[7] In contrast to *agape*, which is God's action toward man, Nygren argues that human love is entirely driven by *eros*. Stemming from the pagan mystery religions and Greek philosophy, the *eros* motif denotes an egocentric desire or yearning for completion, an upward motivation to establish oneself as immortal and be like God. As such, *eros* constitutes the "born rival" of *agape*, such that the two are "diametrically opposed to each other."[8] By *eros* man seeks to ascend to God in order to have fellowship with God at his level—the human is lifted up to the divine. By *agape*, God descends to the human level and communes with man as a fellow-sinner. The pure notion of divine *agape* appeared first in the New Testament, but was soon corrupted by the pagan notion of *eros*. This adulterated idea of love passed into and was developed further in the patristic and medieval church under the name of *caritas*. *Caritas* is basically a self-contradictory conflation of pagan *eros* and Christian *agape*. This false synthesis, established by Augustine and carried to its logical conclusion by Thomas, was smashed by the genius of Luther.

5. Ratzinger, *Principles of Catholic Theology*, 225–26.
6. Hegel, *Philosophy of History*, 349–50.
7. Nygren, *Agape and Eros*.
8. Ibid., 81.

More recently, "post-Christian" theologian Daphne Hampson has published a substantial study in which she similarly poses the Lutheran *morphologie* in almost strict antithesis to both late medieval and modern Catholic thought.[9] Hampson very acutely exposes the failure on the part of many non-Lutheran theologians to comprehend accurately Luther's fundamental theological vision. At the same time however Hampson paints a picture of Luther in colors provided by some of the chief protagonists of idealist and existentialist philosophy, proposing deep substructural connections between Luther, Hegel, and Bultmann. Drawing on the work of Wilfried Joest and Gerhard Ebeling, Hampson claims that Luther "discarded" the classical medieval substance-ontology for a more relational, dynamic conception of human being. In such a schema, the drama of the individual's redemption takes place almost entirely outside the realm of the natural, personal and bodily. The Christian's true "self" is ultimately a discarnate reality, with only a negative or even nullifying relation to the corporeal, personal, and social "self" whose particular history and existence I experience as my very own.

Yet the question remains whether these accounts provide an altogether complete portrayal of Luther's theology, and indeed, whether they properly take into account the deeply sacramental, incarnational and ontological basis of Luther's biblical realism which cannot profitably be omitted from any attempt to summarize his theology in terms of a single paradigm.[10] No one who has read a little more widely across Luther's vast *oeuvre* can fail to notice his robust insistence on objectivity and externality in matters of faith and religion, his commitment to seeking God nowhere except in the flesh of Christ, his conviction that "God will not deal with us except through his external word and sacrament," and therefore his sense that the root of all idolatry consists in spiritual enthusiasm and in unauthorised service of God. As Philip Cary rightly observes, "Luther's understanding of the power of the gospel depends on a Catholic notion of sacramental efficacy, which places salvific power in external things."[11] The image of Lutheranism as fundamentally stained by a hermeneutic of rupture and disjunction has been challenged by several new readings of Luther's theological legacy, which may be summed up in the words of acclaimed Luther scholar Oswald Bayer: "Despite its radically new orientation, the Reformation is linked with the tradition of the church, both its history and its theology."[12] For those who

---

9. Hampson, *Christian Contradictions*.

10. Against the theory that Luther rejected traditional metaphysics, see Juntunen, "Luther and Metaphysics," 129–60.

11. Cary, "Why Luther Is Not Quite Protestant," 449.

12. Bayer, *Theology the Lutheran Way*, 1.

have come to know Luther and the Lutheran Reformation by way of idealist philosophy, secular historical studies, polemical characterization, or the Protestant ecclesial "spirit," this traditional core of Luther's theology largely remains an enigma. Yet it is this incarnational realism which has been the focus of a growing body of Luther studies, most notably those conducted since the 1970s under the initiative of Helsinki University Professor Tuomo Mannermaa, and, in North America from the 1990s, by such figures as David S. Yeago and Reinhard Hütter, sometimes characterized respectively as the "Finnish school" and the "Thomistic turn."[13] By citing these scholars, I do not here intend to advocate any particular "school" or theory of Luther interpretation. However it must be acknowledged that these theologians have precipitated a welcome shift in Luther studies by paying renewed attention to a much-neglected and by no means peripheral theme in his theological worldview. That such a shift continues to be necessary is indicated for example by Hampson's perfunctory treatment of Luther's sacramental theology, an omission that results in a failure to detect the deeply "catholic turn" of Luther's thought, or what Yeago refers to as his "mystical theology of uncreated grace, the purifying encounter with God in His very Godhead, . . . anchored to the preaching and ritual of the Church as the concrete locus of God's certain, undialectical presence."[14] We can perhaps be less severe in our criticism of Nygren: he was writing in the 1930s before any of this work had been done. But while Hampson indeed acknowledges the so-called Finnish school of Luther studies, it is all said and done in one paragraph, and makes little noticeable impression on her selection or analysis of the texts.[15]

Incarnational Spirituality

It can hardly be disputed that there are present in Luther various behavioral tendencies and deep-seated theological impulses that have justly given rise to the kinds of interpretation and criticisms outlined. But it seems significant that other Protestants often consider the Lutheran Reformation to have failed for not going "far enough." In their eyes, Lutheran spirituality has remained "too catholic." This criticism suggests something about the "conservative" nature of the Lutheran reforms. The ecclesial communities which

---

13. For a summary of Mannermaa's work, see Braaten and Jenson, *Union with Christ*; Marquart, "Luther and Theosis." Relevant material by David S. Yeago can be found in "A Christian, Holy People" as well as "The Catholic Luther" and "Gnosticism, Antinomianism, and Reformation Theology."

14. Yeago, "Catholic Luther," 41.

15. Hampson, *Christian Contradictions*, 19–20.

allied themselves with the 1530 *Confessio Augustana* (CA) were seeking not only to retrieve and faithfully embody biblical and patristic Christianity, but also, by maintaining the rich wealth of spiritual disciplines and customary liturgical traditions the church had acquired over the centuries, to retain the legal protection afforded by the term "Catholic." In contrast to many other Protestant churches, and despite Luther's somewhat severe initial revision of the Mass, Lutheran spirituality is marked by and large by a conservative attitude to liturgy, ritual, ceremony, custom, and other traditional practices that are perceived to have evolved in continuity with the scriptural witness. This at least forms a constant refrain in the statements put before the emperor in Augsburg: "Our churches are falsely accused of abolishing the Mass. Actually, the Mass is retained among us and is celebrated with the greatest reverence. Almost all the customary ceremonies are also retained" (CA 24.1–3). "No novelty has been introduced which did not exist in the church from ancient times, and no conspicuous change has been made in the public ceremonies of the Mass . . ." (CA 24.40). "We gladly keep the old traditions set up in the church because they are useful and promote tranquility. . . . We diligently maintain church discipline, pious ceremonies, and the good customs of the church" (CA Apology 15.38–44).

While the forces that occasioned the Lutheran Reformation were multitude and complex and had been in existence in Europe for a long time, two factors stand out in the early theological writings of various reformers. First, there was dissatisfaction with the complex philosophical categories of late medieval scholasticism, and a call to return to the ancient sources of the faith, made possible by a widespread renaissance in biblical and patristic studies. Second, there was a reaction to longstanding pastoral and ecclesial abuses, in which light one can read the Reformation as a movement springing from deeply moral and pastoral concerns. One of the more obvious areas of abuse lay in the area of penitential practice. Documentation of abuses in penitential practice before and up to the sixteenth century can be found in all the sources, not just those with a Protestant bias. Scholars list such matters as forced and extorted confessions, obsession with sexual sins, and an overemphasis on satisfactions, merit, and avoiding hell.[16] Add to that the wider litany of abuses in the church of the late Middle Ages, including the secularization of ecclesial practice; the arrogation of political power by ecclesial office holders; simony; nepotism; mandatory church taxes; the

---

16. On the obsession with sexual sins, which is of relevance for our analysis of Luther's doctrine of marriage: "The ecclesiastical discourse on sex of the thirteenth through the sixteenth centuries was quantitatively important. . . . Never had an entire civilization been subjected to such an investigation of sexuality, especially within marriage." Delumeau, quoted in Rey-Mermet, *Moral Choices*, 112.

proliferation of paid private masses; and last but not least, the scandal of immoral behavior by clergy and popes, including widespread, undisguised concubinage.

This background must be supplemented by reference to fierce intra-ecclesial battles waging at the time: papalists versus conciliarists, Thomists versus Scotists, medievalists versus humanists, champions of the *via antiqua* versus champions of the *via moderna*, battles between schools and even battles between streams within individual schools. And so in the Neoscholasticism of the late medieval period we find an emerging Semi-Pelagian stream, represented by such figures as William of Ockham and Gabriel Biel. It was in this Pelagian piety that Luther himself was formed in his Augustinian Order, strongly influenced by Biel and the famous scholastic axiom: God will not deny grace to him who does what is within him (*faciendi quod in se est Deus non denegat gratiam*).[17] It was only natural that, having discovered the gospel of gratuitous divine mercy, Luther should react against this formative piety and its theoretical underpinnings, and it is in the light of this conflict that we must assess his theological failures and achievements. Any neglect on our part to take note of the intensely polemical, pastoral, and non-systematic character of Luther's theology, embedded in a highly idiosyncratic style marked by rhetoric and hyperbole, can only result in misunderstanding.

The Self-Localization of God

Two primary factors stand out as influencing Luther's views on the physical and external character of God's Spirit-filled operations in human history. One was his Christocentric and incarnational reading of biblical theology, while the other was his confrontation with various spiritual enthusiasts who invoked the authority of the Holy Spirit on purely subjective grounds.

The controversy over spiritual enthusiasm can be traced back to the ministry of Thomas Müntzer (1488–1525). One of Luther's earliest and most impassioned followers, Müntzer took up the post as preacher at St Mary's Church in Zwickau in Saxony in 1520. His radical approach to church reform and spiritual inspiration found numerous adherents. Among them was the weaver Nicholas Storch who, according to Bornkamm, "had brought some of his sectarian ideas from Bohemia and further developed

---

17. See further Oberman, *Harvest of Medieval Theology*; McSorley, *Luther Right or Wrong?*, 191–215. I am yet to follow up the thesis that part of the reason for the emergence of this Semi-Pelagianism was the late medieval Church's ignorance of the Second Council of Orange and of its condemnation of Semi-Pelagian errors.

them with visions and revelations he claimed to have received directly from God." Müntzer publicly praised Storch from the pulpit as a man "truly trained in the Spirit."[18] In short time Müntzer's social fanaticism sparked such violent opposition that the town council had him expelled. Three of his followers—Storch, Thomas Drechsel, and Mark Stübner (or Thomae)—shifted to Wittenberg near the end of December, 1521. These three became known as the Zwickau Prophets.

At this time, Luther was hidden away in the Wartburg castle. Troubled by the unrest caused by various aspects of the Zwickau prophets' teaching (most notably their questioning of infant baptism), Melanchthon appealed to Luther for advice. In reply, Luther urged Melanchthon to test their spirit. The chief matter to be determined was whether the three could attest their divine calling, "for God has never sent anyone, not even the Son himself, unless he was called through men or attested by signs.... I definitely do not want the 'prophets' to be accepted if they state they were called by mere revelation...."[19]

After some time in Prague, Müntzer moved to Allstedt in Electoral Saxony. There with his iconoclastic approach to worship and radical ethics (including total continence in marriage) he gained no small following. From the safety of Allstedt Müntzer wrote to Luther and Melanchthon and personally charged them with worshipping a "dumb God," one who no longer communicates revelation to his elect. "Beloved, make the effort to prophesy, otherwise your theology isn't worth a red cent."[20]

Müntzer's call for the princes and the populace of Allstedt to take up arms in the fight against unbelief and idolatry headed towards an apocalyptic climax. It was Müntzer's claim that "the Spirit of God is now revealing it to many that a 'first-rate, unbeatable, future-oriented reformation' is needed." He saw himself as a "new Daniel," a visionary prophet sent by God to the German princes to guide them to victory.[21] The conflict came to a head in the Peasants' War in May 1525, in which Müntzer was arrested, tried and executed for his role in inciting civic violence.

The second phase of the controversy arose in connection with the teaching of Andreas Karlstadt (1480–1541). Before his death Müntzer had cultivated a warm alliance with Karlstadt based on "an ecstatic brand of

---

18. Bornkamm, *Luther in Mid-Career*, 56–57.

19. Luther to Philip Melanchthon from Wartburg, January 13, 1522, in *Luther's Works*, 48:364–66. (Hereafter *Luther's Works* will be abbreviated LW followed by volume and page numbers.)

20. Bornkamm, *Luther in Mid-Career*, 150.

21. Ibid., 160–61.

mysticism, relying on revelation through visions and dreams."[22] In 1524 Luther, now back in Wittenberg, expressed deepening concern about the alliance, whose increasingly numerous members "boast that they are being moved by pure spirits, without the testimony of Holy Scripture."[23]

It was early in 1525 that Luther finished composing a lengthy treatise directed against Karlstadt's spiritualism. In it Luther criticized Karlstadt and "his prophets" with respect to two main problems. First, "they run and teach without a call," a practice condemned by God in Jer 23:21 ("I did not send them, yet they ran. I did not speak to them, yet they prophesied"). And second, while Karlstadt and the prophets claim to possess the Spirit, they "avoid, run away from, and are silent about the main points of Christian doctrine," having "no idea how a good conscience can be gained or ought to be constituted."[24]

According to Luther, both errors stem from inverting the proper relation between the Spirit's activity and the divinely appointed external means. The inward experience of the Spirit properly "follows, and is effected by" the outward means of grace. "God has determined to give the inward to no one except through the outward. For he wants to give no one the Spirit or faith outside of the outward Word and sign instituted by him. . . ."[25] By contrast, Karlstadt and his prophets had set up "a contrary order," subordinating God's outward order to "an inner, spiritual one." For Luther, Karlstadt's repeated appeals to the Spirit's direct and inward inspiration finally amounted to the exaltation of his own idiosyncrasies over Holy Scripture.[26] Luther's teaching against the spiritual enthusiasts in the 1520s became a standard which later Reformers recalled whenever they encountered persons publicly teaching on the basis of an alleged inward call or private revelation given by the Holy Spirit. In 1537 at Schmalkald, Luther repeated the basic principles he had outlined over a decade earlier:

> In these matters, which concern the external, spoken Word, we must hold firmly to the conviction that God gives no one his Spirit or grace except through or with the external Word which comes before. Thus we shall be protected from the enthusiasts—that is, from the spiritualists who boast that they possess the Spirit without and before the Word and who therefore judge, interpret, and twist the Scriptures or spoken Word according to

---

22. Ibid., 151.
23. Luther to Nicholas Gerbel from Wittenberg, May 6, 1524 (LW 49:82).
24. Luther, *Against the Heavenly Prophets* (LW 40:222–23).
25. Ibid., 146.
26. Ibid., 157.

their pleasure. Müntzer did this, and many still do it in our day who wish to distinguish sharply between the letter and the spirit without knowing what they say or teach.[27]

As mentioned earlier, besides Luther's confrontation with the affair of the Zwickau prophets, there was his development of an incarnational and sacramental hermeneutic of the Scriptures. In his career as a biblical lecturer, Luther increasingly manifested a concern to discern rightly and with certainty the material means or spatial *loci* in which God wills to be sought, apprehended, and worshipped. Luther was particularly captivated by the prominent Old Testament theme of God's self-localization in such places as the ark, the tabernacle, and the Temple in Jerusalem.[28] He found it characteristic of God to "clothe" or "cover" himself in tangible, accessible forms, to hide his naked divine majesty and limit himself to specific, circumscribed avenues of apprehension, designated and recognized as such exclusively by his sovereign but explicit word. Any attempt to know God "outside" these divinely instituted means must be doomed as prideful arrogance. Idolatry consists not just in worshipping the wrong God, but also in worshipping the right God in the wrong way, that is, by self-invented rather than divinely appointed means. On this basis Luther lumps Muslims, Jews, and papists together with pagans in so far as they attempt to find God "outside his Word and promises, according to the thoughts of their own hearts."[29] They worship a "vague God," attempting like the ancient philosophers to find him absolutely, "as he is in himself."[30] God's express desire, by contrast, is to give himself to be found in certain outward, tangible signs, wrapped with veils and clothing, masked with human flesh. Recalling the way Israel's worship in the old covenant was to be confined to the divinely instituted place of God's name, and reading the Deuteronomic regulation christologically, Luther argues that God is to be sought and worshipped nowhere except in the flesh and blood of Christ, who precisely in his humanity is our only mercy seat. In the old covenant, the Jerusalem Temple was the place "where God at the time dwelt bodily." He continues:

> Therefore all who lived in the land or outside the land were obliged to address their prayers and fix their hearts to the place where God sojourned bodily through His Word, to assure that they would worship no other God than Him who sat enthroned

---

27. Smalcald Articles VIII.3, in Tappert, *Book of Concord*, 312.

28. See Kleinig, "Where Is Your God?" This article has been republished more accessibly in Wenthe et al., *All Theology Is Christology*, 117–31.

29. Luther, *Commentary on Psalm 51* (1538), LW 12:312–13.

30. Ibid., 352.

over the cherubim on the mercy seat. All prayers had to be directed thither, just as today in the New Testament our petitions must be addressed to Christ, who is our mercy seat, lest we acknowledge any other god, pray to him, and worship him besides Him who dwells bodily in the Man Christ Jesus. And, in fact, there is no other God.[31]

According to Old Testament scholar John Kleinig, in this and numerous similar passages "Luther was working out the implications of Christ's incarnation exegetically and liturgically. His basic conviction was that God dealt with us physical beings physically."[32] Nor was this concern peculiar to the mature Luther. It is true that before the early 1520s, in opposition to the almost total politicization and materialization of the church's liturgical forms, Luther says that God may be worshipped anywhere.[33] It is especially after the spiritualizing excesses of such radicals as the Zwickau Prophets that Luther more firmly advocates stricter adherence to the divinely commanded and traditionally revered sacramental and ecclesial forms. Even so, Yeago has argued that even before his actual break from the papacy following his meeting with Cajetan in 1518, Luther's basic question was not Roland Bainton's celebrated "How can I get a gracious God?" so much as "Where can I find the real God?"—a question that suggests that Luther was already then thinking in sacramental and incarnational categories.[34] It is not that Luther thought of God's divinity as substantially confined to a circumscribed time and space. Rather, it is that outside of the person of Christ there is no certainty that what we call "God" is in fact God at all, or at least "God for us"; and even if it were, God is not an object for disinterested speculation, but the divine creator and Father who commands our fear, love, and trust, in short, our total worship, and who in the flesh of Christ alone has permanently instituted the exclusive means of creaturely participation in and union with himself. Luther knows that God, being God, is indeed present everywhere, yet "he does not wish that you grope for him everywhere. Grope rather where the Word is, and there you will lay hold of him in the right way. Otherwise you are tempting God and committing idolatry."[35]

---

31. Luther, *Lectures on Jonah* (1525), LW 19:80.
32. Kleinig, "Where Is Your God?" 94.
33. Luther, *Commentary on Psalm 68* (1521), LW 13:33–36.
34. Yeago, "Catholic Luther," 38.
35. Luther, *The Sacrament of the Body and Blood of Christ—Against the Fanatics* (1526), LW 36:342. See also Luther's *Lectures on Genesis: Chapters 15–20* (1539), LW 3:272–77.

With this word "participation" we touch upon the early church's doctrine of deification, and while this is not uncustomary language for the church in Luther's time, the specifically incarnational aspect of the Fathers' teaching on deification finds in Luther's theology an unparalleled renaissance. For deification—humanity's real participation in the life of the triune God—is always depicted by the Fathers as a direct and reciprocal corollary of God's humanization in Jesus Christ. Where the Fathers used the Greek *theopoiein* and its parallels, Luther uses the verb *vergotten*, structurally binding this participation to the hypostatic union of the divine and human natures in Christ. In Christ "human flesh is united with the Godhead; it is made divine."[36] Luther often uses the ancient illustration of a rod of iron penetrated by the burning properties of fire. In the same way, "the divine power is present bodily in the humanity of Christ and does what God naturally does."[37] This interpenetration or communication of the properties of the divine nature to Christ's human nature is no less true when it comes to Christ's humanity as it is physically present on the altar in the sacrament: "God is in this flesh. It is God's flesh, a Spirit-flesh [*Geistfleisch*]. It is in God, and God is in it." For this reason "it lives and gives life to all who eat it, both to their bodies and to their souls."[38] When Jesus requires his followers to eat his flesh and drink his blood, he is basically saying, "If you touch My flesh, you are not touching simple flesh and blood; you are eating and drinking flesh and blood which makes you divine."[39]

What role does faith play in this dynamic? Is the Reformer promoting an entirely materialistic naturalism? For Luther, faith functions as the cementing and unifying power which joins the believing subject to Christ so closely that the two are no longer two, but one. In fact faith "couples Christ and me more intimately than a husband is coupled to his wife."[40] Faith brings about an identity between the believer and the object of faith, a true formal *identity*, whose material effects begin in the here and now; so if the object of faith is God, as it should be, "faith makes a man God."[41] Luther is fond of the patristic notion, ultimately derived from 2 Cor 5:21, of the "wonderful exchange" (*fröhlicher Wechsel/admirabile commercium*). In the real union effected by faith, God becomes man and man becomes God.

36. Luther, *Sermons on the Gospel of St. John: Chapters 6–8* (1530–32), LW 23:125.

37. Ibid., 124.

38. Luther, *That These Words of Christ, "This Is My Body," etc., Still Stand Firm Against the Fanatics* (1527), LW 37:124–25.

39. Luther, *Sermons on the Gospel of St. John: Chapters 6–8* (1530–32), LW 23:122.

40. Luther, *Lectures on Galatians: Chapters 1–4* (1535), LW 26:168.

41. Ibid., 100. "[Faith] consummates the Deity; and, if I may put it this way, it is the creator of the Deity, not in the substance of God, but in us" (ibid., 227).

The righteous one becomes a condemned sinner and the condemned sinner becomes righteous. In this sense faith seems to incorporate the operations ascribed by scholastic theology to the other theological virtues, especially love, though as Luther vehemently argues, Christ, not love, is the "form" of faith. So where the scholastics speak of love,

> we speak of faith. And while they say that faith is the mere outline but love is its living colors and completion, we say in opposition that faith takes hold of Christ and that He is the form that adorns and informs faith as color does the wall. . . . It takes hold of Christ in such a way that Christ is the object of faith, or rather not the object but, so to speak, the One who is present in faith itself [*in ipsa fide Christus adest*].[42]

If Luther emphasizes the role of Christ's humanity in providing a concrete object for faith, it is not because he lacks an orthodox understanding of his divinity. Philip Watson was entirely correct when he stated that "Luther's entire theology can be said to stand or fall with the divinity of Christ. Nothing is more important to him than the Nicene *homoousios*."[43] However it should also be added, as Watson notes, that it is by no means possible for unaided natural reason to discern the divine nature in Christ. If the power and majesty of the divine nature are "hidden" in creation, so that they are only discerned with difficulty, how much more is the divine majesty concealed in the lowly, suffering humanity of Christ. The self-localization of God in the flesh of Christ brings about no automatic, self-evident disclosure. On the contrary, God is most "masked," most deeply concealed in Christ and especially in his crucifixion, where the natural eye can see only injustice, despair, and death. This "revelation under opposites" is what Luther means by the "theology of the cross." God's glory consists precisely in his descent "to the very depths, into human flesh, into the bread, into our mouth, our heart, our bosom."[44] Faith alone penetrates the outer veil, consisting of Christ's flesh and blood, and takes hold of him as true God. Indeed, Luther goes so far as to say that Christ's humanity "would be of no

---

42. Ibid., 129. This passage raises a question often debated by scholars as to what extent Luther and Melanchthon agreed on the doctrine of justification. Melanchthon's view (with that of later Lutheran orthodoxy) is typically held to be "forensic" or "juridical," whereas Luther is said to maintain a more "dynamic" or "organic" conception of the relationship between justification and sanctification, Christ "for us" (*pro nobis*) and Christ "in us" (*in nobis*). My view on the matter is that such antagonism is forced, and makes more of the terminological differences than is warranted given the authors' distinct rhetorical contexts and linguistic styles.

43. Watson, *Let God Be God*, 102.

44. Luther, *"This Is My Body,"* etc., LW 37:72.

use, if the divinity were not in it; yet on the other hand, God will not and cannot be found except through and in this humanity."[45] It is therefore one thing to take hold of Christ's flesh; it is another to take hold of it with faith. In both cases we are taking hold of God himself, but only by faith can such an encounter become a life-giving, salutary union.

Since the physical contact with Christ's flesh in the sacrament (properly) presupposes the existence of faith, such contact can only deepen and enrich the already-existing union of the believer with God. In this regard John R. Stephenson suggests the Virgin Mary as "the paradigm of the worthy communicant," since she is physically and spiritually pregnant with the same Fruit.[46] Indeed, this is how Luther also regards Mary. At the annunciation the whole Christ comes not only into her heart, but also into her womb "as she hears, grasps, and believes" the angel's message.[47] Faith itself is causally dependent on hearing the word, but faith also becomes the means for the believer's increasing impregnation with the incarnate Christ. Not that Christ is reincarnated in each Christian at the supper; but through it he does begin to take ever more concrete form within the Christian's life, so that any assertion that Christ cannot be received or grasped by physical means is definitively negated.

This further reminds us that the word "Christ" when used by Luther as always means the flesh and blood God-man, the eternal Logos who remains permanently united to the flesh of his assumed human nature, taken from his mother. There is a definite order, ordained by God himself, in our coming to know him: "Christ must be grasped first as man and then as God, and the cross of his humanity must be sought after and known before the glory of his divinity. Once we have taken hold of Christ the man, that will soon bring with it the knowledge of him as God."[48] Thus whenever Luther speaks of "Christ" or of our being "in Christ" or of Christ's presence "in faith" or "in us," we should never take the words in a vague, ethereal or immaterial sense, but always as referring to the Son of God in his physical humanity and its word-bound, sacramental extension in the world. For Luther it is not wrong to speak of Christ's "spiritual" presence as long as by it we do not mean immaterial. Only the super-spiritualists think that "spiritual" consists in nonmaterial, nonphysical, inward realities. In view of their misguided

---

45. Quoted by Watson, *Let God Be God*, 102.

46. Stephenson, "Holy Eucharist," 159.

47. Luther, *The Sacrament of the Body and Blood of Christ—Against the Fanatics* (1526), LW 36:341.

48. Luther, *Commentary on Psalm 5* (1519), 204.

use of John 6:63 ("The Spirit gives life; the flesh counts for nothing"), Luther calls for a total redefinition of what is typically meant by "spirit" and "flesh":

> We do not call "flesh" that which can be seen by the eyes or touched by the fingers, as the fanatics do when they call Christ's body useless flesh; but . . . all is spirit, spiritual, and an object of the Spirit, in reality and in name, which comes from the Holy Spirit, be it as physical or material, outward or visible as it may be; on the other hand, all is flesh and fleshly which comes from the natural power of the [sinful] flesh, without spirit, be it as inward and invisible as it may.[49]

Luther's stance on this matter is driven not only by polemical concerns over the real presence of Christ's body and blood in the Eucharist. Of course outward things which are not explicitly instituted by God as effective means of his gracious divine activity "are of no avail." But the fact is "you find no word of God in the entire Scriptures in which something material and outward is not contained and presented. . . . [Such] outward things connected with God's Word [i.e., by divine command and promise] are salvation and blessedness, because they inhere in the Word and bind our faith."[50] God's word alone, which for Luther is nothing else than the tangibly written and orally spoken words of Holy Scripture, determines what is "spiritual" or "Spirit-filled," and so capable of conveying divine life.

The Bodily Word of the Gospel

The texts we have selected so far seem to make it clear that Luther believed in the bodily presence of Christ in the sacrament not on account of some prior general theory or inner experiential feeling. Luther rather keeps on returning to the explicit words of Christ and his authorized heralds in the Bible, by which God has determined where our faith is to "hang its hat," so to speak. Only God determines which concrete, objective forms we are to attach ourselves to with certain, conscience-binding confidence.

This helps to explain Luther's dogmatic and hard-headed refusal, in his Marburg debate with the Swiss reformers Zwingli and Oecolampadius, to relativize, qualify, or explain away Christ's words articulated at each celebration of the Eucharist: *hoc est corpus meum*. Here is not the place to detail exegetical arguments about the *ipsissima verba* of the historical Jesus. Suffice to say, it is this "Lutheran *est*," as Karl Barth disparagingly called it, which

---

49. "*This Is My Body*," etc. (1527), LW 37:99.
50. Ibid., 135–36.

continues to scandalize adherents of those forms of Christian transcendentalism which, in the attempt to guard divine sovereignty, place God beyond the bounds of any creaturely media. Following Luther, the Lutheran confessional writings speak in terms of a paradoxical but real *identification*, not merely a dialectic, between such realities as the Bible and God's word, the bread and Christ's body, Christ and God, human absolution and divine forgiveness. When Christ's duly called servants proclaim the gospel, administer the sacraments, and exercise the keys of the kingdom, *thereby* (*dadurch*) sins are forgiven, the Holy Spirit creates faith, and human beings are united to God. Together, the rich complex of divinely ordained verbal, sacramental, and ritual enactments constitute "the bodily word of the gospel" (*das leiblich Wort des Evangelii*). This pregnant phrase, coined by Luther and enshrined in the crucial fifth article of the Augsburg Confession, dogmatically unites objective justification and its subjective appropriation in an ecclesial, liturgically constituted act, a divine act permeated with human physicality.[51] The outward, physical words and ritual actions are not mere conduits; they establish a kind of "mediated immediacy" between God and man. In both his Genesis commentary and his sermons on John's Gospel, Luther vividly teaches that in the church's public preaching and sacramental ministry we "feel," "grasp," and "touch" God himself, "not only with our hearts but also with our eyes and our hands."[52] Of course this was not an insight unique to Luther; it was the common legacy of medieval Catholicism. One need only recall the eucharistic hymn ascribed to Thomas Aquinas, later rendered by Gerard Manley Hopkins:

> Visus, tactus, gustus, in te fallitur,
> Sed auditu solo tuto creditur:
> Credo quidquid dixit Dei filius
> Nihil veritatis verbo verius.
>
> Seeing, touching, tasting are in thee deceived;
> How says trusty hearing? that shall be believed;
> What God's Son has told me, take for truth I do;
> Truth himself speaks truly or there's nothing true.

Luther's special contribution however lies in the fact that he recognized in this dynamic a pervasive biblical motif, a kind of hermeneutical key that unlocks the whole salvific vista of God's revelatory dealings with human beings. That the realities communicated by "the embodied word" may not be

---

51. Article 5 of the Augsburg Confession, 58. See Bayer, *Leibliches Wort*.

52. Luther, *Sermons on the Gospel of St. John: Chapters 1–4* (1537–40), LW 22:420. See also LW 22:526–29; *Sermons on the Gospel of St. John: Chapters 14–16* (1537), LW 24:64–73.

accessible in their full opacity to the testimony of the senses in no way calls into question the fact of their objective presence and operative efficacy. Just as true faith is not scandalized by Christ's humanity, neither is it blinded by the humility of the physical means of the Spirit.

This is why we must disagree with Hampson when she asserts that for Luther "it could never be that the elements somehow become *in and of themselves* the body and blood of Christ," or that since it is the word that is all important, the outward material signs simply lend "greater assurance."[53] It is to be admitted that strains of this thought can be detected in Luther's earlier writings, especially in the great tracts of 1520. But as Swedish Luther scholar Tom G. Hardt has demonstrated, while Luther always denied allegations that he held a "Capernaitic" or cannabalistic understanding of the real presence, he increasingly pressed what many Lutherans today would consider extreme language into the defence of the Cyrilline, sacramentally realist view, namely, that the consecrated bread is Christ's body and the consecrated wine his blood, *vere et substantialiter*, so that what is seen with the eyes on the altar, held in the hand of the priest, received into the mouth and chewed with the teeth by every recipient, believing or unbelieving, worthy or unworthy, is the risen Christ's real flesh, "full of divinity."[54] Luther was not particularly perturbed by the Roman doctrine of transubstantiation, in which the substance of the bread and wine are said to cease to exist after the consecration, though he felt that it was most unwise to rest the case for the real presence on such tenuous philosophical grounds. Still, he expressed a distinct preference for having "mere blood" with the papists over "mere wine" with the enthusiasts.[55] "Identical predication," he reasons, "is no obstacle to us." What before the recitation of the words of institution is ordinary (*schlecht*) bread and wine becomes "body-bread" (*leibsbrod*) or "flesh-bread" (*fleischbrod*) and "blood-wine" (*blutswein*).[56] Hardt has further argued that Luther's personal and public belief that the sacrament may validly be adored "is a fact that is almost unanimously confirmed by research scholars; albeit the fact is often lamented."[57] And finally one might recall the well-known incident in the last year of his life when Luther castigated one of the assisting deacons in the church in Wittenberg for publicly treating consecrated and unconsecrated elements as the same thing.[58]

53. Hampson, *Christian Contradictions*, 23.
54. Luther, *"This Is My Body," etc.*, LW 37:129–30. See Hardt, *Sacrament of the Altar*.
55. Luther, *Confession Concerning Christ's Supper* (1528), LW 37:317.
56. Ibid., 303.
57. Hardt, *Sacrament of the Altar*, 29.
58. Related by Stephenson, *Lord's Supper*, 94.

Repeatedly in Luther's writings on the Lord's Supper we find him returning to its christological basis in the deified flesh of Christ born of Mary. While he was reluctant to interpret Jesus' words in the Fourth Gospel about eating his flesh and drinking his blood along eucharistic lines because the Zwinglians made use of exactly the same passage to argue for a figurative interpretation of the *verba*, his 1532 sermons on these verses are nevertheless redolent with eucharistic overtones. On account of the personal union Christ's flesh possesses qualities above and beyond those of ordinary flesh: "it will imbue you with godlike power, with godlike virtues and works. It will wipe out your sin; it will deliver you from the devil and death; it will free you from all wretchedness."[59] Quoting from Tertullian against Marcion and Irenaeus against Valentinus, Luther points out that these Fathers assume precisely what the reformed opponents deny, namely, that Christ's real body is physically consumed in the sacrament in such a way that it bestows on the body an immortal character, "though hidden in faith and hope until the Last Day."[60] Zwingli and Oecolampadius had frequent recourse to Augustine's reflections on "sign" with its accompanying and subtle theory of language and symbol. The relationship between a sign (*signum*) and the thing it signifies (*res*) is mysterious and complex, and in Augustine's earlier thought it is possible to detect a certain disjunction between the two. But as his sense of the literal continuity between the Old and New Testaments waxed in opposition to the Manichaean tendency to separate them, Augustine increasingly acknowledge a definite conjunction between a sign and what it signifies, so that the reality is "placed within the sign" (*in signo esse positum*). As Augustine scholar Michael Cameron observes, "This conjunctive understanding bound a reality of the spiritual world to its sign in such a way that, despite their incommensurability, the effective understanding of the reality depended on the particularity of the sign."[61] Luther, sensing his opponents' shaky argumentation, replies that Augustine cannot be used to support the conclusion that the sacrament consists in mere bread and wine or only a "spiritual" (immaterial) presence of Christ, for with Augustine "one can say that Christ's body is invisibly present under a visible sign."[62]

Once we recognize the fact that Christ's flesh is none other than the flesh of God, it is Luther's view that we should look for God nowhere else. Here is a theology of revelation consonant with the tradition of mystical theology bequeathed to the medieval west by Dionysius the Areopagite, for

---

59. Luther, *Sermons on the Gospel of St. John: Chapters 6–8* (1530–32), LW 23:122.
60. Luther, "*This Is My Body*," etc., LW 37:118.
61. Cameron, "Sign," 795.
62. Luther, "*This Is My Body*," etc., LW 37:104.

whom God wills to conceal himself and be found under contrary symbols. Both Dionysius and Luther know that in himself God dwells in the darkness of incomprehension; no one can see God in his unconcealed divinity and live (Exod 33:20).

> Therefore it was necessary for God to hide, cover, and conceal Himself, thus enabling us to touch and apprehend Him. He must disguise Himself in flesh and blood, in the Word, in the external ministry, in Baptism, in the Sacrament of the Lord's Supper, where He gives us His body in the bread and His blood in the wine, to eat and drink. He must conceal Himself in forms to which He adds His Word, in order that we may recognize Him.[63]

For this reason, if a person really wants to find the true God, he or she will seek him nowhere else than in the flesh and blood of the man born of Mary, "for that is where he dwells. In the Son of Man you will encounter God."[64] Luther condemns any attempt to locate God by introspective, imageless contemplation. Christ's humanity is the key that alone opens the way to communion with the holy Trinity:

> You should say that you know no God except the one who was in Mary's womb and sucked at her breasts. Wherever that God Jesus Christ is, the whole of God is there with all his divinity; there the Father and the Holy Spirit are found. Outside this Christ, God is nowhere and not found anywhere.[65]

Marriage and Social Ethics

Notwithstanding the great evils that unfolded in the sixteenth century in the form of wars, social disintegration, and ecclesial schism, numerous good fruits can be credited to the Reformation churches at the grassroots level of moral theology and practice. Luther's doctrine of faith emphasized the primacy of internal moral transformation: only a good tree bears good fruit; change in behavior requires a change in heart, and only the Spirit-filled word of the Gospel can change human hearts. His doctrine of vocation affirmed the value and holiness also of non-clerical forms of ecclesial, family, social and professional service. One does not need to become a monk

---

63. Luther, *Sermons on the Gospel of St. John: Chapters 6–8* (1530–32), LW 23:123.
64. Ibid., 129.
65. Translated by Kleinig, "Where Is Your God?" 102–3.

or priest or a celibate to please God or be saved. The humble milkmaid or soldier or farmer or magistrate who fulfills the mundane duties of his or her calling with true faith and unfeigned love pleases God more than a thousand faithless monks with shaved heads, starved bodies, and scarred backs. Luther's Small and Large Catechisms (of 1529) did much to strengthen domestic and parish morality, with their explicitly biblical ethics embodying an understanding of the Christian life as a continual return to and living out of one's baptism. In short, Luther's ethics are Christocentric, sacramental, interpersonal, and vocationally practical.

Nygren's portrayal of Luther as archenemy of *eros* raises an important question as to Luther's understanding of affectivity and desire and their respective role and appropriation in marital sexuality. The standard Catholic account of the impact of the Protestant Reformation upon traditional Catholic theology and practice of marriage, all in all, paints a pretty gloomy picture. It goes something like this. Martin Luther was a troubled and psychologically disturbed young man who, against all good counsel, decided to become a monk. Finding himself trapped in a vocation to which he was ill suited, he rebelled against his superiors and the church and set himself up as a leader of an antipapal reform movement for German Christians. As part of his new theological program, Luther overturned the church's longstanding teaching on the sacraments, including the sacramentality of marriage. In its place he introduced a secularized theory of marriage severing it from the realm of the sacred. This theoretical position led Luther to sanction all kinds of abuses in marriage: divorce, remarriage, and even bigamy. He himself abandoned the priesthood, indulged his sensual passions, and married a runaway nun. All of this can be traced to two main sources: Luther's own mixed up experiences as a boy, then monk, priest, professor, husband and father, and his pessimistic theological account of human nature, seen as totally depraved and corrupted by sin. Luckily, in spite of Luther's well-meaning but misguided ravings, the Council of Trent stepped in, responding to all these problems in the nick of time and providing the church with much needed theological and pastoral clarity in a time of danger and confusion.

That's the standard account. We find elements of it briefly expressed, for example, in the text on marriage in the teaching of the Magisterium by Raymond Garcia de Haro: "Luther and Calvin rejected the teachings of the Church on marriage." Luther holds that *"marriage is nothing else than the institution destined to satisfy concupiscence."* At root this perverse judgment and the rupture it occasioned can be traced to the Lutheran idea "of the corruption of nature and of justification as a merely extrinsic reality."[66]

---

66. De Haro, *Marriage and the Family*, 66–68.

There is another way of reading the evidence, however. As already mentioned, Luther was formed and raised in a distinctly Pelagian monastic piety. His later recollections of the effects of this Pelagian formation, against which he reacted, help explain certain dominant aspects of his theology, above all its emphasis upon the spiritual incapacities of human nature and the overwhelming prevenience of divine grace. Consider for a moment the following remarks, and what kind of spiritual disposition they manifest:

> I was always thinking, when will you do enough that God will be gracious to you? Such thoughts drove me to the monastery.
>
> I myself was a monk. For twenty years I tortured myself with prayers, fasting, vigils, and freezing; the frost alone might have killed me. It caused me pain such as I will never inflict on myself again, even if I could. What else did I seek by doing this but God, who was supposed to note my strict observance of the monastic order and my austere life? I constantly walked in a dream and lived in real idolatry. For I did not believe in Christ; I regarded him only as a severe and terrible Judge, portrayed as seated on a rainbow. Therefore I cast about for other intercessors, Mary and various other saints, also my own works and the merits of my order. And I did all this for the sake of God, not for money or goods.
>
> When I was a monk I made a great effort to live according to the monastic rule. I made a practice of confessing and reciting my sins and always with prior contrition. . . . Nevertheless my conscience could never achieve certainty, but I was always in doubt and said, "You have not done this correctly, you were not contrite enough, you left that out of your confession."[67]

Luther's thinking about marriage was often directed in explicit opposition to two contrary positions. The first, which Luther attributed to "the papists," devalued and denigrated marriage "as though it had been condemned by God" and instead exalted virginity as the only certain road to holiness. The second, which Luther attributed to the worldly culture of the unbelieving populace, also denigrated marriage, but did so by reducing it to sexual pleasure.[68]

While considering personal factors that impacted upon Luther's theology of marriage, special mention should also be made of his marriage to the well-educated refugee nun Katharina von Bora (b. 1499). Almost as soon as

---

67. These quotes taken from George Yule, "Luther and the Ascetic Life," 230–31.
68. See, for example, Luther, *Lectures on Genesis* (LW 5:30–33).

it happened, Catholic polemicists made Luther's marriage to Katharina the object of castigation, vilification, and ridicule. "Although Luther was by no means the first cleric of his time to marry, his prominence, his espousal of clerical marriage, and his prolific output of printed anti-Catholic propaganda made his marriage a natural target."[69] Even as late as the early twentieth century the influential Dominican historian Heinrich Denifle argued that it was not the doctrine of justification that lay behind the Protestant Reformation, but Luther's sensuality and immorality, which reached its climax in his marriage to this brazen runaway nun.[70]

But there is another side to the story. Like many girls in her time, Katharina had been entrusted by her family to a convent at the age of five. In the wake of evangelical preaching and piety encountered in her early twenties, she and several other nuns wrote to their families seeking release from the cloistered life they had not chosen for themselves. When they were refused, Katharina fled with eleven other nuns, finally (in April 1523) ending up in Wittenberg where, after two years of mixing amongst many of Luther's friends and associates, she attracted the Reformer's attentions.[71] This came over as a surprise to his colleagues. Even though he had defended the marriage of priests in principle, Luther himself was in no rush to marry. Bornkamm explains: "His work overloaded him. His poverty was so grinding that it made support of a family seem foolhardy. Besides, he had a lurking anxiety lest by marrying he throw his confrontation with the Roman church into a false light."[72] In a letter to an interested potential mate, penned in 1524, he expressed the additional fear that his life was destined soon to come to a violent and unhappy end.[73] So when in June 1525 Luther did marry Katharina rather suddenly, he had some explaining to do. He gave two reasons: his father's desire for grandchildren, and his own real affection for Katharina, "for I am neither amorous nor in heat, but I love my wife."[74] Above all, he regarded his marriage as an *opus Dei*, "a work of God."[75] His relationship with her was good-humored and happy, and he affectionately gave her several nicknames, including "my Katy," "Lord Katie," and the "Morning Star of Wittenberg." "I wouldn't give her up for France or Venice,"

---

69. Smith, "Katharina von Bora through Five Centuries," 754.
70. Denifle, *Luther and Lutherdom*, 312.
71. Brecht, *Martin Luther*, 235–40; also Smith, "Katharina von Bora."
72. Bornkamm, *Luther in Mid-Career*, 401.
73. The woman was Argula von Grumbach, an adherent of Spalatin. Quoted by Bornkamm, *Luther in Mid-Career*, 401–2.
74. Cited in Bornkamm, *Luther in Mid-Career*, 406.
75. Ibid., 410.

he commented in 1531. Katharina outlived him by six years (d. 1552, aged 53); she bore six children (two of whom died in childhood), suffered at least one nearly fatal miscarriage, and adopted and nursed a vast brood of needy children and boarders.[76]

To understand Luther's way of thinking about marriage, and before we examine specific ideas, we first have to situate his thought against the broad background of his biblically worked out doctrine of the "three estates" or "hierarchies" or "works of God." They are (*a*) household/family (*oeconomia*), (*b*) politics/society (*politia*), and (*c*) ministry/church (*ecclesia*). Oswald Bayer describes these three estates as "three basic forms of life that are God's disposition for humanity."[77] For Luther, these three estates express the three primary structures or social forms God has instituted and explicitly empowered and sanctified to be the means through which he exercises his providential and saving rule in the world and history. In one way or another these divinely instituted social forms embrace all human beings of all cultures and religions. Each is marked by certain sets of ordered relationships and vocations of responsibility and obligation. For Luther, the order of marriage and family (*oeconomia*) is the most foundational of all three estates, brought into being at the beginning of creation, and the foundation of every person's existence. Without it there would be no society, indeed, no church, for marriage is the origin and nursery of the church. As one of the three holy estates instituted by God, marriage is a permanent reality of the temporal order, pleasing to God and necessary for human well-being. It is therefore to be regarded as sacred or holy, even if it does not of itself save those who enter it.[78]

---

76. As an aside, it is interesting in this connection to consider the comments of Pope Benedict XVI on the question of priests who want to marry. Following discussion of the Legion of Christ scandal, in which it was discovered that the founding priest secretly had a *de facto* spouse and children, the pope had this to say: "Anything involving lies and concealment should not be. . . . When a priest lives together with a woman, one must examine whether a real will to marry is present and whether they could build a good marriage. If that is the case, they must follow that path. If it is a question of a failure of moral will, but no real interior union is there, one must try to find paths of healing for him and for her." Benedict XVI, *Light of the World*, 39–40.

77. Bayer, *Living by Faith*, 61. In connection with the doctrine of the three orders, Bayer comments, "The astonishing feature of Luther's pre-Reformation theology is not . . . the lasting significance of the spiritual, but the increasing significance of the worldly, primarily of marriage and parenthood. . . . The history of Luther's discovery of the positive significance of the worldly and the natural has not yet been written . . ." Bayer, "Nature and Institution," 134.

78. Luther, *Confession Concerning Christ's Supper*, 1528 (LW 37:365).

The second thing we need to do to understand Luther's doctrine of marriage is to relate it to his doctrine of vocation.[79] For Luther, Christianity does not extract a person from the world, but plunges him or her deeper into it. Each Christian is called to live out the life of faith "in vocation," that is, in his or her God-given set of relationships and life circumstances. Through the apparently "unspiritual" means of various human vocations, whether student or farmer, mother or magistrate, priest or parishioner, God reaches into the world with his wisdom, providence, and blessing. Luther calls these vocations "masks of God": through them God meets me, serves me, and calls to me for my willing and faithful response. In this light, marriage places a man and a woman into a new vocation: that of husband and wife, and, if God wills, that of father and mother. Meanwhile they do not cease to be, but still remain, in their vocations of son and daughter, brother and sister, citizen and parishioner, manager and servant, and so on. It is within the concrete relational dynamics, obligations, and opportunities of these multiple vocations that they are to co-operate with God, seek holiness of heart and life, and discern God hiddenly but graciously present to them.

One of the best known passages in which Luther treats the subject of marriage arises in his early polemical tract of 1520, *The Babylonian Captivity of the Church*. In it Luther famously denies that marriage is a sacrament. It was against this denial that the Fathers of Trent directed their first canon of Session 24 (November 11, 1563): "If anyone says that marriage is not in a true and strict sense one of the seven sacraments of the gospel dispensation, instituted by Christ, but a human invention in the church, and that it does not confer grace, let him be anathema."[80]

It should be pointed out that following the more radical reforms of the super-spiritualist Reformers, Luther returned to a more explicitly sacramental theology than is suggested by these early tracts. Even so, we can still ask the question: What was Luther's rationale for denying the sacramentality of marriage? Following the controversy that had erupted with the publication of his *Ninety Five Theses* in 1517, Luther increasingly wanted to bring all such questions back to a single query: by what authority does one make any theological claim? Given his judgment about numerous claims made in the name of divine right, the only final authority he allows is the word of God, made objectively explicit in Scripture. From this, he finds several conclusions that follow.

---

79. The classic work on this is Wingren, *Luther on Vocation*. See also, more briefly, Veith, "Masks of God."

80. Tanner, *Decrees of the Ecumenical Councils*, 2:754.

First, a sacrament is an efficacious divine promise of grace attached to and communicated by means of an external element or sign. Scripture nowhere promises saving grace to those who marry, nor does marriage bear any divinely instituted element or sign in the way that baptism and the Eucharist do. Marriage may be a type or figure of something invisible, but this does not make it a sacrament in the strict sense of an efficacious means of saving grace. Second, marriage exists, and has always existed, among non-believers. Thus it cannot be called a sacrament of the New Law or the exclusive prerogative of the church. Third, the attribution of the term *sacramentum* to the union of Christ and the Church in the Latin version of Eph 5 simply translates the Greek word *mysterion*, which means something secret or hidden. Luther comments: "Christ and the Church are, therefore, a mystery, that is, a great and secret thing, which it is possible and proper to represent by marriage as by a certain outward allegory, but that is no reason for calling marriage a sacrament."

Fourth, while marriage may not be a sacrament, it is instituted by divine law, which says, "What God has joined together let no man put asunder." Thus the joining together of a man and woman in marriage is binding, "however it may conflict with the laws of men, which must give way before it without hesitation." Hence if any pope, bishop or official annul any marriage because it was contracted contrary to the laws of men, he is antichrist, he does violence to nature, and is guilty of lese-majesty toward God, because this word stands, "What God hath joined, let no man separate." For Luther, this meant that vows made by religious and priests to live a celibate life should not annul marriage vows. "He who has plighted his troth to a maiden ought not to take a monastic vow, but is in duty bound to keep faith with her, which faith he cannot break for any tradition of men. . . . No marriage of deacon, priest, bishop, or any other order can be annulled. . . . Between a priest and his wife there exists a true and indissoluble marriage, approved by the divine commandment."[81]

It was also in this early tract that Luther first expressed his preference for bigamy over divorce: "For my part I so greatly detest divorce that I should prefer bigamy to it."[82] Later on Landgrave Philip of Hesse sought and cited Luther's opinion to justify his own act of bigamy. This event has long proved a matter of some embarrassment to Protestants, and Luther's opponents have happily highlighted the event to this day. However the situation was a little more complex than first appearances might suggest. Philip of Hesse, Prince of Saxony, had married the woman assigned to him by political and

---

81. Luther, *Babylonian Captivity*, 218–19.
82. Ibid., 223.

economic expedience. As he took no pleasure in her, he followed the custom of keeping several mistresses in tow. When later stricken in conscience, but unwilling to cleave to his wife, it occurred to him whether it might be permissible for him to follow Old Testament precedent and take a second wife. In 1526 he wrote to Luther and, without mentioning his situation, put it forward as a hypothetical scenario. Luther replied with these words:

> It is my faithful warning and counsel that Christians should not take more than one wife, not only because it is scandalous, and no Christian causes scandal but most diligently avoids it, but also because there is no word of God for it that it is pleasing to him by Christians. Heathen and Turks may do what they please. The ancient Patriarchs had several wives, but they were driven to this by necessity. And accordingly kings received as by inheritance the wives of their friends according to the law of Moses. But it is not sufficient for a Christian to be satisfied with the work of the Patriarchs. He must have a divine word for himself, that makes it certain for him. . . . Therefore I cannot advise it (taking more than one wife), but strongly advise against it, especially to Christians, unless it might be a case of strong necessity, such as that the wife was leprous or similarly afflicted.[83]

As it turned out, it was this phrase "unless it might be a case of strong necessity" that Philip of Hesse latched on to. Years passed, during which time arose the case of King Henry VIII in England, to whom Luther and Melanchthon (in 1531) directed a letter conceding the permissibility of bigamy in order to provide the nation with an heir to the throne. In 1539, Philip of Hesse sent an urgent letter to Wittenberg requesting Luther's blessing to take a second wife. Luther replied, making the following substantial points: (*a*) no public law should be passed allowing bigamy; (*b*) God has instituted marriage as a society between two persons alone, and not more; (*c*) Lamech was the first example in Scripture to have more than one wife, and Scripture speaks of this "as bringing in something against the first rule"; (*d*) Christ reiterated this first rule given from the beginning; (*e*) there may be cases where special dispensation can be given, as long as these are not made public "as a law which others might follow"; (*f*) since bigamy in Prince Hesse's case could not be kept private and would surely cause scandal, it is best avoided; (*g*) sins against marriage and chastity should not be thought of as slight, but grave; (*h*) if the Prince insists on taking a second wife, he should do so secretly, under the appearance that she is only his concubine,

---

83. Luther to Philip of Hesse, 1526, quoted in Faulkner, "Luther and the Bigamous Marriage," 207.

a publicly accepted practice, confiding the truth only to his confessor and nearest confidants.[84]

This brings me to the end of my summary of the more controversial aspects of Luther's teaching on marriage. But there are other aspects of his thought on the topic that anticipate the developments in marital theology that have come to fruition in the integration of more personalist and biblical categories in Vatican II's Pastoral Constitution *Gaudium et Spes* and in the theology of the body of Pope John Paul II. A number of brief comments may be made. First, in the very first part of his treatise *The Estate of Marriage* (1522), Luther begins by grounding marriage in the creation of human beings as male and female, affirming the goodness and integrity of our physical, sexual constitution. God has divided mankind into two sexes, "namely, male and female, a he and a she":

> This was so pleasing to him that he himself called it a good creation. Therefore, each one of us must have the kind of body God has created for us. I cannot make myself a woman, nor can you make yourself a man; we do not have that power. But we are exactly as he has created us: I a man and you a woman. Moreover, he wills to have his excellent handiwork honored as his divine creation, and not despised. The man is not to despise or scoff at the woman or her body, nor the woman the man. But each should honor the other's image and body as a divine and good creation that is well-pleasing to God himself.[85]

Second, Luther takes the command "Be fruitful and multiply" (Gen 1:28) as "more than a command." Rather it expresses a natural necessity, "a divine ordinance [*werck*] which it is not our prerogative to hinder or ignore."[86] The inclination to sexual coupling and procreation is not simply a matter of free choice, but is so deeply bound up with the human constitution that to resist it, except in extraordinary cases of a special call and grace, can only result in harm to the human sexual powers and perversion in sexual practice.

Third, Luther's study of the Bible, especially the Old Testament, led him to praise the value of mutual love and expressions of tender and happy affection between spouses. "[Marriage] is a lawful union not only of bodies but also of hearts."[87] "A husband should conduct himself in a friendly

---

84. From the letter reproduced and translated in Faulkner, "Luther and the Bigamous Marriage," 213–16.

85. Luther, *Estate of Marriage* (LW 45:17–18).

86. Ibid., 18.

87. Luther, *Lectures on Genesis* (LW 5:32).

and gentle manner toward his wife, not only in the bedroom but also in public."[88] "It's the greatest blessing of God when love continues to flower in marriage. The first love is ardent, an intoxicated love which dazzles us and leads us on. When the intoxication has been slept off, the connubial love of the godly is genuine, while the ungodly have regrets."[89]

Fourth, Luther's argument that priests or religious should be free to marry[90] needs to be read in light of two things: first, it was Luther's perception that many who had become priests or religious in his day had done so not out of a sense of divine calling but out of disdain for married life. Second, it was his understanding that marriage is by and large a universal calling and therefore the normal vocation for all men and women, with only a few exceptions. Luther finds this claim substantiated by the scriptural phrase "be fruitful and multiply." For him these words of God do not simply express a command to the first couple. "It is more than a command, namely, a divine ordinance, which it is not our prerogative to hinder or ignore. . . . And wherever people try to resist this, it remains irresistible nonetheless and goes its way through fornication, adultery, and secret sins, for this is a matter of nature and not of choice."[91]

Having said as much, Luther goes on to say that God has exempted three categories of people from this ordinance of creation, according to Matt 19: eunuchs from birth (= the physically handicapped or impotent), eunuchs made by men (= "the castrates," "an unhappy lot . . . plagued with a desire for women, but are unable to consummate their desire"), and eunuchs for the sake of the kingdom (see below). "Whoever does not fall within these three categories should not consider anything except the estate of marriage. . . . Don't let yourself be fooled on this score, even if you should make ten oaths, vows, covenants, and adamantine or ironclad pledges. For

88. Ibid.
89. Luther, *Table Talk* (LW 54:223).
90. Cf. Luther on 1 Cor 7, 1523: "Faith and the Christian life are so free in essence that they are bound to no particular order or estate of society, but they are to be found in and throughout all orders and estates. Therefore, you need not accept or give up any particular estate in order to be saved. On the contrary, the estate in which faith and the Gospel find you, there you may stay and find your salvation. Therefore it is not necessary that you give up marriage and leave your non-Christian spouse for the sake of your faith and salvation. On the other hand, it is not necessary for you to be married, either to a Christian or a non-Christian spouse, for the sake of faith and salvation" (LW 28:39–40). Bayer comments that in this passage we note "a certain polemical element" in Luther's championing of the value of the three orders. "This is a polemic against the favoring, as a matter of principle, of one particular order [e.g., priesthood or celibacy] as a special spiritual station over the temporal stations, which allegedly are of lesser value in terms of their importance for salvation." Bayer, "Nature and Institution," 136.
91. Luther, *Estate of Marriage* (LW 45:18).

just as you cannot solemnly promise that you will not be a man or a woman . . . , so you cannot promise that you will not produce seed or multiply, unless you belong to one of the three categories mentioned above."[92]

What does Luther say about the third category, virgins for the sake of the kingdom? This category, he writes,

> consists of those spiritually rich and exalted persons, bridled by the grace of God, who are equipped for marriage by nature and physical capacity and nevertheless voluntarily remain celibate. Such people put it this way: "I could marry if I wish, I am capable of it. But it does not attract me. I would rather work on the kingdom of heaven, i.e., the gospel, and beget spiritual children." Such persons are rare, not one in a thousand, for they are a special miracle of God. No one should venture on such a life unless he be especially called by God, like Jeremiah [16:2], or unless he finds God's grace to be so powerful within him that the divine injunction, "be fruitful and multiply," has no place in him.[93]

In short, the extraordinary vocation to consecrated celibacy calls for careful discernment aimed at confirming that one has been granted this special grace.

Fifth, despite the bigamy scandals, Luther counseled spouses in difficult marriages to stick it out with Christlike forgiveness. For example, where an accident or illness renders a man's wife incapable of sexual intercourse, Luther commends perseverance in patience and faithful love:

> May he not take another to wife? By no means. Let him serve the Lord in the person of the invalid and await his good pleasure. Consider that in this invalid God has provided your household with a healing balm by which you are to gain heaven. Blessed and twice blessed are you when you recognize such a gift of grace and therefore serve your invalid wife for God's sake. But you may say: I am unable to remain continent. That is a lie. If you will earnestly serve your invalid wife, recognize that God has placed this burden upon you, and give thanks to him, then you may leave matters in his care. He will surely grant you grace, that you will not have to bear more than you are able. He is far too faithful to deprive you of your wife through illness without at the same time subduing your carnal desire, if you will but faithfully serve your invalid wife.[94]

92. Ibid., 18–19.
93. Ibid., 21.
94. Ibid., 35.

Finally, what does Luther have to say about formally regulating marriage? One of the key issues raised by the Protestant Reformation, and that subsequently needed to be responded to by the Council of Trent, was the relation between divine and human law. The Protestants felt a clear line needed to be drawn between the two, with flexibility built into the latter. Moreover, any law claimed to be divine and binding on conscience needed not just papal or conciliar assertion but the explicit support of Scripture. For the Protestants, marriage vows clearly fulfilled this criterion, and thus fall into the category of unchangeable divine law. For them, marriage is a divine ordinance, since Scripture explicitly testifies to its divine institution and its binding character. Faithfulness to marriage vows is binding on pain of sin. On the other hand, what was the status of vows to celibacy? Were these divine or human? Unable to find any explicit scriptural warrant for holding vows to celibacy to be binding and irrevocable on pain of sin, the Protestant Reformers regarded it as a usurpation of divine authority to regard them as more binding than and of superior precedence to vows of marriage. A celibate person, even one who has vowed himself to the celibate vocation, should be free, in certain pressing circumstances, to renounce his vows for the sake of marriage.[95] Whereas someone who is married, even to an unbeliever, is by no means free simply to renounce marriage for the sake of the human vow of celibacy, but is bound by his vows before God.

What about other legal matters pertaining to validity? Initially, in his rejection of absolute papal authority Luther also rejected the absolute authority of canon law. Luther believed that especially in marriage, where "questions of law were at the same time questions of conscience," one had to approach things pastorally and evangelically, not just legally.[96] But soon Luther was flooded with a wave of concrete problems in answer to which he and his colleagues had to formulate their own *de facto* canon law. In a short tract written in 1522, Luther reduced the range of forbidden degrees and impediments to marriage, vastly simplifying the complex regulations in Gratian's *Decretum*, the twelfth-century codification of canon law. Luther listed fourteen forbidden relationships (of consanguinity and affinity) drawn from Leviticus 18, and retained coercion and impotence as valid impediments. "As to other forbidden persons or degrees of relationship, our clerical tyrants have forbidden them for the sake of money. This is evident from the fact that, for money, they turn right around and sell permission

---

95. Note that in the sixteenth century many children were committed to monastic life by their parents, while many took binding vows in a state of passion, fear, or ignorance.

96. Bornkamm, *Luther in Mid-Career*, 109.

for prohibited marriage, and if no money is forthcoming they break up the marriage, contrary to God and every sense of justice."[97]

While it is commonly thought that through such measures Luther relaxed the church's teaching on the indissolubility of marriage,[98] he himself claimed not to support marital breakup or separation. In his 1522 treatise *The Estate of Marriage*, Luther gives three grounds that, by dissolving the marriage, render separation and remarriage permissible (though not obligatory): impotence, adultery, and persistent or longstanding refusal to fulfill the conjugal duty. Separation, but not remarriage, is additionally permissible in cases where spouses find cohabitation unbearable or dangerous.[99]

For all these good intentions, it may be asked how successful the Lutheran approach ended up being in regulating marriage. On the one hand, the Lutheran household became the new sphere for a Christian form of life akin to monastic culture, marked as it was by regular times of divine reading, prayer, and catechesis, with father and mother as co-teachers and priests, and entrusted with the common project of co-working with God in worship and in the world. On the other hand, legal and canonical oversight of betrothal and marriage was by and by handed over to local civic authorities, subsequently nationalized, and as states became secularized, was exercised only in an instrumental way. But it is too simplistic to put the blame for this eventual secularization of marriage on Luther. Devoutly following his theology, pastors in the Lutheran communities remained closely involved with couples and families with a deep sense of urgent responsibility, and while they may have lacked legal power, they certainly retained a high level of moral and spiritual influence. As for secularization, the Protestant Reformation unfolded within a much longer and complex process of secularization whose history goes back at least to the late medieval and renaissance world. It is not just within Protestant Christian culture that history has come to witness the widespread practice of multiple divorces and remarriage and a practical rejection of marriage's inherent indissolubility. At most it could be argued that in desacramentalizing marriage, Luther did not so much directly secularize it, but rather, as Young aptly summarizes, "lowered its resistance to the pressures of the secular world."[100]

---

97. Luther, *Persons Related by Consanguinity* (LW 45:8).

98. "Luther and Calvin alike maintained that scriptural proof could be found for the lawfulness of divorce for adultery and for desertion: and the liberty thus accorded soon received a very wide extension." Joyce, *Christian Marriage*, 387–88.

99. Luther, *Estate of Marriage* (LW 45:30–35).

100. See Young, "Reformations of the Sixteenth and Seventeenth Centuries," 274.

An Ambiguous Legacy

Since the sixteenth century Luther's theological legacy has been vulnerable to multiple and ambiguous interpretations, not least because words of his often intended to address a specific issue or used with rhetorical force in a polemical context are wrongly taken as systematic and definitive pronouncements. Thus, against his Catholic opponents he will assert that faith alone justifies, but against the Protestant Antinomians he will deny it, asserting instead that we are saved only by that faith which is also operative in works of love. What may be stated with confidence is that his abiding concern was to consider all things from the perspective of God's word, to judge reality by what God sees (*coram Deo*), a perspective made known by the inscripturated word whose only infallible interpreter is the Holy Spirit, present with his holy Church in the concrete, tangible means of grace, through which the realities indicated by that word are effectively realized.

None of the momentous crises which led to the formal separation of the ecclesial communities of northern Germany from the Catholic Church took place out of the blue. Some kind of schism between the papal leadership and the German churches had been a long time coming. For at least a century the German prince-bishops had enjoyed relative independence from the papacy. The exercise of ecclesiastical authority thus had become increasingly diffuse and parochial. Combined with this there ran within German Christian piety itself a strong strain of anticlericalism and, within its universities, openness to the new "modern" humanist learning.[101] The political and intellectual climate thus offered a supportive, catalytic context for the Lutheran movement and effective asylum for its chief protagonists. As Harvard medievalist Steve Ozment observes, "many communities believed the Reformation to be an aid not only to long-term providential blessing but also to be a certain democratizing of local government. . . . In many instances cities and territories found direct economic and political benefits in breaking with the ecclesio-commercial complex that had long served the distant interests of Rome."[102]

In conclusion, we may return to consider a number of important questions raised by the interpretations of Nygren and Hampson. Conspicuously absent in Nygren's thesis is any substantial doctrine of creation, along with any plausible account of the relation between creation and redemption. His sole concern is with man the sinner, to the virtual exclusion of man the creature. But this means that, in the end, Nygren's ideal of agape-love

---

101. See further Tillinghast, "An Aborted Reformation."
102. Ozment, *Reformation in the Cities*, 117.

is unrealistic. It fails to make sense of the actual conditions of human life and creaturely experience which constitute "the indispensable subsoil from which agape will be able to blossom."[103] For Nygren, there seems to be no possibility of any correspondence between human desire and divine revelation, between nature and grace. He "never considers the fact that, even though Christian revelation has radically changed the spiritual attitude on which salvation depends, it has not changed human nature and removed it from its ontological laws as they ensue from the creative act."[104] Eros-love, understood as the metaphysical substructure of all creation and as the tendency towards fulfilment in God implicated in every free human act, is not something we can, or should want to, get away from. As C. S. Lewis observed, it would be "a bold and silly creature that came before its Creator with the boast, 'I'm no beggar. I love you disinterestedly.'"[105] Eros has its workings "in our very instincts, appetites and recreations," wherein Love—divine agape—"has prepared for Himself 'a body.'"[106]

It is quite possible that this rupture between man the sinner and man the creature reflects a schism in Luther's own theological vision, although if so, given the strongly anti-Pelagian logic of his thought, it amounts to a shortcoming that can be accounted for. Yet it is disturbing that Nygren finds in the heretic Marcion a kind of early precursor of Luther's revival of the agape motif. "Here at last someone has understood how absolutely new the Christian message is, someone who has perceived what its newness ultimately is."[107] Yet this understanding rests on Marcion's proposed antithesis between the Creator-God and the Father of Jesus Christ, between creation and redemption.

> The thought of the absolute newness of Christianity is intimately connected with Marcion's basic idea of the contrast between the God who created us, and the God who in Christ effected our salvation. The world we live in bears clear testimony to the weakness and imperfection of its Maker; it is crude and impure, and Marcion, like the Gnostics, has nothing but contempt for it. But what is true of the world in general ... applies equally to man; he too, body and soul, is a work of the Creator-God, and his weakness

103. Lubac, "Eros and Agapē," 88.

104. Ibid.

105. Lewis, *Four Loves*, 9. For further critical analysis of Nygren's thesis, see Osborn, *Eros Unveiled*; Mascall, *Recovery of Unity*, 75–86; Pieper, *Faith, Hope, Love*, 207–81; De Andia, "Eros and Agape"; Benedict XVI, *Deus Caritas Est*, §§1–18; Schindler, "Redemption of *Eros*."

106. Lewis, *Four Loves*, 122.

107. Nygren, *Agape and Eros*, 317.

and infirmity are convincing evidence of his Maker's inferiority. . . . It is easy to see why Marcion so stresses the idea that the Highest God, the Father of Jesus Christ, has nothing to do with the creation, but is an entire stranger to us. He is plainly concerned for Agape. The more he emphasizes that God is the Stranger, the greater is the miracle of the Divine love, the greater the paradox of God's Agape.[108]

For Nygren it is no wonder that connected with Marcion's interest in *agape* "is his violent opposition to the Old Testament." He finds in it "a totally different spirit from that of Christianity." Our relation to the old covenant "is not to be one of co-ordination but one of conflict . . . their relationship is purely antithetical."[109]

In this light, Hampson seems all the more likely to be onto something when she takes issue with "the whole Lutheran depiction, from Luther forwards, as to what it means to be a human being." In particular Hampson is critical of the notion of self depicted in Hegelian idealism and Bultmannian existentialism according to which "we are only grounded in God as once and again we break the self as we naturally know it to be and consent to dependence upon another."[110] It is this "break," this obliteration of human nature, an idea apparently derived from Luther and allegedly consonant with the structure of Lutheranism, with which Hampson takes issue. If the Christian's true identity is found totally outside himself, if revelation disrupts any possible continuity between created and redeemed humanity, who or what precisely is the object of justification? Who or what is redeemed?

It seems to me that a way towards an answer to these important questions lies in what we have outlined in Luther's doctrine of the believer's vivification through Christ's flesh. In his Christology and sacramental theology, Luther knows Jesus Christ to be the immortal God who, through his flesh, imparts eternal life to (otherwise) mortal humanity. The fact that he took flesh from Mary in a supernatural manner by no means negates nature. "For grace does not destroy or impede nature and nature's works; indeed, grace improves and promotes them."[111] Moreover, this teaching, which arises from and remains permanently bound to the contingent particulars of the historical Jesus, "is the article of justification."[112] Thus we see for Lu-

---

108. Ibid., 318. Nygren quotes Harnack's observation that the name "the Stranger" remained the Marcionite Church's preferred name for its God (ibid., 323).

109. Ibid., 321.

110. Hampson, *Christian Contradictions*, 237, 245.

111. Luther, *The Gospel for Christmas Eve, Luke 2[:1–14]* (1522), LW 52:12.

112. Luther, *Sermons on the Gospel of St. John: Chapters 6–8* (1530–32), LW 23:129.

ther that human nature *per se* is not the problem. Death, universally active in human nature, is the problem. Christ comes as the divine physician to restore mortally afflicted humanity to life. To the question, "Who or what is redeemed?" Luther has a definite answer: mortal human nature, humanity under the power of sin, humanity bounded by death.

To my knowledge Luther never rejected the common medieval doctrine of secondary causes (*causae secundae*), which ennobles the contingent, causative operations of the physical universe, including those of human beings, by coordinating them with the uninterrupted and providential operation of God, who is present and active in them. Nor, for all his hostility to the Aristotelian philosophical legacy, did he disparage humanity in its creaturely and physical goodness. On the contrary, he held that human beings are created in God's image and therefore endowed with what he called "the majesty of reason," a power that distinguishes them from the irrational beasts. Nor was this majesty lost after the fall. To be sure, few have used more pessimistic language than Luther to describe the impact of sin's crippling influence on the human intellect, will, and sensitive powers. Yet we can still find him admitting that reason remains "that most beautiful and excellent of all creatures . . . even after sin."[113] The crisis becomes apparent when we discern that this near-divine being is subject to death. In relation to himself, and in relation to others, the human being is capable of remarkable progress in virtue or "civic righteousness." This is human nature as we know it from philosophy.[114] But this kind of righteousness cannot spare him from death, which afflicts the virtuous and evildoer alike. Death manifests empirical man's deep dysfunction in relation to God, who created him for immortal life. Luther rejected the Ockhamistic doctrine that there is some kind of neutral territory in which human beings can cultivate a just and ultimately fruitful life untouched by the doom which attends their unbelief towards God. Each day a person is either one step nearer to God, or one step further away.[115] In this sense Luther can conceive of the Christian life as a progressive journey or process: the believer, righteous as far as the judgment of God is concerned, is not yet righteous in

---

113. Luther, *The Disputation Concerning Man* (1536), LW 34:138–39. Luther's famous statement in 1517 that "the whole of Aristotle is to theology as darkness to light" must be interpreted within the context of the renewed prominence of (Ockhamistic) Semi-Pelagianism. As Steven Ozment comments, "In its context, this statement rejected neither reason nor Aristotle per se; it was rather a plea to keep syllogisms, even of a higher order, and inordinate speculation on the conditions of revelation out of the sphere of faith." See Ozment, *Age of Reform*, 238.

114. Thus Luther affirms a legitimate though qualified role for Aristotelian ethics and its notion of acquired justice. See *Lectures on Galatians: Chapters 1–6* (1519), LW 27:219.

115. Luther, *Disputation Concerning Man* (1536), LW 34:140; Luther, *The Disputation Concerning Justification* (1536), LW 34:155.

embodied, concrete actuality, "but is in the very movement or journey toward righteousness."[116] Union with the life-giving flesh of Christ, therefore, takes on corporeal contours in holy works performed within each believer's particular vocation, a cooperative process of willing transformation which necessarily accompanies faith.[117]

Hampson's remaining difficulties may stem more from her rejection of the uniqueness of Jesus, the universal claims of Christian revelation, and Christian theology's preoccupation with questions of no apparent meaning in the modern, post-Darwinian world. She follows Bultmann in judging the traditional confession of Jesus' bodily resurrection as rationally meaningless, for, quite apart from the fact that no universal consequences could follow from such a "small" and isolated historical occurrence, "no such peculiar events exist."[118] Hampson here betrays her compliance with an epistemological method that rules out *a priori* the possibility of there being events in history having universal or absolute significance. The result is a narrow, predetermined philosophical consciousness from which certain kinds of reality are definitively excluded. But "if we cannot pass beyond the limits to human perception set by Kant, then faith will necessarily atrophy, simply for lack of breathing space."[119] The Christian gospel cannot be abstracted and detached from its inherently realist foundations without self-destruction. Even so, while its veracity is bound up with facts that have been seen, heard, and touched (1 John 1:1), in order to have faith—in Luther's sense of *fiducia* or confidence—it is not necessary to have had the same sensory experiences, but only to accept their truth on the basis of someone else's testimony. It belongs to the historical contingency of the Christian religion that we have no *immediate* access to the events that gave it birth. As philosopher Josef Pieper has remarked, "the witness and guarantor on whose word the believer relies is God himself, and we do not encounter him directly."[120]

In a way Cajetan was right: Luther did build a new church. For as Ratzinger has commented, following his excommunication, Luther "not only

---

116. Luther, *Disputation Concerning Justification* (1536), LW 34:152.

117. On the role of the believer's willing co-operation with the Holy Spirit after conversion, see the Formula of Concord: Epitome II (Tappert, *Book of Concord*, 469–72). That this transformation also includes a certain kind of self-denial and "death to self" belongs not just to Lutheranism but also to the teaching of Christ in the Synoptic Gospels. Even the Thomistic construal of the *ordo salutis* implied some kind of sacrificial sublimation of the lower appetites, "so that the passage to the supernatural order, even for an innocent and healthy nature, could never take place without some kind of death." Lubac, *Mystery of the Supernatural*, 28.

118. Hampson, *Christian Contradictions*, 236.

119. Ratzinger, *Truth and Tolerance*, 135.

120. Pieper, *Problems of Modern Faith*, vii.

categorically rejected the papacy but he also deemed the Catholic teachings about the Eucharist (Mass) as idolatry because he interpreted the mass as a relapse into the law and, thus, a denial of the gospel."[121] If this break began in his theology, it was actualized only by decisive external actions, whose precipitation owe as much to Luther's irascible personality and the accidents of history as they do to any inexorable logic. This is not to dispense Luther from responsibility. As he knew, outward communion in the church's material and institutional forms can never be regarded by theology as an incidental or peripheral detail. Within a decade of Cajetan's solemn pronouncement, protesting congregations in northern Germany, under Luther's leadership and with his approval, had elected and ordained their own priests, adopted radically revised liturgical forms, established their own orders of *de facto* episcopal oversight, and come to see themselves—precisely in their separation from the bishop of Rome—as the authentic heirs of the Catholic tradition.

Bibliography

Bayer, Oswald. *Leibliches Wort: Reformation und Neuzeit im Kinflikt*. Tübingen: Mohr Siebeck, 1992.

———. *Living by Faith: Justification and Sanctification*. Translated by Geoffrey W. Bromiley. Grand Rapids: Eerdmans, 2003.

———. "Nature and Institution: Luther's Doctrine of the Three Orders." *Lutheran Quarterly* 12 (1998) 125–59.

———. *Theology the Lutheran Way*. Edited and translated by J. G. Silcock and M. C. Mattes. Grand Rapids: Eerdmans, 2007.

Benedict XVI, Pope. *Deus Caritas Est*. San Francisco: Ignatius, 2005.

———. *Light of the World: The Pope, the Church, and the Signs of the Times; A Conversation with Peter Seewald*. Translated by M. J. Miller and A. J. Walker. San Francisco: Ignatius, 2010.

Bornkamm, Heinrich. *Luther in Mid-Career, 1521–1530*. Edited by Karin Bornkamm. Translated by E. Theodore Bachmann. Philadelphia: Fortress, 1983.

Braaten, Carl E., and Robert W. Jenson, eds. *Union with Christ: The New Finnish Interpretation of Luther*. Grand Rapids: Eerdmans, 1998.

Brecht, Martin. *Martin Luther: The Preservation of the Church, 1532–1546*. Minneapolis: Fortress, 1993.

Cameron, Michael. "Sign." In *Augustine through the Ages: An Encyclopedia*, edited by Allan D. Fitzgerald, 793–98. Grand Rapids: Eerdmans, 1999.

Cary, Phillip. "Why Luther Is Not Quite Protestant." *Pro Ecclesia* 14 (2005) 447–86.

De Andia, Ysabel. "Eros and Agape: The Divine Passion of Love." *Communio* 24 (1997) 29–50.

De Haro, Raymond Garcia. *Marriage and the Family in the Documents of the Magisterium*. San Francisco: Ignatius, 1993.

121. Ratzinger, "Luther and the Unity of the Churches," 213–14.

Denifle, H. *Luther and Lutherdom*. Translated by R. Volz. Somerset: Torch, 1917.
Faulkner, John Alfred. "Luther and the Bigamous Marriage of Philip of Hesse." *The American Journal of Theology* 17 (1913) 206–31.
Gilson, Etienne. *The Spirit of Medieval Philosophy*. Translated by A. H. C. Downes. Notre Dame: University of Notre Dame Press, 1991.
Hampson, Daphne. *Christian Contradictions: The Structures of Lutheran and Catholic Thought*. Cambridge: Cambridge University Press, 2001.
Hardt, Tom G. *The Sacrament of the Altar: A Book on the Lutheran Doctrine of the Lord's Supper*. Translated by E. L. Rye. Fort Wayne, IN: Concordia Lutheran Seminary, 1984.
Hegel, G. W. F. *The Philosophy of Right; The Philosophy of History*. Translated by J. Sibree. Great Books of the Western World 46. Chicago: W. Benton, 1952.
Joyce, George Hayward. *Christian Marriage: An Historical and Doctrinal Study*. London: Sheed and Ward, 1933.
Juntunen, Sammeli. "Luther and Metaphysics: What Is the Structure of Being according to Luther?" In *Union with Christ: The New Finnish Interpretation of Luther*, edited by Carl E. Braaten and Robert W. Jenson, 129–60. Grand Rapids: Eerdmans, 1998.
Kleinig, John W. "Where Is Your God? Luther on God's Self-Localisation." In *Perspectives on Luther: Papers from the Luther Symposium Held at Luther Seminary, Adelaide, South Australia 22–23 March, 1996 Commemorating the 450th Anniversary of the Reformer's Death*, edited by M. W. Worthing, 91–103. North Adelaide: Faculty of Luther Campus, 1996.
Lewis, C. S. *The Four Loves*. London: Fontana, 1960.
Lubac, Henri de. "Eros and Agapē." In *Theological Fragments*, translated by R. H. Balinski, 85–90. San Francisco: Ignatius, 1989.
———. *The Mystery of the Supernatural*. Translated by R. Sheed. New York: Crossroad, 1998.
Luther, Martin. *The Babylonian Captivity of the Church*. Translated by A. T. W. Steinhäuser. Revised by Frederick C. Ahrens and Abdel Ross Wentz. In Martin Luther, *Three Treatises*, 123–78. Rev. ed. Philadelphia: Muhlenberg, 1960.
———. *Commentary on Psalm 5* (1519). In *Luther's Commentary on the First Twenty-two Psalms*. Translated by Henry Cole. Edited by John Nicholas Lenker. Sunbury, PA: Lutherans in All Lands, 1903.
Marquart, Kurt E. "Luther and Theosis." *Concordia Theological Quarterly* 64 (2000) 182–205.
Mascall, Eric Lionel. *The Recovery of Unity*. London: Longmans, 1958.
McSorley, Harry J. *Luther Right or Wrong? An Ecumenical-Theological Study of Luther's Major Work*, The Bondage of the Will. New York: Newman, 1969.
Nygren, Anders. *Agape and Eros*. Translated by Philip S. Watson. London: SPCK, 1953.
Oberman, Heiko. *The Harvest of Medieval Theology: Gabriel Biel and Late Medieval Nominalism*. Cambridge: Harvard University Press, 1963.
Osborn, Catherine. *Eros Unveiled: Plato and the God of Love*. Oxford: Clarendon, 1994.
Ozment, Steven. *The Age of Reform, 1250–1550*. New Haven: Yale University Press, 1980.
———. *The Reformation in the Cities: The Appeal of Protestantism to Sixteenth-Century Germany and Switzerland*. New Haven: Yale University Press, 1975.
Pelikan, Jaroslav, and Helmut T. Lehman, eds. *Luther's Works*. American ed. 55 vols. St. Louis: Concordia, 1955–86.

Pieper, Josef. *Faith, Hope, Love*. San Francisco: Ignatius, 1997.

———. *Problems of Modern Faith: Essays and Addresses*. Translated by J. van Heurck. Chicago: Franciscan Herald, 1985.

Ratzinger, Joseph. "Luther and the Unity of the Churches: An Interview with Joseph Cardinal Ratzinger." *Communio* 11 (1984) 210–26.

———. *Principles of Catholic Theology: Building Stones for a Fundamental Theology*. Translated by Mary Frances McCarthy. San Francisco: Ignatius, 1987.

———. *Truth and Tolerance: Christian Belief and World Religions*. Translated by H. Taylor. San Francisco: Ignatius, 2004.

Rey-Mermet, Théodule. *Moral Choices: The Moral Theology of Saint Alphonsus Liguori*. Translated by Paul Laverdure. Liguori, MO: Liguori, 1998.

Schindler, D. C. "The Redemption of *Eros*: Philosophical Reflections on Benedict XVI's First Encyclical." *Communio* 33 (2006) 375–99.

Smith, Jeanette C. "Katharina von Bora through Five Centuries: A Historiography." *Sixteenth Century Journal* 30 (1999) 745–74.

Stephenson, John Raymond. "The Holy Eucharist: At the Center or Periphery of the Church's Life in Luther's Thinking?" In *A Lively Legacy: Essays in Honor of Robert Preus*, edited by Kurt E. Marquart et al., 154–63. Fort Wayne, IN: Concordia Theological Seminary, 1985.

———. *The Lord's Supper*. St. Louis: Luther Academy, 2003.

Tanner, Norman P., ed. *Decrees of the Ecumenical Councils*. 2 vols. Washington, DC: Georgetown University Press, 1990.

Tappert, Theodore G., ed. and trans. *The Book of Concord: The Confessions of the Evangelical Lutheran Church*. Philadelphia: Fortress, 1959.

Tillinghast, Pardon E. "An Aborted Reformation: Germans and the Papacy in the Mid-Fifteenth Century." *Journal of Medieval History* 2 (1976) 57–79.

Veith, G. E. "Masks of God." http://www.lcms.org/Document.fdoc?src=lcm&id=607.

Watson, Philip S. *Let God Be God: An Interpretation of the Theology of Martin Luther*. London: Epworth, 1947.

Wenthe, Dean O., et al., eds. *All Theology Is Christology: Essays in Honor of David P. Scaer*. Fort Wayne, IN: Concordia Theological Seminary Press, 2000.

Wicks, Jared, ed. and trans. *Cajetan Responds: A Reader in Reformation Controversy*. Washington, DC: Catholic University of America Press, 1978.

Wingren, Gustaf. *Luther on Vocation*. Translated by Carl C. Rasmussen. 1957. Reprint, Evansville, IN: Ballast, 1994.

Yeago, David S. "The Catholic Luther." *First Things* 61 (1996) 37–41.

———. "'A Christian, Holy People': Martin Luther on Salvation and the Church." In *Spirituality and Social Embodiment*, edited by L. Gregory Jones and James J. Buckley, 101–20. Oxford: Blackwell, 1997.

———. "Gnosticism, Antinomianism, and Reformation Theology: Reflections on the Costs of a Construal." *Pro Ecclesia* 21 (1993) 37–49.

Young, R. V. "The Reformations of the Sixteenth and Seventeenth Centuries." In *Christian Marriage: A Historical Study*, edited by Glenn W. Olsen, 269–301. New York: Crossroad, 2001.

Yule, George. "Luther and the Ascetic Life." In *Monks, Hermits and the Ascetic Tradition*, edited by W. J. Sheils, 229–39. Studies in Church History 22. Oxford: Blackwell, 1985.

6

Alasdair MacIntyre's Hermeneutics of Tradition

CRAIG HOVEY

I

IT MAY WELL BE that, as the eminently terrestrial, Hebrew philosopher Qohelet says, "there is nothing new under the sun" and that "what has been is what will be" (Eccl 1:9 RSV). Nevertheless, we are perennially enraptured with *newness* and captivated by the thought that to whichever bleak and otherwise intellectually sterile stock we may owe our provenance, the horizon still promises that at least some of that may finally be left behind. History may repeat itself in the lives of others, but not in mine. Nobody, it seems, wants to think that everything we do has been done before, or at least, not in this particular way, with this particular emphasis, motivation, and so on. Yet neither will it do brazenly to assert our absolute freedom from the past, particularly as such assertions are only the thinly veiled reachings of desperation. It is true that Qohelet magnificently and commendably lacks the starry-eyed optimism of the modern spirit, but every honest description of the human situation must surely locate us in the same place: under the sun.[1]

Our situation is always somewhere in the middle. To be *middle* is simply to be creaturely: less than God and yet dependent on God and others; it is to have a past that will not easily be discarded but also to participate in the hope that not all time is past to us, which is to say that the future will

---

1. I am grateful to Dan Olson for this concept.

not easily be postponed (it quickly becomes present). The middle status of Christians reflects this. It is a matter of *identity* and *task* and both of these are known, transmitted, enabled, and brought to flourishing through the ways that the church inhabits (and thereby simply *is*) a tradition in good working order. We ineluctably inhabit the middle space carved out by an active and ongoing dialectic between the future-oriented exercise and meaning of freedom and the constraining identity-granting presence of the past.

Still, as Alasdair MacIntyre notes, we only know how to describe what a tradition is by looking back on it.[2] We are in the middle but also forward of our forebears in the same tradition and thereby better able to see and name the challenges they faced as challenges to the tradition we share with them. Likewise, those of us in the present who live by and in a tradition are in the middle of our own challenges that it will be up to future generations to identify with better precision than we are now able to do. A tradition's identity-forming aspect is therefore prominently confirmed by honesty, which is to say, by the recognition that who I am is larger than my present actions and other attempts at self-definition. It recognizes that how I now act, if it is to be intelligible to me as an action of one sort as opposed to another, owes to connections (linguistic and otherwise) that others have made before me. My acting in these intelligible ways, then, also demands that I honestly identify the continuities between these others and myself. I am one of them, I then say, through nothing more than the tacit belief that what I do and say has some continuity with the other things that I do and say.

I have begun this way in order to emphasize how the ways we conceptualize the self will be most genuine when we neither seek to evade the traditions of which we are a part, nor shrink from the active life of inhabiting them. Hannah Arendt defined tradition in the strong sense of enabling identity: I know how I am because I come from a people who have thought of and known themselves in this particular way. MacIntyre's use of tradition involves with greater emphasis the agent in the tradition's present-tense hermeneutical activity.[3] In order for a tradition to be living, it must be in dispute. It must be able to be identified as that which has produced ways of thinking, doing, and living that are themselves challenges to the tradition's

---

2. MacIntyre, *God, Philosophy, Universities*, 165.

3. Arendt worried about "repetition" of the past, a quality she adduced ought to be absent from politics, thus in a sense opposing the *vita activa* to tradition (see *The Human Condition*, chap. 1). Max Weber relied on a similar understanding when he typologized, as three bases of political legitimacy, tradition, faith, and enactment. In this case, tradition appeals to something's validity as "that which has always been" and frequently enforces conformity to it through superstition and psychological inhibition. Weber, *Economy and Society*, 36–37.

self-identity. These are the most significant pressures that will be exerted against the outer edges of what constitutes a tradition. The internal critic does not simply ask, "What lies beyond?" Instead, she asks, "How can what lies beyond be brought inside?" Like the ever-expanding universe, a tradition that is at the height of its health and in sheer command of its critical faculties will be actively renegotiating its boundaries. It will, paradoxically, refuse to take for granted the absoluteness of its inheritance for the sake of the debt it owes to that very inheritance; it will rebuff every suggestion that a word uttered ought to be the last word.

MacIntyre refers to this dynamism and draws attention to the ongoing nature of a tradition by defining it as "an argument extended through time in which certain fundamental agreements are defined and redefined in terms of two kinds of conflict: whose with critics and enemies external to the tradition who reject all or at least key parts of those fundamental agreements, and those internal, interpretative debates through which the meaning and rationale of the fundamental agreements come to be expressed and by whose progress a tradition is constituted."[4] The ability to name one's ongoing participation in a tradition as participation in a *living* tradition will depend on the extent of the tradition's own success in addressing things as counterintuitive as the very means it employs to determine success.

II

Alasdair MacIntyre's well-known and influential recovery of tradition within the discourse of moral philosophy serves as a prominent counterpoint to the dominant modes of reasoning that the Enlightenment produced as well as the ones that its heirs only half-heartedly discarded when they thought they were well rid of them. For the broader aims addressed by the essays in this volume, MacIntyre's account may neatly be divided heuristically according to three sets of related questions. In the remainder of this essay, I will focus mostly on the second and third. First, there are questions relating to what a tradition is, particularly when viewed from the outside. What distinguishes movement and activity within the tradition from movement and activity independent of it? How much change can a tradition bear and still be recognizable as the same thing? These questions are commonly asked of a tradition when it is fragmenting or, for whatever reason, is in poor working order.

---

4. MacIntyre, *Whose Justice? Which Rationality?*, 12.

Second, there are questions about how a tradition engages itself from within. How much rests on the tradition's ingenuity in producing satisfactory responses to its most trenchant challengers? What, in short, are the hermeneutical options that govern maneuvers amidst a tradition's assorted self-understandings? The second set of questions relate most directly to the virtues, those classic marks of character chiefly associated with Aristotle and, in Catholic moral thought, with Thomas Aquinas. MacIntyre's recovery of virtue in the late twentieth century initiated a distinct challenge to the dominant philosophical options: Kant and his best-known critics, universal moral codes and their despisers, moral duty and those whose ethic grandiosely repudiates such things. It was a calculated attack on the Enlightenment's imposing assemblage of clique-morals (universality, autonomy, individuality) that only benignly paraded themselves as all-encompassing but are now roundly acknowledged to have been harboring all along a most insidious violence encoded in the outliers's irrationality and savagery. Yet it was just as much an exposé directed against the Enlightenment coterie's celebrated opposites (particularity, subjectivism, relativism) which befall MacIntyre's reprimand just to the extent that their vaunted status trades in merely reproducing in mirror images the very supply of options they purport to rebuff.

This kind of critique must, of course, always be on its guard lest it succeed more in being clever than in being true. For MacIntyre, both the Enlightenment and its strident detractors have in common one thing that unites them more than they realize: their disdain for tradition. It is a disdain both of particular traditions and of tradition simply as such. Immanuel Kant famously asked, "What is enlightenment?" to which he supplied his own answer: "man's emergence from his self-incurred immaturity" and the courage "to use one's own understanding without the guidance of another."[5] *Sapere aude!—Dare to be wise!* This self-confident contempt for all things traditional not only undergirded the massive Enlightenment project with its unprecedented value for doubt and novelty, its notoriously sweeping claims about the capacities and inferences of reason, and its coolheaded political achievement of distance from every medieval (or worse) petty superstition. It also lies at the heart of the subsequent claims on the same topics, the postmodern fear of commitment that sets in with such force once the old, conquering hopes of reason have been dashed. And what of the final set of questions?

Third are questions about how traditions relate to each other. What must traditions share in order to have a debate over the nature of goods

---

5. Kant, "Answer to the Question: 'What Is Enlightenment?'" 54.

and the means of achieving them? Must they have in common a critical mass of background beliefs in order to make claims on each other? These are questions of communication and have particular interest to Christian thought so long as Christianity can never rest content with a superior tradition (rationally or otherwise) that merely serves those whose it is. If the Christian tradition (and here the plurality of Christian traditions must be recognized, to be addressed later on) is bearer of the good news by which it is constituted, then its primal impulse will always be drawn on as one of extension and engagement, which means that a gospel that is intrinsically already *communication*—God's to the world in Christ; Christ to the world in and as the church—then Christianity's outward forces will be most genuine and true to its task when they refresh and enliven rather than threaten and imperil the tradition of which they are a part.

Until now, I have avoided explicitly naming the false choice between conservative and progressive. MacIntyre disagrees with Edmund Burke's politically invested appeals for tradition over against reason—new thinking—and the peace and stability of tradition over against conflict.[6] Burke was doing with the *idea* of tradition what he saw that a people ought to do

---

6. MacIntyre, *After Virtue*, 206. There is some question over how to read Burke in this regard. In some ways, MacIntyre seems closer to Burke when it comes to natural rights. For Burke, such "pretended rights" are not the "*real* rights of men" (*Reflections on the Revolution in France*, 58). The question of what we understand rights to be cannot be answered through appeals to what is self-evident and natural but "it is a thing to be settled by convention." Therefore Burke asks, "how can any man claim, under the conventions of civil society, rights which do not so much as suppose its existence? rights which are absolutely repugnant to it?" (58). Burke prefers the conventions of civil society to the stridently sure metaphysicality of natural rights theorists since they are morally and politically closer to the kinds of balances and compromises that he thinks ought to characterize such societies: "the rights of men are in a sort of *middle*, incapable of definition, but not impossible to be discerned" (61, emphasis original). Though antidemocratic, Burke in this kind of appeal seems to be a classic liberal for rejecting appeals to a natural and eternal order, and if so he is not very far from MacIntyre, who famously claimed of natural rights that "there are no such rights, and belief in them is one with belief in witches and unicorns" (*After Virtue*, 69). MacIntyre does qualify this statement to ensure that he is not misunderstood as dispensing with all rights whatsoever: "By 'rights' I do not mean those rights conferred by positive law or custom on specified classes of person; I mean those rights which are alleged to belong to human beings as such . . . as natural rights or as the rights of man" (68–69). Christopher J. Insole argues that Burke only seems to be "modern" in his efforts to tie rights only to convention and that these efforts really grow out of Burke's more fundamental judgment that convention is the politically most appropriate way to encode and root a society in eternal law (*Politics of Human Frailty*, chap. 1). If, therefore, MacIntyre is consistent in his distancing from Burke's account of tradition, he does so as one who is as much a historicist as he is one who longs for the premodern, which, while leaving more to say about how MacIntyre negotiated the options, nevertheless goes some distance toward explaining why progressive and conservative for him represent a false choice.

with and to their own tradition: appeal and adhere to it. But to MacIntyre, this serves a truncated and falsely attenuated function. The reason is simply that the dialectic between adherence and activity is not only a characteristic of every living tradition, but may even be said to be nothing other than the tradition itself, the confrontation of new realities only recognizable as such because of the depth of a commitment to what is not new.

For MacIntyre, "all reasoning takes place within the context of some traditional mode of thought, transcending through criticism and invention the limitations of what had hitherto been reasoned in that tradition."[7] As an example, in its founding documents, a university may state its reasons for existing and its mission. Over time—and very quickly, in fact—these things will create a tradition and part of what it will subsequently mean to live and work as part of that tradition is to argue about the university's existence as times change and new challenges arise that were not spelled out by the founders. Life in the university's tradition will thereby be a *hermeneutical life*. The living tradition's life is, by definition, a contested life; it is a life of contestation *over* definitions, simple descriptions, and monolithically patent propositions. When that life ceases to be a hermeneutical life, the tradition that purportedly makes the institution an institution will cease to be vital to it. "Indeed, when a tradition becomes Burkean, it is always dying or dead."[8] People will ask, but will have no way of answering, "What are these buildings here for?"

Now, how can one tell whether disagreements are salutary and point to a tradition's vibrancy and health or whether they are a sign of its decline or even absence? After all, we would easily be misled if we assumed that every debate signals that a tradition is in good working order. Indeed, in a characteristically powerful excess of rhetoric, MacIntyre diagnoses the modern moral predicament as one that we know to be "after virtue" because of the interminability of contemporary debates over war, abortion, and so on, drawing, as they do, on fragments of the ruined moral traditions of the past. A people may deceive themselves into feeling quite moral, in fact, on account of their engagement in such debates when what is really going on is the exchange of a lot of hot air generated by loose rational associations and sheer personal preference.[9] Still, as Jeffrey Stout observes, just because ethical debates are still going on does not mean that they are interminable—the nineteenth-century debates over the abolition of slavery came to an end

---

7. MacIntyre, *After Virtue*, 206.

8. Ibid.

9. The extended metaphor of this "disquieting suggestion" animates the first two chapters of *After Virtue*.

and presumably their doing so points to the work of one or more moral traditions.[10] Another answer to the question about debate actually side-steps it by adducing that the real importance lies not with the tradition but with the story that can be told of harmony and disharmony across time (and not with the coherence of embodying it).

Disharmony and discontinuity are the watchwords of much postmodern discourse but they still depend conceptually on their opposites. Put simply, the discontinuities stand out against a more fulsome background of continuities. The flux can only be said to be "flux" because not everything is in flux; most of the time, most things are not. One of the metaphysical tensions in Nietzsche's thought is precisely the unintended conservatism implied in the eternal recurrence of everything; the ability to name *change* disappears from meaningful vocabulary when change is all that there is: change as a groundwork of all existence is very difficult to specify as what exists.

MacIntyre therefore finds in the postmodern "genealogists" (Nietzsche, Foucault, Deleuze) a particular version of the dialectic between change and stasis, though with this twist. "From the genealogist's standpoint the problems are not ones of discontinuities within continuities so much as of continuities within discontinuities."[11] To MacIntyre, this reversal evinces a lack of honesty and gratitude toward the continuous since even though Foucault, for example, never claimed to *enact* or *cause* discontinuity but only to identify such ruptures in history, Foucault himself was engaged in a criticism whose continuity is partially extended and strengthened in direct proportion to its success in finding discontinuity.[12] So by taking for granted the priority of discontinuous things (and whether this taking-for-granted evinces a metaphysical faith in it remains an interesting question to debate), Foucault can be said even to weaken his own method of investigation. Says MacIntyre: "For if the genealogist is inescapably one who disowns part of his or her own past, then the genealogist's narrative presupposes enough of unity, continuity, and identity to make such disowning possible."[13] These are all aspects of one of the questions with which we began: how a tradi-

---

10. Stout, *Democracy and Tradition*, chap. 5. Stout points out that, as much as MacIntyre rejects liberalism for being a tradition founded on disdain for tradition, it is nevertheless still a tradition (see *Whose Justice? Which Rationality?*, chap. 17: "Liberalism Transformed into a Tradition"). For Stout, liberalism is best exemplified as democracy and by a set of proper names (Emerson, Dewey, etc.) that do not appear in MacIntyre's genealogy of liberalism.

11. MacIntyre, *Three Rival Versions*, 214.

12. Foucault theorizes about discontinuity in *Order of Things*, chap. 7.

13. MacIntyre, *Three Rival Versions*, 214.

tion engages itself from within. The owning and disowning are part of that engagement.

III

It is therefore possible, on MacIntyre's critique, that these thinkers are quite simply fooling themselves and just so are falling into a trap that was set before they got there. They cannot finally be "post-" to the traditions they think they are rejecting since their very mode of rejecting them employs skills afforded by them. What is the meaning of this? MacIntyre famously tells a modern declension narrative in which the nadir is a very deliberate and decisive trap-setting by the eighteenth-century German philosopher, Immanuel Kant. A principal goal of Kant's philosophy was to argue that morality is independent of religion and cannot be derived from it. He reasoned that claims such as "Jesus Christ is perfect," while sounding as if they carry the force of revelation nevertheless depend rather more prosaically on prior rational notions of perfection. Attributing perfection to Jesus Christ, then, lays a religious claim athwart a moral one that was independently and previously conceived.

By this strategy, though, Kant thought he was doing Christianity a favor by saving it (or at least "its" morality) from the charge of subjectivism. Religion *is* piety and the subjective experience of God via nonrational encounter, Kant happily allows; but this is no threat to morality. It is not possible to know whether something is morally right because God commands it. And when revealed religion also accords with rational (prior, independent) morality, so much the better for revealed religion; but such accordance is never anything more than icing on the metaphysical cake.[14]

From what, exactly, did Kant think he was saving Christianity? The answer is that he saw the need to save it from becoming a form of speaking, living, and acting that was perpetually turned in on itself, providing for itself at every turn the sufficient reasons for everything that it does and claims.

---

14. As Gilles Deleuze observes, "Kant often reminds us that the moral law has no need at all for subtle arguments, but rests on the most . . . common use of reason. . . . We must therefore speak of a moral common sense. . . . Moral common sense is the accord of the understanding with reason, under the legislation of reason itself. We rediscover here the idea of a good nature of the faculties and of a harmony determined in conformity with a particular interest of reason." Deleuze, *Kant's Critical Philosophy*, 49–50, cited in Connolly, *Why I Am Not a Secularist*, 172. Kant's universalizing was just the overreaching assertion of the particular, hence his reliance on "we" and "common," concepts that have come under extreme ridicule in recent years as evidence of his failure.

But this will quickly be written off as an utterly meaningless religion caught up in tautologies about God's goodness and every other claim it wishes to make:

> A: "God is good."
>
> B: "What does 'good' mean?"
>
> A: "We know what good means by looking at what God is like."
>
> B: "Then you are just claiming 'God is what God is like.' Pathetic."
>
> A: "Darn."

Kant's way out guards against this fatal disappointment and it is, quite literally, a "way out": what is outside to religion is the realm of moral and other reasoning that owes nothing to religious confessions in order to be true. MacIntyre is a characteristic critic of this kind of reasoning: "In so endowing moral rules with objectivity one is in danger of deifying them, of setting them up as standards by which God himself can be brought under judgment. Kant does not flinch at this prospect; but even a casual reader of the Bible ought to be aware of the blasphemy involved."[15] It is the surest way to encourage the worship of idols. In fact, in accepting Kant on this score, the only way to say anything true and non-idolatrous of God ("God is good" clearly will not qualify) is to say nothing at all.[16]

It is almost certainly pointless to ask whether, in all of this, Kant remained Christian. He certainly thought he did. A more fruitful question is to ask what kind of modification to the Christian moral tradition Kant represents. It is fair to say that the independence of Kant's morality created something other than Christian morality—but this was not its precise goal. Its precise goal was not the *creation* of an alternative morality but the *demonstration* that all morality is necessarily independent of religion. It only takes, then, the existence of a rival to blow the entire enterprise wide open and to expose its pretentious neutrality and universality. This is not the place to detail how this has been done (to do so would in some sense simply be to recount the history of philosophy since the Enlightenment). Nevertheless, this very point describes a great deal of MacIntyre's lifelong project: arguing that reason cannot be the way out of particular traditions since reason itself is always *constituted* by traditions, even those traditions against which reason sets itself most doggedly in the attempt to be free of them.

---

15. MacIntyre, *Difficulties in Christian Belief*, 105.

16. The contemporary revival of negative theology certainly represents a way of refusing this alternative.

With considerable irony, we may observe that the greatest threat to Kant's universalizing does not even come from "outside" in the sense that anthropology, for Kant's own day, was soon to make plain. Rather, there is a considerable Christian inside to Kant's outsiding. As William Connolly summarizes Gilles Deleuze, "From this alternative perspective Kant can now be interpreted first to project persisting elements of a Christian culture into a 'common sense' projected as a constitutive universal and then to invoke this projected accord of the faculties to justify a Christian-inspired rendering of the moral life. Common sense is projected as an unschematized universal; it then functions to place beyond critical review a particular interpretation of morality."[17] Kant's solution was merely a bluff waiting to be called, a stop-gap amidst early modernity's flight from yet another bluff (Kant thought)—the dogmatic and insular medieval period. But the way forward can prove difficult when its breaking free of the past really only reintroduces the old particulars in shiny new (universally rational) garb. Kant's most critical failure was lack of gratitude toward the moral rationality he dressed up.

Kant's crucial mistake, according to MacIntyre, was assuming that the moral tradition he had inherited (Christianity) needed to be rescued from what others would later call relativism (or nihilism). Reason was summarily exalted above not only the Christian tradition, but over every tradition whatsoever. Its superiority and priority over tradition lie precisely in its not owing anything to it so as to be immune to the fates traditions inevitably face as they develop through time. What makes appeal to tradition dangerous is both its inherent instability and its temporality. If a rational argument only makes sense in terms that have been employed by a particular tradition and that are therefore terms with their own flux-history, then Kant reasoned that the argument's conclusion is no more stable than the history to which it has united itself for its intelligibility.

Again, MacIntyre's crucial claim, if correct, is a disaster for Kant: all reasoning is tradition-constituted.[18] Kant's reasoning is no different from anyone else's in this respect. Its universality was scrupulously ornamental but it did not go all the way down. In a cruel twist of history, his fantastic failure has probably been more responsible than anything else for the currently fashionable false humility and monotonous reduction of morality to mere taste and preference in today's society. But there is also no reason that

---

17. Connolly, *Why I Am Not a Secularist*, 173.

18. MacIntyre asks, "Of what did the Enlightenment deprive us? What the Enlightenment made us for the most part blind to and what we now need to recover is, so I shall argue, a conception of rational enquiry as embodied in a tradition . . ." (*Whose Justice? Which Rationality?*, 7).

the alternative to Kant ought to be his mirror image. MacIntyre notes that the crucial decision we now face on this side of the Enlightenment's collapse is "Aristotle or Nietzsche?"[19] MacIntyre himself has developed considerably as a distinctively Christian philosopher since he asked that question and presumably now would ask, "Thomas or Nietzsche?" But why Nietzsche?

Nietzsche is one genealogist who was keenly aware of some critical facts that MacIntyre accepts: not only that Kant did not do Christianity any favors, but also that Kant's independent and autonomous morality remains deeply associated with Christianity, even for those who, unlike Kant himself, at least ostensibly want nothing to do with it. Nietzsche's appeal for a revaluation of morality, for example, was a response to what he perceived to be the atheists' loss of nerve, the refusal finally to take leave of everything god-like, the failure to greet the idols' twilight with ardent anticipation of their replacements. MacIntyre begins *The Religious Significance of Atheism* by observing how much a great nineteenth-century radical atheist like Ludwig Feuerbach, in his careful refutation of Christianity, nevertheless sought to retain its core moral principles and yet without its transcendent metaphysics.[20] Feuerbach was just a pagan version of Kant, but still too Christian to be a good pagan. To Nietzsche, any philosophy that holds on to notions like Christian justice without God or ethics without metaphysics is not only insincere or cowardly; it is also in obvious cahoots with its enemy and so cannot help talking out of both sides of its mouth. Untrue to itself, it lacks the philosophical abandon appropriate to the whole of life conceived according to utter faithfulness to temporality and terrestriality (and that pervades Nietzsche's inimitable style of writing). When Zarathustra repeatedly counsels, "Be faithful to the earth," his target audience is never the serene religious who are content with their faith in otherworldly assurances and goals, but always the tortured and schizophrenic irreligious who, having conceived of a space without God, nevertheless withhold their lives from it. Nietzsche's gospel to them is the perfectly hard truth but poison to their ears: that space is really nothing other than the earth itself and you constantly betray it by your half-hearted embrace of God's death.

---

19. *After Virtue*, chap. 18.

20. MacIntyre and Ricoeur, *Religious Significance of Atheism*, 4. Interestingly, MacIntyre goes on to suggest that in our time (the late 1960s), such dependence on and confusion over the task of atheism has disappeared. There is a great deal of irony and certainly a historical argument to be made in the fact that this dependence has re-emerged in recent years with a vengeance in the quasi-serious writings of Richard Dawkins, Christopher Hitchens, Daniel Dennett, and Sam Harris. For critique of Sam Harris, in particular, see my *What Makes Us Moral?*

By staring into the void and confidently walking forward, Nietzsche presents, for MacIntyre, the only genuine alternative, not only to tradition-as-such (itself an extremely problematic notion as I will soon show), but to the god-tradition that prizes morality itself. Nietzsche understood the way that great traditions work and he sympathized with people's desire to be part of them. The way that the West has never ceased to venerate Ancient Greece, however, did not please him at all. In fact, such veneration only masqueraded itself as respect for tradition; it was really just a cover-up for a fundamental timidity, a root anxiety that life might ever ask us truly to be a part of it. Nietzsche claimed that the Ancient Greeks—in their noblest moments—never gave a thought to their legacy, nor concerned themselves with fidelity to their past. Instead, their life was staunchly present-tense. They were creators rather than protectors. Their only care was in knowing whether present acts maximize the creative impulse. Subsequent generations appeal to these Greeks in direct proportion to their effete resignation to pasts that will almost certainly be more glorious than the future.[21] They sustain and cultivate only the most tenuous and plain connections with this heritage but they cannot endure it as their own. They forsake the moves that would truly make them Greek-kin: a blithe disregard and utter contempt of tradition. *That* is the only way to share in it.

Greek tradition exhibited for Nietzsche what political philosopher, William Connolly, describes as a "politics of becoming."[22] With such a politics, new political possibilities—ways of life—are thrust into being through discordance and in particular through disturbance of the old laws and identities. As such, any commensurate ethic will lack the simplicity that Kant sought; instead there will be ambiguity and the most prominent mark of the use of reason will not be agreement and stability but debate and reformulation. For Nietzsche, "We can destroy only as creators."[23] A Greek disregard for unity may have ironically produced a united nobility, but if it did so, then is was *because of* an ironic attachment to the goods that that tradition would produce, which is to say, its primary concern with living a discordant life,

---

21. Nietzsche therefore remarks that "we moderns have nothing whatever of our own" in contrast to the Greeks who "kept a tenacious hold on their unhistorical sense" (*Untimely Meditations*, sec. 4). This is the ultimate paradox for a people who want to claim to be free of tradition and yet constantly assemble fragments of others' pasts for want of knowing who they actually are. Nietzsche continues: "Only by replenishing and cramming ourselves with the ages, customs, arts, philosophies, religions, discoveries of others do we become anything worthy of notice, that is to say, walking encyclopaedias, which is what an ancient Greek transported into our own time would perhaps take us for."

22. Connolly, *Why I Am Not a Secularist*, 172.

23. Nietzsche, *Gay Science*, sec. 58.

of overcoming the self-deception that leads to prematurely assuming that disparate things display a greater degree of organization than they actually do. Instability was not the goal but the given. The attendant ethic is one that is determined to live and create in the face of it. And while this kind of ethic may give the appearance of staid greatness, it is only an appearance afforded by the ethic's refusal to stop moving lest it become the "gravedigger of the present."[24]

IV

It should be obvious now why Nietzsche represents an improvement over Kant and a striking difference—not only of degree or emphasis, but of real content. Nietzsche is unafraid to extol a particular tradition; he even thinks he is being exceedingly more faithful to it than his contemporaries. The tradition furnishes him with thoughts about how to inhabit, live within, and thereby extend a tradition—granting the deep ironies that this holds. He in fact cares very little for theorizing about tradition-as-such since the primary function of a tradition is to enable a kind of life and Nietzsche famously had scant patience for the distances created by philosophical inquiry into the nature of things that are most properly to be exercised rather than talked about. Even when true, talking gets in the way of living, though it will always be less true the more it is *only* talked. Put simply, Nietzsche does not need a theory about the superiority of tradition as a mode and resource for moral reasoning because he has something better: a superior tradition.

MacIntyre acknowledges that Kant has laid a trap that has an extremely strong gravitational pull. Kant's implicit challenge to every would-be opponent is to meet him on his own turf: *Show me a universally demonstrable morality that defeats my universally demonstrable morality.* It is, of course, a setup since Kant's real agenda is to show the superiority of the rational-as-universal. Even if Kant loses on these grounds, he has still won. This setup has led many to assume that the thing that Kant saves us from is inevitable once his scheme ceases to save. Nietzsche knew otherwise and so discharged a full-scale attack on nihilism. MacIntyre's way out shares some characteristics with Nietzsche, although also some great differences. It shares a certain flippancy toward Kant's rigorous neutrality. This *must* be the way of proceeding in order to evade Kant's trap. Any claims about the superiority of tradition must themselves arise from a particular tradition, otherwise the claims are self-defeating: they fail the more they succeed. For

---

24. Nietzsche, *Untimely Meditations*, sec. 1.

this reason, MacIntyre cannot be said to proffer tradition-as-such, although book titles can be misleading on this point.

This is also the reason why MacIntyre cannot be said to be a relativist. A relativist knows something that a relativist is not finally entitled to know: that no scheme, moral or otherwise, is superior to another. MacIntyre describes the "relativist challenge" this way: "Every set of standards, every tradition incorporating a set of standards, has as much and as little claim to our allegiance as any other."[25] It is never a descriptive claim; it is always normative and therefore (in utter contradiction) *absolute*—the very thing it supposes it avoids. In truth, the relativist is an ironist, a master of detachment. But the relativist does not need great knowledge of anything. Perhaps we have therefore come too far in this essay without describing how the specifics of Christianity justify appeals to *this* tradition (again, rather than tradition-as-such). MacIntyre's history of Catholic moral thought is the description of reasoning within an Aristotelian-Augustinian-Thomistic tradition of the virtues.

Whereas holding on to fragments of moral traditions may give one the impression that she is engaged in moral justification, fragments are the freefloating snippets that they are due to their disassociation from questions about what life is for. Virtues in the tradition MacIntyre extols are ordered to precise answers to such questions. What drops out in modernity is—and this is by Kant's design—the *telos* of human life: life yearning and stretching after God, participation in whose life constitutes the final consummation of all motion, desire, and hope. Nietzsche too and much more famously sought an ethic purged of *teloi*, instead claiming that "the goal of humanity cannot lie in its end but only in its highest exemplars."[26] This modern disdain common to Kant and Nietzsche obviously cannot be shared by Christianity for which union with God completes the kind of life that human life is. In MacIntyre's words:

> In Kant's morality, the divine commandments can play no role because to do right is to abide by certain standards whose validity is independent of religious belief; in Christian morality God must play a role because he created our nature and he alone knows what in the end will make us happy. And thus the Kantian arguments show not that morality as such is independent of religious belief, but that the morality which is so independent is an alternative to the morality which is not. To attempt to

---

25. MacIntyre, *Whose Justice? Which Rationality?*, 352.
26. Nietzsche, *Untimely Meditations*, sec. 9.

the title "morality" for the one and to deny it to the other would be merely to play with words.[27]

It may sound as though in affirming the existence of multiple "moralities" that MacIntyre is adopting a neutral standpoint with respect to all of them. But he intends the exact opposite. The other moralities can be recognized as moralities precisely because of his adherence to a particular one in the same way that religious people will generally be more skilled at knowing what a religion is than those who are outside to all of them.[28] It is worth reflecting on how contrary this is to the spirit of modernity, both with regard to moralities and religions. MacIntyre sharpens the point even more: "Certainly we can and do affirm that Christian morality is more adequate than non-Christian; but in doing this we rely on Christian standards of judgment. We merely affirm in another way our adherence to Christian morality."[29] In other words, to claim that there are moralities out there that are not Christian and to call them by their appropriate name are, for MacIntyre, but one and the same movement of a Christian avowal.

What MacIntyre is describing is a process of naming, of calling things by the right name. "Morality" is one such name that can only ever be as absolute as the willingness of an adherent to one morality to be so closely identified with it that she stakes her account of the rest of them on it. Consider the magnitude of such devotion: it forsakes all ground of ironic detachment in declaring that *this* morality cannot simply be a choice among many since it is also the means by which one goes about claiming that one knows what a morality is. To lose that devotion is therefore to be thrust into a vertigo worthy of Nietzsche—"What did we do when we unchained this earth from its

---

27. MacIntyre, *Difficulties in Christian Belief*, 107. Playing with words in this exact sense is what John Milbank does in "Can Morality Be Christian?" MacIntyre, of course, wants to avoid setting morality over against Christianity as much as setting Christian morality against whatever we agree to call Kant's program once we have decided it is something other than morality for its not being Christian.

28. And this can be done without essentializing religion but by exercising the skill of noticing what Wittgenstein called "family resemblances." What the academy knows under the label "religious studies" is, after all, a thoroughly modern, essentializing construction. See, for example, Fitzgerald, *Ideology of Religious Studies*, which argues that "there is no coherent non-theological theoretical basis for the study of religion as a separate academic discipline" (3).

29. MacIntyre, *Difficulties in Christian Belief*, 108. Elsewhere, MacIntyre specifically says as much regarding the virtues; their content as particular virtues with normative application precedes the concept of virtue: "To understand that generosity or courage or thrift is a virtue is to understand that one ought to be generous or brave or thrifty, and this 'ought' has a force prior to any choice of moral standards that we make" (such as the choice to be virtuous, presumably). MacIntyre, *Secularization and Moral Change*, 51.

sun?"³⁰ But it is not and cannot be, however conceived, a giddy slide among morality's variety pack ironically festooned with hangers-on to which one, however unentitled, nevertheless holds on to for expedience sake. This morality may certainly be contested—and it is the activity of the tradition that does not let it be immune from this for too long—but one cannot be free of it and then search for a better one since "morality" has lost its meaning if the moral object of devotion is truly discarded.

Therefore, MacIntyre is not only proffering conclusions about the nature of moral and rational traditions. He is doing these things from within a particular tradition and is frank about the necessity that he do so. It cannot be enough to adduce arguments such as "there can be no rationality as such"³¹ since in claiming that rationality is tradition-dependent we are just as surely presented with the fruits of some kind of reasoning which would simply and automatically refute themselves if they did not plainly display the tradition to whose debt they owe. Here, the temptation to regard tradition with contempt—shared by the thinkers of the Enlightenment as much as the genealogists—is fraught with incoherence.

V

Genealogy is a distance-preserving form of storytelling. It simultaneously seeks explanation while abjuring the pretense (and traps) of making a priori definitional claims. But doesn't genealogy therefore simply want to have it both ways? According to MacIntyre, a serious problem arises in the way that genealogy undergoes its work. On the one hand, its story rests on a radical disjunction or rupture. Perhaps the new discovery fatefully codifies disgruntled past failures into exalted values in which the slaves now revel. On the other hand, with supreme irony, there is surely something profoundly slavish about the genealogist's story in this regard since it is always told against (in MacIntyre's nomenclature) the self-images of the age. The telling is all that is needed to subvert what it tells; and its ability to tell such a story, in practice, undermines the triumphant story it wants so badly to tell.

> The genealogist has up till now characteristically been one who writes *against*, who exposes, who subverts, who interrupts and disrupts. But what has in consequence very rarely, if at all, attracted explicit genealogical scrutiny is the extent to which the

---

30. Nietzsche, *Gay Science*, sec. 125. This is what MacIntyre terms an "epistemological crisis." See his "Epistemological Crises, Dramatic Narrative, and the Philosophy of Science."

31. MacIntyre, *Whose Justice? Which Rationality?*, 352.

genealogical stance is dependent for its concepts and its modes of argument, for its theses and its style, upon a set of contrasts between it and that for which it aspires to overcome—the extent, that is, to which it is inherently derivative from and even parasitic upon its antagonisms and those toward whom they are directed, drawing its necessary sustenance from that which it professes to have discarded.[32]

It is one thing to make this accusation and another to demonstrate it. MacIntyre approaches a demonstration of this problem by showing that an agenda burdened to show discontinuity and to disown a past by identifying rupture nevertheless relies on ways of naming the discontinuities as such that in turn depend on continuity of identity and concepts, at least so as to enable the disowning. Even though the genealogist tells a story, it is not meant to be the kind of story that tells me who I am. It may tell me who I *was* as one who accepted and believed and acted according to norms that the genealogy has now disclosed were not fixed but were merely features of a particular history parading themselves as absolutes and attended by a convenient loss of memory. But MacIntyre adduces that the genealogist's successes are more apparent than real since the very act by which it reveals one thing covers up another, namely, any continuity of the self, the continuing presence of this past to myself in and as my own identity.

Practically speaking, this means that the genealogist cannot truly own up to a terrible past and certainly cannot admit to a guilty one. (MacIntyre's example of this is Paul de Man and attempts by his apologists to exculpate his anti-semitic leanings in the early 1940s.)[33] No genealogy will help you live with your past. Nor is this its purpose, which is precisely the opposite: to enable distance from the past that the genealogy tells. Likewise, absent from the genealogist's toolkit is any ability to narrate those multifarious changes that a tradition undergoes short of rupture and discontinuity but after the decisive break that it is the genealogy's primary function to illuminate—its evolutionary and plastic elements of which the genealogist herself is a part. (This helps MacIntyre explain Nietzsche's early departure from Basel and presumably also his henceforth non-traditional mode of contact with academia as an outsider.)

Still, the genealogist is not therefore simply left without an identity. Rather, as a consummate writer of histories as fictions, the genealogist can make of his own past whatever he wishes and optionally and masterfully speak of it in the dulcet tones of irony. After all, "We are creators!" And,

---

32. MacIntyre, *Three Rival Versions*, 215.
33. Ibid., 212.

at that, our creating into the future will always, as necessary, involve the creation of a commensurate past. This is because the noble and triumphant will governs both. Yet can anyone live with a past that is morally their own creation? It is only at the cost of a will, not to truth, but to *self-deception*. Nietzsche recognized this as a question of what we take pride in: Pride presides over memory: "'I have done that' says my memory. 'I cannot have done that' says my pride, and remains inexorable. Eventually memory yields."[34] The most basic problem MacIntyre finds here has to do with the way that a thoroughgoing genealogy project is self-defeating (meaning it can never truly be thoroughgoing). It faults Kant and other moderns for solidifying and codifying much older moralities of *ressentiment* but in doing so confidently invokes the power of narrative against it at the cost of losing all narrative ability to hold onto anything.[35]

For MacIntyre, one of the major contributions of any tradition is found in its language. Every tradition attempts to describe the world as well as our acting within it. And it is common now to acknowledge that we exist dialectically within the world we linguistically inhabit. Iris Murdoch typified this with her assertion that we can only act in the world that we can see; and our seeing is a function of what we are enabled to say.[36] A tradition's speech is its linguistic inheritance, and as such what counts as the tradition involves the ability to speak on behalf of it, within it, and on account of it. One's linguistic encounter with the world is therefore as much world-constituting as it is world-representing; in fact, the former is more fundamental than the latter since I can represent using language only the reality that the linguistic resources of my tradition allow me to see.

If this is so, then it is of little use attempting to evaluate the suitability of a linguistic tradition by matching it up against a reality that is conceived independently of the way that that reality comes to us linguistically. *Interpretation* of things and events, rather than things and events in themselves, ascends to the place of primary concern. Reality mediated through language parallels with and merges into the cultural sanctions that supervene on a

34. Nietzsche, *Beyond Good and Evil*, sec. 68, cited in MacIntyre, *Three Rival Versions*, 211.

35. A number of questions remain for me that must be left unanswered in this essay. Is this *necessarily* the case for genealogy or has it merely happened to be the case for the inheritors of Nietzsche (e.g., Foucault, Deleuze)? After all, MacIntyre happily concedes that a time may come when genealogy may either discover or put to use resources it has thus far neglected. Moreover, if much of this is MacIntyre's own refutation of nihilism, then is it a fair critique of Nietzsche himself? Or was Nietzsche, in fact, able to anticipate a postmodern *ressentiment* of subversion?

36. Murdoch, "The Idea of Perfection." The second clause owes to Stanley Hauerwas's well-known appropriation of Murdoch's insight.

people's memory, which is to say what counts not only as *their* history but of any history so long as they are the ones who remember and tell it. Marshall Sahlins no doubt speaks for all of modern anthropology in claiming that "an event becomes such as it is interpreted. Only as it is appropriated in and through a cultural scheme does it acquire historical *significance*."[37] Events only have meaning if they can be granted significance, and both of these can only happen if there is some larger complex of significations that a people use to interpret what they do and what happens to them.

The recognition that this is so is thoroughly Nietzschean, especially when it attempts to face with honesty the reality of cultural (tradition-linguistic) mediation without doing so in order to evade it. Nietzsche responds to the positivism "which halts at phenomena" and which declares the mere and root existence of facts. "No, facts is precisely what there is not, only interpretations. We cannot establish any fact 'in itself': perhaps it is folly to want to do such a thing."[38] There is always an interpretation *behind* facts, including facts like "Everything is subjective" and even "there is always an interpretation behind facts." Knowledge has no meaning apart from the desire of power to dominate and still the ambiguity though bold assertion—Kantian confidence!

All of this is a political contest that Nietzsche precisely names:

> It is our needs that interpret the world; our drives and their For and Against. Every drive is a kind of lust to rule; each one has its perspective that it would like to compel all the other drives to accept as a norm.[39]

Likewise, Foucault built a career around the insight that knowledge and power operate together. Yet language trades in something more subtle than knowledge since it is possible to speak things like confessions that admit unknowing as much as knowing and that, like Augustine's magisterial account of the Trinity, are humbly only ways to keep from being completely silent.[40] Genealogy is subversive in the literal sense of attending to what lies beneath the dominant, often ahistorical accounts in order to tell a historical story of how it came to be this way and what has been excluded along the way.

37. Sahlins, *Islands of History*, xiv, quoted in Lear, *Radical Hope*, 9.
38. Nietzsche, *Will to Power*, sec. 481.
39. Ibid.
40. "Silenced" is the lot of those who lack power rather than those who lack knowledge. Yet Foucault's insight is that what passes for knowledge is what can go unchallenged by the alternate accounts of those who either gain no hearing or who have held their tongues for so long they have forgotten what they knew.

VI

Where does this leave those who want to talk about the Christian tradition? And what is there to say about how one tradition relates to others? If genealogy tells stories in order to subvert the substance of the story it tells, then Christianity is at odds with it, not only given its sanguine dwelling within and as a tradition of discourse. Christianity is also charged with more complex story-telling than the genealogist. It is surely the mark of a degenerate way of speaking if one only has something to say when there is something to overcome and—lest we sidestep an element that constantly accompanies these discourses—someone to *conquer*. Nietzsche is right that Kant clings to a subtle but very real violence. It is true that the encounter of one tradition with another will be one of conflict since each will tell narratives that are grander than the stories of one tradition. They are not just accounts of reality that are "true for me" since only a callow and fantastic ironist could actually live with this kind of thoroughly undernourished, suburban jingle.[41] The fact that many people do in fact live with it ringing in their ears only means that they are hiding something, a more basic set of commitments to which they feel they are not entitled. These commitments are therefore usually unreflective, conservative, deeply entrenched, and malevolently absolutist. "True for me" is the product of postmodern, fascist sloganeering. Postmodern nations still conquer traditional ones.

One reason Burke favored his static account of tradition lies in what he took to be its ability to achieve social stability and peace. The dreamers of the Enlightenment who disagreed with Burke about tradition nevertheless also dreamed of peace. If modernity promised peace through reason, then a century of one unbridled monstrosity after another tempered that hope. Modernity exchanged one form of carnage for another—that of tribes for that of nations—while vastly expanding the scope of its justification. Yet postmodernity makes nearly-equivalent promises, only this time in the wake of the devastating legacy of the Enlightenment. If unity through essentialist accounts of what it means to be human is really only a cuddly, modern affectation, then the diversity of such accounts—indeed diversity of everything—surely stands as the renewed, if postponed, promise of peace.

---

41. MacIntyre discusses this postmodern attitude in the nomenclature of emotivism. In an early work, he writes, "It is quite clear that when I use moral concepts I do at least try to make a claim which goes beyond the expression of my choices or feelings" (*Secularization and Moral Change*, 52). Any attempt to apply moral concepts to others ("You ought to do this") assumes a shared moral vocabulary within a moral community. When that moral community is lost, other communal commitments rush in to take its place even though they will not readily be acknowledged as such.

An ironic people will always lack the discipline that true peace requires since they afford themselves the luxury of holding all of their commitments at arm's length. Such commitments are easily discarded (and the ones that remain will not admit to self-conscious acknowledgment). What is the alternative?

The inverse of a traditional identity that can only with great difficulty be discarded without considerable loss is the discipline that remaining with the tradition entails. It is surely a sign of our postmodern times that "true for you too" connotes ultimate domination and elicits suspicion of *all* encounters. And yet the conflict of traditions can only be avoided through insularity or disdain for traditions. Such conflict may be a genuine alternative promise for peace; and it may not. Whatever it will be will quite simply depend on the tradition itself. What then will be the marks of a peaceable tradition? I propose two and appeal to Christianity's local language in doing so.

1. Paradoxically, it knows that the identity of those who embody it is at stake but also they are not prepared to ensure its victory at all costs. Only a tradition that contains within itself a determined dependence on a source other than itself will be willing to sacrifice what is known for what is promised. This requires the theological virtue of hope. It will not equate survival with life because it believes that its life must be cross-like, freely yielding up survival for the hope of the life that resurrection brings. The martyrs die joyfully, knowing that it was never up to them to secure the future that might have been brought by a greater willingness to compromise with their obdurate killers. The future is God's *especially* for the people God has created and who look back over this tradition and can attribute its most genuine victories to a kind of success and faithfulness so counter-intuitive that it requires a knowledge brought by God that would not be available otherwise. the church's memory of martyrs also reminds it that "victory at all costs" is a pagan slogan if ever there was one.[42]

---

42. I confess that I do not know what MacIntyre would make of this set of comments. However, Jonathan Lear, whose *Radical Hope* is obviously profoundly influenced by MacIntyre, provides a clue. Lear's account of the Crow Nation in its final years is part real history and part thought experiment about what happens when one tradition encounters another. It is also about the virtues necessary for entertaining the thought "change or die" when the change required by a people can only be imagined in vague generalities, but the specifics are literally unimaginable. Lear's counterpoint in the story he tells of the Crows' successful change through the leadership of their chief, Plenty Coups, is the Sioux and their chief, Sitting Bull, who held on to a kind of "messianic" hope of deliverance from the American conquerors. Lear writes, however, that "the point here is not whether one was for or against working with the white man or learning from him. Rather, it is that Sitting Bull used a dream-vision to short-circuit reality

2. It believes that its truth is universal but that it has not seen nor heard the end of it, has not yet fully grasped it, and fully expects unheard parts of it to appear in the mouths of even its most dogged enemies. Its love for truth expresses itself in a perpetual movement that seeks after the truth's depths and that mines it for greater and greater fullness. It no more distrusts true accounts it has inherited any more than it can live without them. But its living *with them* and *by them* unlocks the way that there is more to life because there is more to the truth than we now know. This points to an important way that faith precedes knowledge (as for Anselm, famously, *credo ut intelligam*): greater faith will mean a greater confidence to look and listen for God apart from the usual places and people and outside the church; less faith will mean that what we now know is all that there is and where there is more to find, we already know where to look. The way of peace is therefore paved with a willingness to accept the ambiguity of things, a ready confession that my ego (my subjectivity) entitles me only to interpretations of reality, a prompt release of the power to control and still with violence the chaos of competing accounts.

Clearly these are marks of Christianity, though just as clearly they are not universally present or everywhere nurtured within the church. Even so, they are present and nurtured in some respects and in some places. And one's determination to discover them even to a small degree in every corner of the church is merely correlative of the determination to recognize when enemies speak and practice the truth, often despite themselves.

I have brought this essay to a place where Christian language presses to speak its own account of its tradition including what can be said of humanity's status as *middle creatures* of the God of Abraham and Jesus Christ. If one tradition relates to the others through conflict, what are we to make of the particular peaceable shape that the gospel gives to those who inhabit its truth? Can we say that peace is the guiding hermeneutic of Christianity?

---

rather than to engage with it" (150). But it is not at all clear to me that Lear's antipathy toward apocalyptic messianism in its Sioux form ought to be shared by Christians. After all, Sitting Bull is only "wishful" if his hope is a false one. "It is a hallmark of the wishful that the world will be magically transformed . . . without having to take any realistic practical steps to bring it about. The only activity in which one is enjoined to partake is a ritual . . ." (150–51). It is true that, for the Sioux, such non-instrumentality did not make them nonviolent; indeed, it gave them perhaps unrealistic reasons to fight. Still, one suspects that what makes wishing and hoping salutary or not cannot finally have anything to do with how much it encourages or discourages engagement with "reality" (itself an intensely culturally imperialistic term). It must instead have simply to do with whether the object of one's wishing and hoping is true. And this is not something that is objectively observable even when you see the wishers get killed. But it is something that a tradition may and must remember as noble death if it is a tradition that shares the same hope. In Lear's case, at least, it is clear that he has vastly different hopes.

Peace hopes that history will make eschatological sense by trusting God and, to the exact same extent, doubting the absoluteness of every self-confident subjective claim to have captured meaning. Meaning is *given*; it is grace in story-form. But it is not a story that we can presume to tell, not least because it is a story we still inhabit as God's creatures. All of creation is a story and the questions it lifts up are natural and good since even our inability to answer them fully in the present only confirms creation's dependence on God for meaning. Even so, this is not the same thing as supposing that creation lacks intelligibility or rationality. Such things are merely wrapped up with the nonrational comportments to which stretching after them gives rise. Faith, that is to say, is appropriate to the lives of creatures whose exercise of it does not conflict with the reachings of reason. "The best so far" (which MacIntyre describes as the highest status that can ever be attributed to a living tradition[43]) is therefore, for Christianity, anything but a defeated concession to the fact of mediated reality. Rather, it is nothing but the confession of middle-creatures whose place in their tradition is determined by a story that is too large to grasp and that is simply still on its way to completion by Jesus and the saints. It is nothing other than the honest reality of good news that still elicits hope.

Finally, what does this mean for Christianity's own speech, its own linguistic inhabiting of tradition? The gospel makes and is the speech of the church just as it is simultaneously both an impulse to speak and an impulse to keep silent, dialectically moving between knowledge and ignorance, revelation and mystery. If it is right to refer to Christianity itself as a tradition, it is also right to grant that it has always been and, short of glory, always will be a tradition made up of lesser ones, of half-baked and half-hearted commitments to the gospel of Christ tempered by disciplines and practices that seep across from other lesser traditions and all with often very little conscious effort to tie them all together or make them rationally coherent. Even so, the fact that, for example, the church is somehow knit around its creeds, confessions, saints, and so on not only means that Christians should expect that there will continue to be new creeds as the gospel encounters new worlds in the world (which is to say new traditions), but the "somehow" that names the mystery by which the church is so knit *is precisely the same mystery* by which it expects the new forms.[44] This is one of the lessons that

---

43. MacIntyre, *Three Rival Versions*, 64.

44. As an example, I have in mind the remarkable creed produced by the Masai in Tanzania that includes the confession that Christ was "a Jew by tribe, born poor in a little village, who left his home and was always on safari doing good, curing people by the power of God, teaching about God and man, showing that the meaning of religion is love" (cited in Donovan, *Christianity Rediscovered*, 148).

liberation theologians have been teaching the rest of the church in recent years.[45]

This is a startling reality against which the language of tradition no doubt strains considerably. The health of the Christian tradition is bound up with consistent pressure that even the most hard-won doctrinal debates throughout its history must be radicalized by those whose lives are part of the tradition's newness in order that we be faced with a reality that we know surpasses our present knowledge, but which we cannot truly know with fullness unless we are faced with it. The reason for this is *not*, MacIntyre is clear to say, a historicist matter of the time-bound nature of all truth but a linguistic matter of particularistic formulations. The historical context of doctrine does not contextualize the truth but situates in time any timeless claims that doctrine makes. "It is [therefore] that such claims are being made for doctrines whose formulation is itself time-bound and that the concept of timelessness is itself a concept with a history, one which in certain types of context is not at all the same concept that it is in others."[46] The fact that timelessness itself has a history and that claims of timeless truth are made in time does not invalidate them; it only spreads the burden of proof and the nature of the engagement across a much wider canvas: not just implacable tidiness of the syllogism that dismantles opponents for being irrational and illogical (and, we may now assert, *historical*), but the attempt at resolving the tension in terms that the traditions will themselves recognize. The attempt may well fail, of course. But it may yield something unexpected to both—as Augustinian Christianity did with Platonism—a confession that nevertheless remains open to refutation so long as it continues to be confessed *in time*, which is surely the only way for middle-creatures to confess anything. In the meantime, the fact of diversity of traditions is not an indication that none of them can be true just as the fact of diversity of rationalities does not indicate that there is no such thing as rationality. Instead, such diversity is, for those who do not despise tradition, an opportunity for a genuinely specific form of engagement.[47]

45. "As part of the lived past of the living church, this [dogmatic] tradition is one manner—valid in itself—of coming to grips with the mystery of Christ. But the unfathomable riches of Christ are not exhausted in ecclesiastical formulas, be they ever so venerable. And this holds not only for the councils of Chalcedon or Constantinople, but even for the various christologies that are part of the New Testament" (Boff, "Images of Jesus in Brazilian Liberal Christianity," 13).

46. MacIntyre, *Whose Justice? Which Rationality?*, 9.

47. "It is crucial that the concept of tradition-constituted and tradition-constitutive rational enquiry cannot be elucidated apart from its exemplifications" (ibid., 10). I must therefore acknowledge that this essay is probably far too *meta* to make the kinds of claims it does. I must simply refer the reader to MacIntyre's own exemplifications from the history of philosophy and theology.

The dialectic of tradition therefore re-emerges at the point of the Christian gospel's surfeit of virtue, its ability—which is surely nothing other than God's own ability—to sustain a people who are alternately grateful for and not yet fully satisfied with the truth of their tradition. Such virtues, I maintain, are themselves part of the communicative impulse of the gospel itself and an elaboration of its nagging inclination toward transcending and expanding the tradition of Christianity. I suspect this is the reason why the history of the gospel is so often fraught with conquering. An encounter of one tradition with another is conquering when it is a *threatening* encounter, however much the gospel's communicative impulse stands above it. And a threat faced in a deficit of faith, hope, and love is supremely compensated when conquering strength overreaches them in order to ensure victory. The gospel in the church may, of course, cower instead in recognition of its lack of virtue. But it surely just as often makes up for its lack by employing a hodgepodge collection of lesser skills, some of which contradict its message and mission.

The virtues that sustain and animate the Christian life as a recognizably Christian life are the ones Thomas described as *infused*—the theological virtues (faith, hope, and love). It is essential that these three give shape to all of the other virtues and that they are the most basic marks of how the Christian tradition understands itself. Therefore the correlative of embracing tradition rather than disdaining it (in either its modern or postmodern styles) will be a combination of gratitude and a slightly chastened impatience—grateful for this "argument extended through time" and eager to join and extend it. Those who therefore speak about and on account of the Christian tradition are truest to its spirit when their critique is matched by love and their ecclesial navel-gazing is matched by impetuous engagements with strangers and enemies.

Bibliography

Arendt, Hannah. *The Human Condition*. 2nd ed. Chicago: University of Chicago Press, 1998.

Boff, Leonardo. "Images of Jesus in Brazilian Liberal Christianity." In *Faces of Jesus: Latin American Christologies*, edited by José Miguez Bonino, translated by Robert R. Barr, 9–29. Maryknoll, NY: Orbis, 1984.

Burke, Edmund. *Reflections on the Revolution in France*. 1790. Reprint, London: Seeley, Jackson, and Halliday, 1872.

Connolly, William E. *Why I Am Not a Secularist*. Minneapolis: University of Minnesota Press, 1999.

Deleuze, Gilles. *Kant's Critical Philosophy*. Translated by Hugh Tomlinson and Barbara Habberjam. Minneapolis: University of Minnesota Press, 1984.

Donovan, Vincent J. *Christianity Rediscovered*. 25th anniv. ed. Maryknoll, NY: Orbis, 2003.
Fitzgerald, Timothy. *The Ideology of Religious Studies*. New York: Oxford University Press, 2000.
Foucault, Michel. *The Order of Things: An Archaeology of the Human Sciences*. New York: Routledge, 2002.
Hovey, Craig. *What Makes Us Moral? Science, Religion and the Shaping of the Moral Landscape; A Christian Response to Sam Harris*. London: SPCK, 2012.
Insole, Christopher J. *The Politics of Human Frailty: A Theological Defense of Political Liberalism*. London: SCM, 2004.
Kant, Immanuel. "An Answer to the Question: 'What Is Enlightenment?'" In *Kant: Political Writings*, edited by Hans Reiss, translated by H. B. Nisbet, 54–60. Cambridge: Cambridge University Press, 1970.
Lear, Jonathan. *Radical Hope: Ethics in the Face of Cultural Devastation*. Cambridge: Harvard University Press, 2006.
MacIntyre, Alasdair. *After Virtue*. 2nd ed. Notre Dame: University of Notre Dame Press, 1984.
———. *Difficulties in Christian Belief*. New York: SCM, 1959.
———. "Epistemological Crises, Dramatic Narrative, and the Philosophy of Science." *Monist* 60 (1977) 453–72.
———. *God, Philosophy, Universities: A Selective History of the Catholic Philosophical Tradition*. New York: Rowman & Littlefield, 2009.
———. *Secularization and Moral Change*. Oxford: Oxford University Press, 1967.
———. *Three Rival Versions of Moral Enquiry: Encyclopaedia, Genealogy, and Tradition*. Gifford Lectures 1988. Notre Dame: University of Notre Dame Press, 1990.
———. *Whose Justice? Which Rationality?* Notre Dame: University of Notre Dame Press, 1984.
MacIntyre, Alasdair, and Paul Ricoeur. *The Religious Significance of Atheism*. New York: Columbia University Press, 1969.
Milbank, John. "Can Morality Be Christian?" In *The Word Made Strange: Theology, Language, Culture*, 219–32. Oxford: Blackwell, 1997.
Murdoch, Iris. "The Idea of Perfection." In *The Sovereignty of Good*, 1–44. New York: Routledge, 2002.
Nietzsche, Friedrich. *The Gay Science*. Translated by Josefine Nauckhoff. Cambridge: Cambridge University Press, 2004.
———. *Untimely Meditations*. Translated by R. J. Hollingdale. Cambridge: Cambridge University Press, 2004.
———. *Will to Power*. Translated by Walter Kaufmann and R. J. Hollingdale. New York: Vintage, 1968.
Sahlins, Marshall. *Islands of History*. Chicago: University of Chicago Press, 1985.
Stout, Jeffrey. *Democracy and Tradition*. Princeton: Princeton University Press, 2004.
Weber, Max. *Economy and Society: An Outline of Interpretive Sociology*. Edited by Guenther Rother and Claus Wittich. 2 vols. Berkeley: University of California Press, 1978.

Part Three

Tradition: Liturgy and Lament

7

Tradition, Truth, and Time
Remarks on the "Liturgical Action" of the Church

ROBERT C. KOERPEL

Introduction

How SHOULD THE CHURCH understand the idea of tradition? How does tradition come to expression in human history and shape human rationality? What is tradition's relation to truth and time? Can the Christian idea of tradition be adduced from Scripture and subsequently identified with it? Or, does tradition rely on non-textual realities and, if so, what are they?

These questions form the speculative backdrop against which the following essay engages the idea of tradition in the thought of the twentieth-century French Catholic philosopher Maurice Blondel. Blondel's account of tradition challenges its readers to consider tradition in terms different than but still attuned to the modern practice of historiography. It does so by articulating tradition as the synthetic living reality, the bond (*vinculum*) which mediates the dialectical tension between history and faith, eternity and temporality, receptivity and kenosis, and deposit and development and represents the *vinculum substantiale* (substantial bond) that exists between Creator and creature established by Christ's hypostatic encounter with the world.[1] The concrete process by which tradition unfolds God's truth in time

---

1. Blondel's idea of tradition as the synthetic bond between history and faith belongs to his appropriation of the metaphysical concept of the *vinculum substantiale* in

is through the faithful action of the church. In Blondel's horizon "faithful action is the Ark of the Covenant" where God's truth represented in doctrine becomes a living reality in the church. In discussing the interconnection between tradition, time, and truth this essay brings into sharper focus the Blondelian insight that through the liturgical action of the church tradition is not only a representation of revealed truth in human history, but also the church's encounter with and participation in revealed truth in time.

By drawing on the thought of contemporary authors who have dealt with the question of tradition, this essay also develops and advances Blondel's key insight into interconnection between tradition, time, truth and liturgical action, while maintaining continuity with and bringing more coherence to his idea of tradition in order to provide readers with a clearer window from which they might view Blondel's contribution to a participationist and representational understanding of the Christian faith revealed to the church and carried through liturgical action in tradition.

1. Between History and Dogma: Blondel's Idea of Tradition

In the context of the positions put forward by his early twentieth-century Catholic interlocutors,[2] Blondel argues the "need for an intermediary between history and dogma, the necessity for a link between them which would bring about the synthesis and maintain solidarity without compromising

---

Leibniz's philosophy. For a detailed discussion of the *vinculum substantiale* in Leibniz's thought and Blondel's appropriation of it, see Grumett, "Blondel, Modern Catholic Theology and the Leibnizian Eucharistic Bond." Blondel's first considers this motif in his Latin dissertation and soon after in the 1893 version of the *L'Action*. After these two works it would unfold as a central theme around which his thought interweaves the trinitarian structure of history, the encounter between infinite and finite being in the eucharistic action of the church, and the notion of tradition as the bond between history and faith. See *De Vinculo substantiali et de substantia composita apud Leibnitium* and the revised edition of the dissertation *Une énigme historique. Le "Vinculum substantiale" d'après Leibniz et l'ébauche d'un réalisme supérieur*. For the impact of Leibniz's account of the *vinculum substantiale* on Blondel's thought, as well as his criticism of Leibniz's account, see *Carnets intimes*, 1:47–48, 2:122–23; and *Lettres philosophiques*, 11–13.

2. Blondel represents his interlocutors as the two early twentieth-century Catholic schools of thought he names, "extrinsicism" and "historicism." The one, extrinsicism, tends to emphasize the juridical, abstract, or conceptual nature of dogmatic statements with little or no reference to the concrete and historical circumstances in which they were formulated, while the other, historicism, tends to reduce dogmatic statements and texts to the individual, unique, and ascertainable facts of the historical situation from which they arise.

[history's and dogma's] relative independence."[3] The synthetic principle of tradition

> must have an original force, and a foundation of its own; for neither facts nor ideas nor reasoning have really succeeded in extricating us from the circle in which were enclosed by the initial question: "How is it that the Bible legitimately supports and guarantees the Church, and the Church legitimately supports and interprets the Bible?"[4]

The notion of tradition must be a metaphysical principle with an ontological value distinct from history and dogma and Scripture and the church and yet, a principle that is able to function as the source of unity between each without eliding the one for the other. In other words, the objective of Blondel's notion of tradition is to understand how tradition unites the fundamental tensions in Christianity while maintaining the distinct integrity of each. To do so requires identifying the space between them, a space that constitutes their unity-in-distinction and that is interwoven into the fabric of the exegetical methods and the speculative doctrines of the church in such a way that it presupposes the ordinary language and grammar spoken in the church. As Blondel notes,

> This vivifying power is known to everyone. It is a commonplace to say that the Church rests on "Scripture and *Tradition*." But what is it precisely? What is its function? What rational justification can be offered for it? How is it that it is linked, on the one hand, to historical facts without being absorbed into history, and that it is bound up, on the other hand, with speculative doctrines though it is not completely absorbed in them.[5]

The task at hand is to liberate tradition from the assumptions that conceal it by describing its role and discovering "the source of its strength, and by virtue of what right it knows history in some respects otherwise and better than the critical historian, and dogma otherwise and better than the speculative theologian."[6]

To begin, Blondel notes that the conventional idea of tradition is that of "transmission, principally by word of mouth, of historical facts, received truths, accepted teachings, hallowed practices and ancient customs. Is that, however, the whole content, is it even, where Catholicism is concerned,

3. Blondel, *History and Dogma*, 264.
4. Ibid.
5. Ibid., 264–65.
6. Ibid., 265.

the essential content of the notion?"[7] The conventional idea of tradition conceives of tradition as an epiphenomenon that emerges in the absence of texts, "supplementing the lacunae," as Blondel puts it. In this way tradition is invoked in distinction to Scripture as revealing a "state of mind" or "ancient custom" prior to the text or even implied in the text, and becomes subject to a double presupposition:

> Tradition only reports things explicitly said, expressly prescribed or deliberately performed by men in whom we are interested only for their conscious ideas, and in the form in which they themselves expressed them; it furnishes nothing which cannot or could not be translated into written language, nothing which is not directly and integrally convertible into intellectual expression; so that as we complete our collection of all that former centuries, even without noticing it, confided to memory—rather like students of folklore noting down folk-songs—Tradition, it would seem, becomes superfluous, and recedes before the progress of reflective analysis, written codification and scientific co-ordination.[8]

Conceiving of tradition in terms of a reality that emerges in the absence of texts neglects the dynamism of tradition, and, as Blondel would note in a later comment on tradition, that "element in tradition which is irreducible and always escapes when we formulate tradition in writing . . . [and which] permits some few particles of the gold of truth to pass from the level of what is implicit in life (*l'implicite vécu*) to the level of the expressly known (*l'explicite connu*)."[9] For Blondel, tradition is a metaphysical principle whose ontological value comes to expression through its mediative and unitive functions. It is a "principle of unity, continuity and fecundity which is both initial, anticipatory and final, precedes all reconstructive synthesis and likewise survives all reflexive analysis."[10] It is the bond that unites the "communion of saints," mediating the living community's contemporaneity with the whole church, both living and dead.

The truth of tradition, then, is attuned to the historical realities of faith, but it transcends the heuristic gaze of critical history, inviting one to participate in the truth that stretches back to the past and into the future

---

7. Ibid. Blondel does not mention the important distinction between apostolic, post-apostolic, and ecclesial tradition.

8. Ibid., 266.

9. Blondel, "Tradition," 1140–41.

10. Ibid., 1141.

from the present.[11] This is the "living reality" of tradition, which operates on the charism of discernment embodied in concrete practice and animates the entire life of the church, drawing into itself a living synthesis of the speculative, historical and moral truths of the church, manifesting and corroborating these truths through the concrete reality of "faithful action."[12]

Here we encounter the central reality of the synthetic bond between action and tradition in Blondel's account. In his well-known work exploring the phenomenon of action, *L'Action*,[13] Blondel laid the groundwork for this bond through a "regressive analysis" of the will's necessary development, which he expressed in the form of a polarity (heteronomy) between the freedom of the will and the necessity of the will through the categories of the *"la volonté voulue"* (willed will) and the *"la volonté voulante"* (willing will). For Blondel, the term "action" connotes a metaphysical reality akin to traditional metaphysic's use of the term "existence" as the most fundamental and originating principle moving the essence to act.[14] Action also represents a shift in the understanding of God's power as the original dynamism of spiritual beings, which resides beyond the intellect and the will, while at the same time functions as the source of power for the intellect and the will. In Blondel's horizon, the will plays "less the role of a faculty among others than that of a *vestigium*. Such a vestige must first recognize itself as such—as a trace—follow its own path, and then traverse itself to find that of which it is the imprint."[15] It is an imprint of the *vinculum substantiale* (substantial bond), the *actus purus* (pure act) from which all reality has its origin and the end toward which all creation moves. The objective of the dialectic at work in *L'Action* is to discover what is necessary in action, the "determinism of action." The determinism of action will reveal the necessity of the supernatural within all willing. Action, Blondel will say toward the end of his work, "is a synthesis of man and God."[16]

11. Cf. Blondel, *History and Dogma*, 268.

12. Cf. Ibid., 274.

13. Blondel, *L'Action (1893)*. There are at least two versions of *L'Action* published by Blondel. The first version was published in 1893 after his doctoral defense at the Sorbonne. The second version was published as two volumes in 1936 and 1937 as part of Blondel's trilogy on thought, being, and action. All references in this essay are to the English translation of *L'Action (1893)*.

14. The reader needs be aware that the metaphysical tradition has never been unanimous in its interpretation and usage of the term "existence." For a historical overview of the pre-Socratic, Platonic, and Aristotelian interpretations of the term, see Sweeney, *Metaphysics of Authentic Existentialism*, 3–63. For an excellent survey of the Aristotelian-Thomist tradition of interpretation, see Gilson, *Being and Some Philosophers*.

15. Marion, "La conversion de la volonté selon *l'Action*," 160.

16. Blondel, *L'Action (1893)*, 343.

The relationship between action and tradition is adumbrated toward the end of the dialectic in *L'Action*, when, in the final stage of the drama of the "life of action" Blondel suggests that "dogmas are not only facts and ideas in act, but also they are principles of action."[17] That is, the full value and meaning of dogma is not understood until it is embodied in practice, and practice becomes the unifying source of action and thought. In this respect, "a tradition and a discipline represent a constant interpretation of thought through acts, offering each individual, in the sanctified experience, something like an anticipated control, an authorized commentary, an impersonal verification of the truth."[18]

In *History and Dogma*, published over a decade after *L'Action*, the interplay between action and tradition unfolds within a more explicitly ecclesial horizon that envisions the disclosure of the speculative truths of Christian doctrine as a process sustained by ecclesial practice.

> "To keep" the word of God means in the first place to do it, to put it into practice; and the deposit of Tradition, which the infidelities of the memory and the narrow limits of the intelligence would inevitably deform if it were handed to us in a purely intellectual form, cannot be transmitted in its entirety, indeed, cannot be used and developed, unless it is confided to the practical obedience of love. Faithful action is the Ark of the Covenant where the confidences of God are found, the Tabernacle where he perpetuates his presence and his teaching. If the essential truth of Catholicism is the incarnation of dogmatic ideas in historical facts, one must add reciprocally that the miracle of the Christian life is that from acts at first perhaps difficult, obscure and enforced, one rises to the light through a practical verification of speculative truths. *Lex voluntatis, lux veritatis.*[19]

What Blondel suggests here is that to discern the content and meaning of God's truth in revelation requires the proper disposition of the will. The ecclesial and liturgical practices of prayer, almsgiving and fasting, that is to say, concrete practices, dispose the community (the church) toward discerning the truth revealed both in Scripture and doctrine.[20] In this way, the practice of tradition offers a constant interpretation of Scripture and doctrine by penetrating its content and implications, and in so doing, illuminating the speculative truths contained in each.

17. Ibid., 372.
18. Ibid., 380.
19. Blondel, *History and Dogma*, 274.
20. Cf. ibid.

From this perspective, Blondel's account of tradition is not an epiphenomenon that appears in the absence of the canonical scriptures. Rather tradition relies on texts and, at the same time, it relies on something else he calls "an experience always in act which enables it to remain in some respects master of the texts instead of being strictly subservient to them."[21] This account of tradition allows it to be more than a force preserving the intellectual aspect of the past in texts, but also a living reality of Christ's presence. Tradition, as Blondel puts it, "frees us from the very Scriptures on which it never ceases to rely with devout respect,"[22] to reach the real Christ who escapes scientific examination without rejecting the practices of exegesis and history.

Since the idea of tradition in the Blondelian framework is not literally dependent upon the church's texts, though it perpetually renews and provides an interpretive horizon for them, tradition has a relative latitude in appropriating other means for expressing the central truths of Christianity, without these other means, whether in their social, cultural or philosophical forms, usurping the theological expression of the principle truths of faith.[23] Of course, it is possible for the normative truth claims of tradition to be obscured by ideology. But, when a living tradition is embodied well in practice the central and enduring truths of that tradition are intelligible to the community which represents the living tradition—and, when embodied poorly, imperspicuous to the community. There obtains, therefore, in the Blondelian framework, a symbiosis between truth and freedom in tradition, where, tradition simultaneously preserves and develops through the ongoing interplay between history and "faithful action." In this way, Blondel writes, "One realizes through the practice of Christianity that its dogmas are rooted in reality. One has no right to set the facts on one side and the theological data on the other without going back to the sources of life and of action, finding the indivisible synthesis."[24] The synthesis is a "Christian knowledge" that attends to history, as well as the "collective experience of Christ verified and realized in us."[25] In other words, tradition is a form of knowledge which situates itself between "those who offer us a Christianity so divine that there is nothing human, living or moving about it, and those who involve it so deeply in historical contingencies and make it so dependent upon natural factors that it retains nothing but a diffused sort

21. Ibid.
22. Ibid., 268.
23. Cf. ibid., 280.
24. Ibid., 286.
25. Ibid., 287.

of divinity."²⁶ Simply put, tradition is the synthetic living reality between history and dogma.

2. The Trinitarian Nature of History and Truth in Tradition

For Blondel, tradition is not the antinomy of critical history, a static, isolated reality untouched by time. Nor is it simply synonymous with the facts established through critical history. Tradition is not some "sacred stone cast down from heaven to be passed on from generation to generation, nor is it an accumulation of sediments from centuries of human thought."²⁷ The object of the study of tradition is not to establish mere causal links between phenomena, since tradition is not bound to historical attestation in the same manner as the modern practice of historiography. In order to avoid making "category mistakes" when one attempts to speak about religious events and their relation to dogmatic claims to truth, Blondel thought one needs to attend to the various linguistic usages of term "fact."²⁸ The categorization of the different kinds of facts suggests that to comprehend the full dimension of religious facts, to discover their internal connections, hierarchical interdependence, and spiritual substance, requires that they be seen through their various and appropriate categories.

> The issue is to bring together simultaneously all kinds of proof, to understand why all facts are not on the same level; how for instance the adoration of the magi, although its "historicity" is less impossible than the virgin birth, is, from the doctrinal view, of infinitely lesser importance and could be considered without guilt, the parabolic illustration of an infinitesimal point.²⁹

Blondel's categorization of the various kinds of facts constitutes the first step in the process of synthesizing history and dogma and in establishing a form of Christian knowledge situated between immanence and transcendence. It also displays how the practice of tradition does not preserve historical facts and speculative aspects of the past, nor does it ignore the way in which the past influences historical and conceptual details. Rather, tradition attests to history by drawing the "living (vital) reality" out of the historical features of

---

26. Ibid., 286.
27. Blanchette, *Maurice Blondel*, 206.
28. Cf. Blondel, "De la valeur historique du dogme," 229–45.
29. Ibid., 241–42.

the past and into a living synthesis that applies to the present and illuminates the future.[30] In this sense, tradition relies on history to "re-present" the vital reality of truth present in the past in order for that reality to form the living synthesis of truth in the present. Here the Blondelian notion of tradition moves beyond the exercise of marshalling evidence of the past in support of religious belief, despite the importance of that task. Instead, tradition's principal task is to facilitate the interplay between the living reality (deposit) of truth received from the past, embodied (action) in the present life of the church, and orientated toward the future (development).

The interplay between deposit, development, and action in Blondel's account of tradition resonates deeply with the Pauline idea of tradition. For Paul and the early church the revelation of God in the person of Jesus Christ is both the origin and the content of tradition, i.e., the *paradosis*, the "linking process in time which is of the historical order, and a non-temporal or supra-temporal reality, fully present here and now."[31] The knowledge of tradition given in the liturgical action of baptism and the ecclesial practice of the church and learned through catechetical training was the principle reality through which one participated in the truth that is genuinely present while at the same time always already beyond one's full comprehension. To be a witness to the tradition of the twelve disciples meant to see, to hear, and to practice, but also to deliver and to transmit (*tradere*) the knowledge that comes from the deposit of faith through tradition. The concept of "deposit" within the Pauline corpus signifies the essence of God's plan to redeem the world through the death and the resurrection of Christ and this event remains the ultimate referent of tradition (2 Tim 1:13–14; 1 Cor 3:11), which discloses itself through each facet of faith, including the episcopal, juridical and institutional.[32] Yet, while this truth remains the enduring and ultimate referent of tradition the practice of interpreting, discerning, and embodying its presence as the pattern of redemption in the world remains open to development and change. That is, within the apostolic economy of tradition exists an ecclesial space in which the content of revelation can be given further interpretation and formulation. While the historical Christ, the living Word of Scripture is the origin of tradition, the ecclesial space of tradition always transcends the material reality of Scripture by the "pneumatic surplus" dwelling at its center.[33] When the phenomenon of tradition opens up

30. Blondel, *History and Dogma*, 267.

31. Congar, *Tradition and Traditions*, 12–13.

32. On the relations between tradition, apostolic succession, and Scripture, see Ratzinger, "Primacy, Episcopate, and Apostolic Succession."

33. Cf. ibid., 18–19. Here the limitations of thinking about revelation in positivistic terms as information instead of transformation become clear when one tries to

a new interpretation and a further explication of revelation it will always transcend the purely historical, as, for example, when the christological interpretation of the Old Testament prescinds from the chronological pattern of the Old Testament.[34] The new interpretation need not be considered completely foreign; rather, it can be seen as a *new understanding of the same revelation* disclosed in a different situation.[35] Here, through the gift of the Holy Spirit, tradition functions as the hypostatic bond between God's concrete and continual action in human history and the historical and literary character of God's revelation in human history expressed in the canonical Scriptures. For Saint Paul and Blondel alike, then, the transmission (*tradere*) of tradition in the church is a participation in the communion of eternal love found in the Trinitarian life of God, which the Holy Spirit initiates, sustains, aids and guides through persons in communion.[36] The transmission of tradition that takes place from person to person in the church is an analogical reflection of the *kenotic* self-giving and the spontaneous receptivity that occurs between the life of the divine persons of the Trinity. In this way the church imperfectly participates in the perfect transmission (*tradere*) of Christ that flows from the incarnation and its finality.

For the church to participate in the receptive and kenotic movements of the economy of tradition, as Blondel's account implies it does, it must remain open to the divine disclosure of truth in tradition. In order to discern the truth of tradition and the possibility of genuine change and development in tradition those actions which represent the truth of persons in communion with God must be directed toward the one who gives the gift of tradition. Thus, discerning the divine disclosure of truth in tradition is an exercise in hope that in faith the church will dispose itself to the gifts of the Spirit and the prospect of embodying a mode of charity that, Blondel declares, "insinuates a new order into the normal order."[37] Here Blondel's own diary captures well the movement of receptivity and kenosis through which human existence enters into the triune Life itself through the divine Mediator and in doing so participates in the new order of charity.

> Being is love; we cannot know if we do not love. The Spirit of God is charity; without the charity that is poured out into our hearts, we cannot rise either to the Son or the Father; We cannot

---

reconcile the claim that no new public revelation is to be expected before Christ comes again with the claim of doctrinal development.

34. Cf. Ratzinger, "Revelation and Tradition," 47.
35. Cf. ibid.
36. Cf. Blondel, *La philosophie et l'esprit Chrétien*, 2:77–88.
37. Ibid., 283.

> understand anything in the world of the Spirit's operations. By the Incarnation, the world was created anew; but in a transcendent and ideal manner. In order for there to be real unity, an immanent life, *vinculum substantiale*, the Spirit of unity and of love must secretly penetrate the interiority of beings and therein complete reality, being; and being is always a presence of God; more than a knowledge, more than a production, it is love. The action of substances upon one another is at one and the same time a subordination of power, an influence of ideal persuasion, and an attraction of love.[38]

Through the death and resurrection of Christ the church participates through grace in the Trinitarian life of eternal love that flows into the world, and the "new order" of love that enters into the historical order of creation. The synthesis of the facts of history and dogmas of faith reflect the effect of this new order. As Blondel puts it, "The synthesis of dogma and facts is scientifically effected because there is a synthesis of thought and grace in the life of the believer, a union of man and God, reproducing in the individual consciousness the history of Christianity itself."[39]

In the Blondelian horizon, then, there is an observable analogy between all human action and the revelation of God's triune life in history. It is through the mysterious dynamic of action that humanity is given a genuine space (*analogia libertatis*) to make history happen.[40]

> In created beings, the mystery of the Trinity is always represented, and the action of each of the eternal persons can be sensed there. The relation of these operations, this bond of the intimate constitution of beings is always synthetic and contingent. We always have need of experience to acquire the science of the real, the work of the freedom of choice; and in the human world, in the rule of the moral will, experience is action.[41]

For Blondel, this space is by no means void, awaiting, as with Kant, the categories of understanding imposed upon it in order to render it intelligible to consciousness. It contains an immanent intelligibility, but the content is mediated between the subject and the world not by "Observing Reason"[42] in

---

38. Blondel, *Carnets intimes*, 1:222.
39. Blondel, *History and Dogma*, 287.
40. Blondel examines the Trinitarian structure of history in more detail in the trilogy on thought, being, and action in *La pensée* (2 vols.); *L'Etre et les êtres*; *L'Action I*; and *L'Action II*.
41. Blondel, *Carnets intimes*, 1:125–26.
42. Cf. Hegel, *Phenomenology of Spirit*, 139–262.

the sense Hegel envisions, where "[Reason] involves the Harmony of Being in its purest essence, challenging the external world to exhibit the same Reason which the Subject (the Ego) possesses."[43] Instead, the content of creation is rendered intelligible by virtue of its created status, which makes it receptive to its full realization through the Incarnate Word. Put another way, the hypostatic bond, which is the site of redemption in creation, mediates redemption in human history in such a way that the natural order need not abandon that which makes it distinctively other to its source of fulfillment, the supernatural. As Blondel writes, "the whole natural order comes between God and man as a bond and as an obstacle, as a necessary means of union and as a necessary means of distinction.[44]

The Trinitarian structure of history raises two distinct but interrelated questions for Blondel's idea of tradition: First, how does the hypostatic bond of the person of Christ furnish the idea of tradition with a concrete form? And second, how can one discern this form as the pattern of redemption in the world? In its multiplicity and diversity, the church (the body) forms together with Christ (the Head) the living subject of tradition by virtue of its relationship of similarity and difference to Christ. As the living subject of tradition, the church is given the content of tradition through its participation in the mission (*missio*) the Father gives to the Son for the salvation of the world, which is disclosed through the Spirit in history at various levels through the prophets, the Incarnation, the Apostles and the church. Yet, while the church is one with Christ (the Head) as Christ's body, and therefore, the living subject of tradition, the church is at the same time other to Christ, as expressed form of the Incarnate Word which cannot articulate itself unequivocally apart from Christ. This unity-in-distinction provides the horizon from which the interplay or polarity between the acts of the church as both body (human) and head (divine) are rendered theologically intelligible, and the framework within which one can begin to understand the relation between liturgical action and time in tradition.

3. After Blondel: The Liturgical Action of Tradition and Time

Blondel's insight into the relationship of time in tradition, where tradition "anticipates and illuminates the future and is disposed to do so by the effort

---

43. Hegel, *Philosophy of History*, 439.
44. Blondel, *L'Action (1893)*, 410.

which it makes to remain faithful to the past,"⁴⁵ is one of the most prescient yet undeveloped insights that Blondel intuitively discloses in his account of tradition, as well as an insight that theologians influenced by Blondel's account of tradition have sought to give theological expression to. In Yves Congar's comments on the transmission of tradition that takes place in the "sacramental order" published roughly a half a century after the publication of *History and Dogma*, he observed that the transmission of tradition that takes place through liturgical action requires a unique understanding of temporality. As Congar put it,

> the sacraments have a peculiar temporal duration, in which past, present and future are not mutually exclusive, as in our chronological time. Sacramental time, the time of the Church, allows the sharing by men who follow [one another] through the centuries in an event which is historically unique and which took place at a distant time; this sharing is achieved not merely on the intellectual level, as I could commune with Plato's thought, or with the death of Socrates, but in the presence and action of the mystery of salvation.⁴⁶

Congar's assertion about the horizon of time within which the sacraments are practiced and give concrete expression to the event of salvation intimate at the interplay between the elements of time Blondel envisioned at play in the liturgical action of tradition.

For liturgical action facilitates the bond uniting the activities of remembering, imagining, and anticipating and through this process the time of tradition is distinguished from chronological time. Through liturgical action the time of tradition becomes a form of time that is not above or alongside chronological time, but rather internal to chronological time.⁴⁷ As an internal aspect of chronological time, the time of tradition allows liturgical action not simply to refer to a contact in the past but to make the past context there again as absent. When considering the temporal character of the liturgical action of tradition it is important to keep in mind that we tend to think presences and absences as spatial features or temporal attributes of the thing, "and often interpret them as the object's being 'here' or 'there,' or 'going on now' or 'all finished' . . . But presence and absence are not fea-

45. Blondel, *History and Dogma*, 268.

46. Congar, *Tradition and Traditions*, 259–60. See also Congar, *Meaning of Tradition*, 134–43.

47. Here we have in mind Husserl's distinction between world time, the time of clock and calendar, and internal time, as the "*Objective temporality that appears* (for example: the temporality of this die) from the '*internal*' *temporality of the appearing* (for example: that of the die-perceiving)." See Husserl, *Cartesian Meditations*, 41.

tures of things, they are modes of presentation."[48] This observation casts into relief the need to attend to the distinction between pictorial representation (pictures) and symbolic representation (symbols), particularly in the dialectic between now and then that obtains in liturgical action. The unique character of pictorial representation is that "pictures do not merely refer to something, but make something present."[49] As this distinction comes to expression in the practice of memory

> I appreciate that what I am remembering is not in the present of my life; I present earlier motions and events as having been lived through, but as not being lived through now, except as absent and "there again." Yesterday's dinner is not being eaten now, but I am now remembering and reidentifying not an image of the dinner, but the dinner itself again, as absent.[50]

In the time of tradition the past, present, and future are encountered in a manner distinct from chronological time. The time of tradition requires a living subject (community) reenact the displacements of time, which are remembered and imagined not in abeyance, nor in the "act of symbolization,"[51] but in the *action* of the event of historical happening. It is in this sense of time that the church's liturgical action participates in the sacrificial action of Christ's death and resurrection as the gift given to the church by Christ from the Father and through the Spirit. It is in faith that the church participates in the fullness of the gift of the Son yet to come.

That the church's liturgical action takes place in time but is not fully dependent upon the ordinary conception of time is reflected in the form in which the liturgical act is mediated.[52] Despite the tendency among modern and contemporary ritual theorists to categorize the form of a liturgical act as "purely formal, secondary, and mere physical expression of logically prior ideas,"[53] a preponderance of meaning resides in the form of the liturgical act itself and not merely its function as a symbolic description of a deeper

---

48. Sokolowski, *Pictures, Quotations, and Distinctions*, 24.
49. Ibid., 21.
50. Ibid., 124.
51. For example, see Chauvet, *Symbol and Sacrament*, 128–40.
52. Here I have in mind Heidegger's critique of the ordinary conception of time in the final section of division two of *Being and Time*, where Heidegger argues that traditional metaphysics imposes the present, as here and now, as the only basis through which being discloses itself. In this horizon, Heidegger maintains, "time shows itself as a sequence of 'nows' which are constantly 'present-at-hand,' simultaneously passing away and coming along. Time is understood as a succession, as a 'flowing stream' of 'nows,' as the 'course of time.'" See Heidegger, *Being and Time*.
53. Bell, *Ritual Theory, Ritual Practice*, 19.

reality that remains hidden.[54] Indeed, the form of the liturgical act is inextricably bound to its content such that the latter is unintelligible apart from the former. The form of the liturgical act, its exterior expression, is both the veiling and unveiling of the content, the interior reality of the liturgical act. The unity-in-distinction between interiority and exteriority discloses the significance of the form of the liturgical act as a "pointer which is indissolubly united to the event which is the actual content of the sacrament."[55] In the case of the eucharistic action of the church, the host mediates the exteriority (distance or otherness) between Christ and the church, which makes possible the church's genuine participation in the divine life of Christ present in the liturgy. But the form of the host as "daily bread" also mediates the community's contingency, its daily dependence on God as the "one who makes [the] gift of bread . . . and finally of existence itself."[56] It is the provisory character of the host that "insures against any taking possession of the present"[57] in a manner akin to the way in which the ordinary conception of time imposes the present on the past and the future as the condition for the possibility of real presence in the eucharistic action. Instead, in mediating the real presence of the Other the form of the consecrated host displays the irreducible exteriority of the eucharistic present, a "properly Christian temporality" which "constitutes the ultimate paradigm of every present."[58]

The form of the liturgical act further reflects the multiple contexts and the temporal forms of the present, past, and future the liturgical action of the church engages in while celebrating the Eucharist. The church's eucharistic celebration establishes a form of the present, past, and future that is chronologically later than the present and the past of Jesus's celebration of the Eucharist. But the church's celebration "takes place within them and blends with them temporally" through the re-enactment of Christ's sacrificial action. Simply put,

> When [the church] reenacts the death and Resurrection of Jesus, it also reenacts the action God performed in the Exodus. The Last Supper invoked the Passover, so when we invoke the Last Supper we also invoke the Passover that preceded and was drawn into it. Our Eucharist thus has a double revival of the

54. For an example of an interpretive method that ignores the form of an action or ritual practice in its effort to discover how an action or practice symbolically represents the cultural ethos and shared value of a community, see Durkheim, *Elementary Forms of the Religious Life*.

55. Balthasar, *Glory of the Lord*, 1:579.

56. Chauvet, *Symbol and Sacrament*, 397.

57. Marion, *God Without Being*, 175.

58. Ibid., 176.

past, with one of its reenacted pasts, the Last Supper, enclosed within the context set by the other, the Passover. The past of our Eucharist is the present of the Last Supper and the sacrifice of Calvary; in a deeper dimension, the past of the our Eucharist is the present of the Passover and the Exodus.[59]

The temporal forms of the present, past, and future that the liturgical action of the church embodies disclose that the past and the future dimensions of liturgical action constitute the condition for the possibility of rendering the present intelligible. That is to say, the past in the eucharistic action (*memoriale passionis Domini*) is only intelligible as the church's present petition and anticipation of Christ's return (*Epektasis*). In this way the "present of the Eucharistic gift is not at all temporalized starting from the *here and now* but as memorial (temporalization starting from the past), then as eschatological announcement (temporalization starting from the future), and finally, and only finally, as dailyness and viaticum (temporalization starting from the present)."[60] As the most visible action of God's encounter with the world, the celebration of the Eucharist is the site where the transmission and the historicity of the truth in tradition is on display as a diachronic living reality.[61] Further, the ontology of the liturgical action of tradition configures the interplay (or tension) between the past, present, and the future, the *anamnesis*, allowing the liturgical action of tradition, as in Blondel's account, to anticipate and to illuminate the future through its fidelity to the past.[62] "We are and we act always 'now,' but our now is always the recapitulation of a past and the anticipation of a future."[63]

As the inner nature of tradition liturgical action displays that the action involved in memory has the unique capacity to be the same action we once perceived, yet, not the same action in perpetuity, since actions are bound to their present and cannot be in another action in the same present.[64] For

---

59. Sokolowski, *Eucharistic Presence*, 103.

60. Marion, *God Without Being*, 172. For Marion, the primacy of the present in the ordinary conception of time imposes itself on the modern interpretation of the theology of transubstantiation, creating and facilitating the conditions for the possibility of Christ's real presence in the eucharistic action.

61. For a discussion of the liturgy as the "site" of the encounter between the finite and infinite, its relationship to the church, and how this encounter and relationship has been spatially construed in modern eucharistic theology, see Pickstock, *After Writing*, 158–66. Also see Lawrence Paul Hemming's critique of Pickstock's interpretation in *Worship as Revelation*, 77–79.

62. Cf. Blondel, *Letter on Apologetics*, 268.

63. Sokolowski, *Eucharistic Presence*, 105.

64. Cf. Sokolowski, *Pictures, Quotations, and Distinctions*, 126.

the same action to appear again in memory requires "'another temporal context' . . . originally given to us when we memorially or imaginatively place ourselves at a time, at a then, different from the one we are in now."[65] Liturgical action discloses a mode of representation in which the self enacts displacements creating for it an interplay or polarity between the present, past, and future that is central to its identity. Indeed, such displacements are the central feature of what it means to be a human being. For through the process of enacting the liturgical displacements of the church the self discovers an anthropology that discloses the radical non-necessity of the self's being[66] and affirms finite reality (creation) to be the location and matter (bread and wine) through which God encounters the world.

> To reach man, God must go through all of nature and offer Himself to [man] under the most brute of material species. To reach God, man must go through all of nature and find him under the veil where He hides Himself only to be accessible. Thus the whole natural order comes between God and man as a bond and as an obstacle, as a necessary means of union and as a necessary means of distinction.[67]

As God's concrete encounter with the world liturgical action is the deepest sense of tradition by which the church, as a synthetic living reality, simultaneously relives (past), embodies (present), and transmits (future) and realizes its identity through the interplay between "deposit" (past) and development (future). Through the liturgical action of the church, the self is reconfigured by being unable to imagine itself as the source of its own existence. In this manner, liturgical action becomes the true source of being and the concrete way in which humanity comes to participate in the eternal life of God. It is the reason Blondel maintained the eucharistic action of the church to be the "act par excellence" which seals the synthesis between God and man in a "true communion."[68]

It is this reality of liturgical action and its relationship to the phenomenon of tradition that prompted Blondel to speak of tradition metaphorically as "an umbilical cord that prevents the Church from being stillborn. Through it, divine blood really flows; and this divine blood feeds the Church and allows the spiritual birth of souls who are called to grow into divine maturity."[69] Here, in the encounter with Christ Blondel sees in tradition an

65. Ibid.
66. For Blondel's reflections on the contingency of self, see *L'Action (1893)*, 314–29.
67. Ibid., 410.
68. Blondel, *L'Action (1893)*, 387.
69. Blondel, *La philosophie et l'esprit Chrétien*, 2:82.

irreducible element that continually eludes literal (and textual) formulation. It is the index that points to the way in which the communal life of liturgical action becomes the vessel through which the truths of tradition transform "what is implicit and 'enjoyed' into something explicit and known."[70]

> The essence of Tradition should not be considered under the material aspect of Scripture or that which can be expressed with words. For what it transmits is precisely what cannot adequately be named or mummified under sensible or intellectual aspects; we are dealing here with a living transmission, not only through words but also through actions, signs, contacts between living persons, gestures that exclude all doubts and hesitations for they surpass mental deliberations.[71]

Tradition, far from being an ersatz form of historiography, a social phenomenon that could be adequately interpreted by the social sciences, or a collection of texts and customs that are invoked to supplement Scripture, "is more a spiritual community in the process of constituting itself historically on the basis of a Revelation and a life that surpasses its own human, historical, and natural capacity."[72] Tradition is the synthetic bond that draws the incarnational and spiritual dynamisms of eternity into the historical life of the church and calls the church to discover God's living presence in human history not merely as facts and linear phenomena or as a social and cultural reality, but as the event of salvation and redemption. It is this richer and deeper understanding of the ontological reality of tradition in the life of each individual Christian within the mystical body of Christ that comes to concrete expression in the liturgical action of the church. Indeed, it is this understanding of tradition which Blondel sought to give expression to and without which, he maintained, the fullness of truth contained in God's revelation could not be represented adequately and fully encountered in human history and the church's dogma.

Bibliography

Balthasar, Hans Urs von. *The Glory of the Lord*. Vol. 1, *Seeing the Form*. Translated by Erasmo Leiva-Merikakis. Edited by Joseph Fessio and John Riches. San Francisco: Ignatius, 1982.
Bell, Catherine. *Ritual Theory, Ritual Practice*. New York: Oxford University Press, 1992.
Blanchette, Oliva. *Maurice Blondel: A Philosophical Life*. Grand Rapids: Eerdmans, 2010.

70. Blondel, *Letter on Apologetics*, 268.
71. Blondel, *La philosophie et l'esprit Chrétien*, 2:80.
72. Blanchette, *Maurice Blondel*, 206.

Blondel, Maurice. *Carnets intimes*. 2 vols. Paris: Cerf, 1961–66.
———. "De la valeur historique du dogme." In *Les premiers écrits de Maurice Blondel*, 229–45. Paris: Presses Universitaires de France, 1956.
———. *History and Dogma*. In *The Letter on Apologetics; and, History and Dogma*. Translated and edited by Alexander Dru and Illtyd Trethowan. Grand Rapids: Eerdmans, 1994.
———. *L'Action (1893): Essay on a Critique of Life and a Science of Practice*. Translated by Oliva Blanchette. Notre Dame: University of Notre Dame Press, 1984.
———. *L'Action I: Le problème des causes secondes et le pur agir*. Paris: Alcan, 1936.
———. *L'Action II: L'Action humaine et les conditions de son aboutissement*. Paris: Alcan, 1937.
———. *L'Etre et les êtres*. Paris: Alcan, 1935.
———. *La pensée*. 2 vols. Paris: Alcan, 1934.
———. *La philosophie et l'esprit Chrétien: Conditions de la symbiose seule normale et salutaire*. Paris: Presses Universitaires de France, 1946.
———. *Lettres philosophiques*. Paris: Aubier, 1961.
———. "Tradition." In *Vocabulaire technique et critique de la philosophie*, edited by André Lalande, 1140–41. 8th ed. Paris: Presses Universitaires de France, 1960.
———. *Une énigme historique. Le "Vinculum Substantiale" d'après Leibniz et l'ébauche d'un réalisme supérieur*. 2nd ed. Paris: Gabriel Beauchesne, 1930.
Chauvet, Louis-Marie. *Symbol and Sacrament: A Sacramental Reinterpretation of Christian Existence*. Translated by Madeleine Beaumont and Patrick Madigan. Collegeville, MN: Liturgical, 1995.
Congar, Yves. *The Meaning of Tradition*. Translated by A. N. Woodrow. San Francisco: Ignatius, 2004.
———. *Tradition and Traditions: An Historical and a Theological Essay*. Translated by Michael Naseby and Thomas Rainborough. New York: Macmillan, 1966.
Durkheim, Emile. *The Elementary Forms of the Religious Life*. Translated by J. W. Swain. London: Allen and Unwin, 1968.
Gilson, Etienne. *Being and Some Philosophers*. Toronto: Pontifical Institute of Mediaeval Studies, 1949.
Grumett, David. "Blondel, Modern Catholic Theology and the Leibnizian Eucharistic Bond." *Modern Theology* 23 (2007) 561–77.
Hegel, G. W. F. *Phenomenology of Spirit*. Translated by A. V. Miller. Oxford: Oxford University Press, 1977.
———. *The Philosophy of History*. Translated by J. Sibree. New York: Dover, 1956.
Heidegger, Martin. *Being and Time*. Translated by John Macquarrie and Edward Robinson. New York: Harper & Row, 1962.
Hemming, Lawrence Paul. *Worship as Revelation: The Past, Present and Future of Catholic Liturgy*. London: Burns & Oates, 2008.
Husserl, Edmund. *Cartesian Meditations: An Introduction to Phenomenology*. Translated by Dorion Cairns. The Hague: M. Nijhoff, 1960.
Marion, Jean-Luc. *God Without Being: Hors-Texte*. Translated by Thomas A. Carlson. Chicago: University of Chicago Press, 1991.
———. "La conversion de la volonté selon *l'Action*." In *Maurice Blondel: une dramatique de la modernité*, edited by Dominique Folscheid. Paris: Editions Universitaires, 1990.

Pickstock, Catherine. *After Writing: On the Liturgical Consummation of Philosophy.* Oxford: Blackwell, 1998.
Ratzinger, Joseph. "Primacy, Episcopate, and Apostolic Succession." In Karl Rahner and Joseph Ratzinger, *The Episcopate and the Primacy*, translated by Kenneth Barker et al., 46–54. New York: Herder and Herder, 1962.
———. "Revelation and Tradition." In Karl Rahner and Joseph Ratzinger, *Revelation and Tradition*, translated by W. J. O'Hara, 26–35. London: Burns & Oates, 1966.
Sokolowski, Robert. *Eucharistic Presence: A Study in the Theology of Disclosure.* Washington, DC: Catholic University of America Press, 1994.
———. *Pictures, Quotations, and Distinctions: Fourteen Essays in Phenomenology.* Notre Dame: University of Notre Dame Press, 1992.
Sweeney, Leo. *A Metaphysics of Authentic Existentialism.* Englewood Cliffs, NJ: Prentice-Hall, 1965.

8

Joseph Ratzinger and the Hermeneutic of Continuity

TRACEY ROWLAND

Changes in the liturgy take on a momentous significance for the believer, for they are changes in his experience of God—changes, if you wish to be Feuerbachian, in God himself. The question whether to make the sign of the cross with two fingers or with three split a Church. So can the question whether or not to use the Book of Common Prayer or the Tridentine Mass.

—ROGER SCRUTON, *THE PHILOSOPHER ON DOVER BEACH*[1]

ROGER SCRUTON IS NOT a Catholic philosopher but it is remarkable how often his sociological insights converge with those of Catholic philosophers and theologians, especially Joseph Ratzinger/Benedict XVI. In this context his Dover Beach essay on aesthetic experience and culture goes to the heart of the philosophical problems associated with the liturgical experiments of the generation of 1968. Scruton appreciates that form cannot easily be separated from content, that mere gestures can effect a change in spiritual understanding and that liturgy is not something that can be fabricated out of some individual's imagination. Liturgical changes are matters of extreme

---

1. Scruton, *Philosopher on Dover Beach*, 115.

delicacy. They may appear to be mere matters of taste but in fact they have the capacity to change a person's understanding of God and entire relationship to Him. As Ratzinger remarked at a liturgical conference at Fontgombault Abbey in 2001, "the Greek Church Fathers understood that the sacrifice of prayer should not be mere speech, but the transmutation of our being into the *logos*, the union of ourselves with it."[2] If this is the point of worship, then liturgical changes do have an enormous capacity to affect an individual's relationship with God. For the current generation of Catholic scholars, writing after the 2007 Apostolic Exhortation *Sacramentum Caritatis*, the theological question is no longer, how do we correlate the liturgical life of the church with trends in popular culture? The question is rather, what are the principles governing a liturgical hermeneutic of continuity where the word "continuity" refers to the church's two millennia of divine worship?

At its most general, the expression "hermeneutic of continuity" is associated with Joseph Ratzinger/Benedict XVI's interpretation of the documents of the Second Vatican Council, as outlined in his Christmas Message to the Roman Curia in 2005 (although in that address he actually used the expression "hermeneutic of reform") in contrast to that of his fellow German *peritus*, Karl Rahner SJ, who spoke of a "decisive break" between pre- and post-Conciliar Catholicism, and whose theological interpretations are thus associated with the "hermeneutic of rupture."[3] The expression using the word "continuity" rather than "reform" is found in Benedict XVI's Apostolic Exhortation *Sacramentum Caritatis* of 2007, a document which is specifically dedicated to liturgical issues and eucharistic theology. Some papal commentators have sought to read some deeper meaning into the use of the word "reform" in one context and "continuity" in another; however, footnote 6 of the Apostolic Exhortation which treats the "hermeneutic of continuity" theme refers readers of the document back to the 2005 Christmas message, suggesting that the two meanings are the same. "Reform" connotes a development that improves upon the status quo and "continuity" carries the nuance of a particular non-revolutionary style of reform such as that which is found in John Henry Newman's *Essay on the Development of Doctrine* in which Newman offered seven criteria by which developments could be judged to be either consistent or inconsistent with an earlier tradition. In the spirit of Newman, this paper sets forth seven principles found in

---

2. Ratzinger, "Theology of the Liturgy," 10–11.

3. Benedict XVI, Christmas address of His Holiness Benedict XVI to the Roman Curia, December 22, 2005. For Rahner's "decisive break" speech, see "Towards a Fundamental Theological Interpretation of Vatican II."

Ratzinger/Benedict's publications for structuring a hermeneutic of continuity in the liturgical context.[4]

1. An Organic Development of a Rite of Apostolic Provenance

Some of Joseph Ratzinger's most forthright statements on the principles governing a hermeneutic of continuity are found in an unusually long preface to Alcuin Reid's doctoral dissertation which was published as *The Organic Development of the Liturgy* by St. Michael's Abbey Press in 2004. In the opening paragraph of the preface, Ratzinger spoke of the liturgy as a "living" organism and used botanical metaphors to describe its development. This is consistent with accounts of the development of tradition found in the works of the late nineteenth-century Tübingen scholars, such as Johann Adam Möhler. Grant Kaplan summarized the Tübingen scholars' account of tradition as a "living truth instead of the transmission of old ideas, the church as an organism instead of a *societas perfecta*, Christ as the incarnate *logos* rather than a mere teacher, and the Holy Spirit as an active participant in human life instead of a departed entity who last engaged in the world's affairs during Pentecost."[5] The central theme here is that tradition is something dynamic and culturally embodied. When applied to the liturgical sphere, the liturgy is seen as something *living* rather than static. It is an organism with the capacity for growth and an event which requires the participation of the entire Trinity. Nonetheless, Ratzinger states that its growth is not possible unless its identity is preserved and proper attention is paid to the inner structural logic of the organism:

> Just as a gardener cares for a living plant as it develops, with due attention to the power of growth and life within the plant, and the rules it obeys, so the Church ought to give reverent care to the Liturgy through the ages, distinguishing actions that are helpful and healing, from those that are violent and destructive.[6]

With reference to paragraph 1125 of the *Catechism of the Catholic Church*, which asserts that "even the supreme authority in the Church may not change the liturgy arbitrarily, but only in the obedience of faith and

---

4. The author is not suggesting that these seven principles are exhaustive of all the insights on this subject, which may be discerned through a close study of Ratzinger/Benedict XVI's publications.

5. Kaplan, *Answering the Enlightenment*, 99.

6. Ratzinger, Preface to *Organic Development of the Liturgy*, 3.

with religious respect for the mystery of the liturgy," Ratzinger went on to emphasize that "the Pope is not an absolute monarch whose will is law, but the guardian of an authentic Tradition."[7] He cannot do whatever he likes with the liturgy and he is duty-bound to oppose the initiatives of those who believe that they can do whatever "comes into their head." He has "the task of a gardener, not that of a technician who builds new machines and throws the old ones on the junk-pile."[8] The various liturgical rites of the church are nothing less than a "living form of *paradosis*—the handing-on of tradition."[9]

Thus one might say that for Ratzinger these Rites cannot be treated like a Gilbert and Sullivan comic opera libretto which is updated with references to contemporary public figures and social events to make it easier for the audience to follow the plot and be entertained. Any legitimate Rite must be an organic development of a Rite of Apostolic Provenance, not something manufactured by a committee of academics, or worse, the parish liturgy team:

> As "feast," liturgy goes beyond the realm of what can be made and manipulated; it introduces us to the realm of the given, living reality, which communicates itself to us. That is why, at all times, and in all religions, the fundamental law of liturgy has been the law of organic growth within the universality of the common tradition. Even in the huge transition from the Old to the New Testament, this rule was not breached, the continuity of liturgical development was not interrupted: Jesus introduced his words at the Last Supper organically into the Jewish liturgy at the point where it was open to them, as it were, waiting for them.[10]

The fact that Ratzinger believed that the liturgy is something living made him open to accepting a plurality of different Rites. He was never attracted to the ideal of bureaucratic uniformity—"a one Rite fits all" attitude. He referred to the pre-Conciliar coexistence of the Ambrosian Rite, the Mozarabic Rite of Toledo, the Rite of Braga, the Rite of Chartres and the Rites of the Carmelites and Dominicans alongside the Roman Rite of Pius V as something unproblematic. Speaking directly of the Dominicans he said, "we had no doubt that their Rite was as Catholic as the Roman Rite, [and] we

---

7. Ibid., 3.
8. Ibid.
9. Ibid.
10. Ratzinger, *Feast of Faith*, 66–67.

were proud of this richness in having many different traditions."[11] While he believes that there can be "no question of creating totally new Rites," "there can be variations within the ritual families."[12] The primary question is always: is this particular Rite an organic development of a Rite of Apostolic Provenance?

2. No Archeologism or Mechanical Rationalism

This raises the question of how we know if something is an organic development. As a matter of logic, there are two types of liturgy that, by their very nature, can never be organic. The first type is what Ratzinger calls "fabricated liturgy"—something that has been constructed in the minds of academics, professional liturgists or people who otherwise organize social events. Ratzinger lists the characteristics of fabricated liturgy as (1) arbitrariness as the necessary form of the rejection of each previously given form or norm; (2) unrepeatability because in repetition there would already be dependence; and (3) artificiality, since the result must be a pure creation of humans.[13]

The second kind of liturgical outlook which is hostile to the notion of organic development is liturgy which seeks to be the primal form, or the form of a particular era, which one way or another expressly excludes the possibility of growth. For example, for some the particular era might be the first century of the church's life, for others, the thirteenth or sixteenth centuries, or even the liturgical books as they stood in 1961. Ratzinger describes the mentality associated with this denial of the living or organic nature of the liturgy as "archeologism."

In his preface to Reid's work, Ratzinger asserted that "liturgical reform is something different from archeological excavation," adding that "not all the developments of a living thing have to be logical in accordance with a rationalistic or historical standard."[14] With reference to the liturgical experiments of the 1960s and 1970s, he also observed that "because historical knowledge cannot be elevated straight into the status of a new liturgical norm, this archeological enthusiasm was very easily combined with pastoral pragmatism."[15] Anything that was not regarded by the historians as "original" was at risk of being eliminated and when these "archeological

---

11. Ratzinger, speech on the tenth anniversary of the Motu proprio *Ecclesia Dei*, October 24, 1998, Rome. http://www.latin-liturgy.org/RatzingerArticle.html.
12. Ratzinger, *Spirit of the Liturgy*, 169.
13. Ratzinger, *New Song for the Lord*, 119.
14. Ratzinger, Preface to *Organic Development of the Liturgy*, 3.
15. Ibid., 5.

remains" seemed insufficient, they were often supplemented with "pastoral insights." In these cases the "liturgical product" embodied the very worst aspects of archeologism and fabrication. Moreover, toward the end of his preface Ratzinger refers to the difficulty of defining "pastoral" and notes that decisions about what is pastorally appropriate are often made by professors with "rationalist presuppositions" who often "miss the point of what really supports the life of the faithful."[16] Here the reference to "rationalist presuppositions" suggests the need for a richer account of the relationship between anthropology and liturgical experience than was commonly available in the 1960s.

An academic study of the archeologism and mechanical rationalism at work in the formulation of the Missal of Paul VI (also referred to as the *Novus Ordo* of 1969), can be found in Catherine Pickstock's *After Writing: On the Liturgical Consummation of Philosophy*. Pickstock notes that the Conciliar generation of liturgists tended to assume that the text of the Roman Rite, which reached more or less its mature form in the Italian Mass books of the eleventh and twelfth centuries, represented a corruption of an original liturgy:

> They often alluded rather mysteriously to earlier times when things were different, when there apparently was no intrusive *Kyrie*, no Preface, no *Hanc Igitur*, not even a *Pater Noster*. And they would then invoke such supposedly pure liturgies as Hippolytus' *Apostolic Tradition* and Justin Martyr's *Apology*, texts which are now almost universally regarded as treatises on liturgy, rather than actual liturgical traditions.[17]

In an interview with Jeffrey Tucker from *Sacred Music*, Pickstock also argued that the post-Conciliar liturgists "misinterpreted the many oral features of the text (such as repetitions) as grandiose rhetorical additions, or even as messy nuisances" and "failed to see them as part of an overall apophatic theology thoroughly medieval in character."[18] They replaced the poetic repetitions with asyndetic or list-like syntax which "encourages the sense that the reality they describe comprises atemporal changeless units of simplified matter."[19] She adds that "such forms of language are useful to politicians and bureaucracies, and it is no accident that political speeches and other jargon make frequent use of these characteristically 'modern' parts of

---

16. Ibid.
17. Pickstock, *After Writing*, 170.
18. Pickstock, "More than Immanent," 64.
19. Ibid., 63.

speech. . . . But the hidden assumptions of these language-forms are wholly hostile to liturgical purpose."[20]

Pickstock concludes that the form of the Missal of Paul VI was modern in the sense of rationalistic and mechanical: "They ironed-out the liturgical stammer and constant re-beginning; they simplified the narrative and generic structure of the liturgy in conformity with recognisably secular structures and rendered simple, constant and self-present the identity of the worshipper."[21] Similarly in his *Worship as Revelation*, Laurence Paul Hemming draws a link between the mechanical character of our contemporary commodity-driven culture and contemporary attitudes toward worship:

> Our current age sees everything as an object of manufacture, as something which can be got hold of and improved, or altered, to produce *better* or *more effective* outcomes. This is our present fate, especially in the West, to understand all things in this way—and it is inevitable that we should transfer even to our sacred worship the same outlook. To learn to be entrained to something that precedes and outlasts us, and that, rather than being shaped by us is what shapes us in God, is a task.[22]

This tendency to treat the liturgy as a product to be manufactured was recognized by Benedict XVI in his address to the Pontifical Liturgical Institute on May 6, 2011. He remarked that it was unfortunate that after the Second Vatican Council, "the liturgy was taken more as an *object* to be reformed rather than a *subject* capable of renewing Christian life."[23]

In an attempt to remedy the effects of such archeological and mechanically rationalist practices, in 2001 the Congregation for Divine Worship issued the instruction *Liturgiam authenticam* on the right implementation of *Sacrosanctum Concilium*, the Constitution on the Sacred Liturgy of the Second Vatican Council. Of particular relevance to the problem of mechanical rationalism were paragraphs 20 and 27. According to paragraph 20,

> While it is permissible to arrange the wording, the syntax and the style in such a way as to prepare a flowing vernacular text suitable to the rhythm of popular prayer, the original text, insofar as possible, must be translated integrally and in the most exact manner, without omissions or additions in terms of their content, and without paraphrases or glosses.

---

20. Ibid.
21. Pickstock, *After Writing*, 176.
22. Hemming, *Worship as a Revelation*, 10.
23. Benedict XVI, Address to the Pontifical Liturgical Institute, May 6, 2011, 6.

Paragraph 27 further expressly prohibits the elimination of phrases merely because they are considered obsolete in daily usage and warns against the hasty tendency to sanitize biblical passages where seemingly inelegant words or expressions are used.

One might therefore conclude that an organic development will normally be one that builds on what is already present, not one that reworks the liturgical practices and idioms in accordance with the latest philosophical fashions. In particular, developments cannot take the form of archeological excavations.

3. Culture-Transcendent Not Culture-Dependent

Implicit within paragraph 27 of *Liturgiam authenticam* is the notion that the liturgy itself generates a culture, or to put the idea more concretely, liturgical language should penetrate the language of daily usage, rather than the language of daily usage penetrating the territory of liturgical language. This stance is contrary to the whole spirit of the late 1960s which was one of correlating the cultural expressions of the Catholic faith to the culture of modernity. A short opinion piece published in 1966 by Gareth Edwards in the Jesuit journal *America* was typical of the mentality. Edwards claimed that the Second Vatican Council's *Constitution on the Liturgy* implied that "the nearer the language of the Eucharist can be brought to modern vernacular, the greater the resulting benefit" and further "that our democratic society and informal habits make it necessary for us to think of God as a friend, not as a king." It would be a great pity, wrote Edwards, "if, at the moment when it bursts out of the strait jacket of Latin, it allowed itself to be enclosed in that of Anglican English. . . . If the Church wants to sweep the world like the Beatles, it must use language as contemporary as theirs."[24]

However not all Catholics were of such a disposition. The contrary argument had been presented some three years earlier by Evelyn Waugh in a letter to his friend Lady Acton:

> If they intend to have versions of the liturgy in the everyday speech of everyone, they will have to have some hundreds of thousands of versions. In civilized countries Norway has two languages, Spain three, Milanese can't understand Sicilian etc. When you get to Asia and Africa it is a Babel. As you know most African languages are quite incapable of conveying theological meanings and some haven't even a word for "virgin." I am told that they have two words for girls, one before and one after

---

24. Edwards, "Modern English in the Mass," 483.

puberty.... Surely it is one of the signs of the Holy Ghost that the half-baked and illiterate do somehow grasp the truths of the Church without understanding [every single] word?[25]

Waugh's point was eventually recognized in 2001 in paragraph 12 of *Liturgiam authenticam*. It acknowledged that there are dialects which do not support common academic and cultural formation and thus cannot be taken into full liturgical use, since they "lack the stability and breadth that would be required for their being liturgical languages on a broader scale."[26] While Ratzinger's statements are couched in somewhat more irenic language, they are much closer to the stance of Waugh than to Edwards. In *Principles of Catholic Theology* he wrote that the church "is an independent linguistic subject that is united by the common basic experience of faith and is thus possessed of a common understanding."[27] This is consistent with what linguistic philosophers call the expressivist theory of language, which emphasizes the primary importance of a common culture for the correct understanding of words and phrases.[28] In the context of a discussion of the 1970s pastoral project of transposing Church teachings into "short formulae" employing contemporary idioms—a project strongly endorsed and promoted by Karl Rahner—Ratzinger concluded that the "theory of short formulas disputes the right of the Church as such to have a language of her own and measures her formulations by the standard of secular comprehensibility (advertising slogans)"![29] Conversely, while he was critical of Rahner's short formulae project, Ratzinger endorsed the Ephphrata rite—the blessing on the eyes and ears at baptism so that the baptismal candidate will be ready to receive the Word of God.[30] This rite expresses the belief that "deafness

---

25. Reid, *Bitter Trial*, 33.

26. Analogous attempts were made with sacramental forms at this time. There were attempts to substitute the elements of bread and wine for more "vernacular" elements such as rice. These experiments were never authorized by the Congregation for Divine Worship.

27. Ratzinger, *Principles of Catholic Theology*, 125.

28. Cardinal Francis George of Chicago referred to the pastoral relevance of the difference between the expressivist and instrumentalist theories of language in his doctoral dissertation *Inculturation and Ecclesial Communion*, 107.

29. Ibid., 125.

30. The issue of the rise of new vocabularies was also addressed by the Russian Orthodox scholar Georges Florovsky (1893–1979) who, taking up a position at polar ends of the spectrum from Rahner, argued that it was no historical accident that the gospel was given to the world in the Greek language. He believed that "in the religious destiny of man there are no accidents" and that when divine truth is expressed in a human language, the words themselves are transformed and sanctified. Therefore the words of dogmatic definitions should not be criticized as historically imprisoned or otherwise

and dumbness can be overcome by the Holy Spirit who acts concretely in the community of the Church to make the process by which the individual becomes capable of speech a part of the process by which he is incorporated into the Church."[31]

While Ratzinger's comments in *Principles of Catholic Theology* were not directed specifically to the use of language in a liturgical context, they do provide evidence of a sensitivity to the issues commonly raised by linguistic philosophers about the difficulty of transposing concepts from one language into another where there is no common cultural heritage—in this context, no heritage of Christian influence. Just as one would not expect to find a word for kangaroo or marsupial in an Eskimo dialect, some dialects "lack the stability and breadth," to borrow the phrase from *Liturgiam authenticam*, to convey theological ideas about such quintessentially Christian "things" as the Trinity and the Incarnation. According to the expressivists, it is through an immersion within a particular culture that one comes to understand the meaning of certain concepts central to that culture. The cultural immersion comes first, and the understanding of language after that.

Ratzinger's reservations about the 1970s enthusiasm for projects of linguistic transposition and his opposition to the "correlation to modernity" pastoral strategies also run parallel with ideas set forth by Henri de Lubac in *The Christian Faith*, by Jean Borella in the *The Sense of the Supernatural*, and by Louis Dupré in *Symbols of the Sacred*. De Lubac wrote that the message of Christ as formulated by the church in the first centuries, "split wide open certain categories, both profane and religious, of pagan and in certain cases even Jewish antiquity," and that this will always be the case with any attempted transposition to new linguistic registers. He concluded that it is "an illusion that makes people demand, for instance, a Eucharistic prayer expressed solely in the language of 'current' or 'everyday life' using only 'familiar concepts.'"[32] The logic of both de Lubac and Ratzinger's position is that it is the liturgical language of Christian centuries that should be penetrating contemporary cultures, not the idioms and practices of contemporary cultures penetrating the church's liturgy. As Matthias Joseph Scheeben expressed the principle more broadly, "Christianity bears within itself an essential determination to bring to particular cultures its religious ideas and

---

limited but should be received as "eternal words, incapable of being replaced." See Florovsky, *On Church and Tradition*, 23. Nonetheless, consistent with Vladimir Lossky and Ratzinger, among others, Florovsky emphasized that revelation is not exhausted in "words" or in the "letter" of Scripture and further, he noted that tradition is best known and understood by participation in the life of the church, not by genealogical research.

31. Ibid., 125.
32. Lubac, *Christian Faith*, 289.

principles in order, through its divine energy, to change them, to penetrate, transform, ennoble and raise them from the natural sphere."[33]

In support of such a position, Jean Borella argues that a sense of the supernatural is a sense of a higher nature or a sense that the possibilities of existence do not limit themselves to what we ordinarily experience. He further argues that in order for this sense to be awakened in people, they need to have an experience of forms which by themselves refer to nothing of the mundane: "While elements of the physical world are always involved—otherwise no experience of it would be possible —they are set aside from the natural order to which they originally belonged and consecrated in order to render present realities of another order."[34] Similarly, Louis Dupré argues that "the purpose of a ritual act is not to repeat the ordinary action which it symbolizes, but to bestow meaning upon it in a higher perspective."[35] Thus, "a reduction of ritual gestures to common activity defeats the entire purpose of ritualisation, which is to transform life, not to imitate it."[36]

In *After Writing: On the Liturgical Consummation of Philosophy*, a work which was critical of the philosophical assumptions at the base of the liturgical changes of the 1960s, Pickstock argued that those who presided over these events were correct to acknowledge a link between the form of the Mass and the cultural matrix from which the form and gestures of the liturgy are derived. However she suggests that they erred in thinking that because there was a close nexus between the culture and liturgy of the medieval period, it automatically followed that "modern man" should have a Mass which incorporates elements from his contemporary culture.[37] For liturgical action to be authentic, Pickstock argues that it must share Christ's own time-transcending and time-transforming character. Ratzinger, de Lubac, Borella and Dupré all agree on this principle. Unlike the culture of Christendom however, the culture of modernity lacks time-transcendent properties. Indeed it is now an academic cliché to say that its most striking hallmark is its neurotic obsession with the present moment. It is also

---

33. Scheeben, "Das allgemeine Concilium und die Wissenschaft," 100ff., cited in O'Meara, *Church and Culture*, 58.

34. Borella, *Sense of the Supernatural*, 59.

35. Dupré, *Symbols of the Sacred*, 13.

36. Ibid.

37. The reference to "Modern Man" here and throughout this essay is a reference to a particular sociological species with certain mental attitudes and sensibilities which seemed to fascinate religious leaders and scholars in the 1960s. Many of the pastoral projects of that era were justified by references to the needs of modern man. The expression therefore is not a synonym for contemporary man, since the contemporary man could very well be a postmodern, rather than a modern.

disenchanted and hostile to tradition. Paul de Man, for example, has argued that the combined interplay of a deliberate forgetting with an action that is also a new origin, reaches its most powerful expression in the idea of modernity.[38] The combination of the need to forget with the need for a new origin runs counter to the whole nature of ritual which recalls the remembering community to a realm which is beyond the temporal. Pickstock concludes that modernity "has produced a parody of the liturgical, a sort of anti-liturgical liturgy that confirms the dominance of politics and art without liturgy."[39] In reaching this conclusion she drew on material in Paul Connerton's *How Societies Remember*:

> The temporality of the market and of the commodities that circulate through it generates an experience of time as quantitative and as flowing in a single direction, an experience in which each moment is different from the other by virtue of coming next, situated in a chronological succession of old and new, earlier and later. The temporality of the market thus denies the possibility that there might exist qualitatively different times, a profane time and a sacred time, neither of which is reducible to the other. The operation of this system brings about a massive withdrawal of creativity in the possibility that there might exist forms of life that are exemplary because prototypical. The logic of capital tends to deny the capacity any longer to imagine life as a structure of exemplary recurrence.[40]

At the time when correlationism was the most popular pastoral strategy, modernity was very much in vogue. The mountains of postmodern publications that have appeared since the late 1980s were yet to be written. Speaking of the Conciliar generation's enthusiasm for all things *moderne*, Kenneth L. Schmitz has reflected that the Catholic scholars of the 60s generation failed to perceive that the "foundations of modernity were beginning to crack under an increasingly incisive attack" and he also observed that they had no cultural concept of "Modernity," merely the historical category "modern philosophy."[41] In the pre-Conciliar theology academies responsible for the intellectual formation of the clergy there was no place in the curriculum for the theological analysis of contemporary cultural practices such as now commonly goes by the name of the theology of culture. While there were a few lay writers interested in this territory—for example,

---

38. De Man, "Literary History and Literary Modernity," 388.
39. Pickstock, "Liturgy and Modernity," 19.
40. Connerton, *How Societies Remember*, 64.
41. Schmitz, "Postmodernism and the Catholic Tradition," 235.

Charles Péguy, Paul Claudel, Christopher Dawson, G. K. Chesterton, and Georges Bernanos—this kind of scholarship had yet to find a respectable place within the clerical theological establishment. The focus was more on systematic, dogmatic and moral theology, not on how various cultural (including liturgical) practices can either thwart or foster the transmission of meaning. In the theology departments liturgy was predominately a subject about rubrics and modern philosophy was a component of the study of epistemology. The links between the two were rarely, if ever, explored. It did not occur to professors to think of the effects of modern philosophy on liturgy since they were accustomed to thinking of liturgy and epistemology in totally different mental compartments. Half a century later however, scholars are examining the impact of modern philosophical assumptions upon the liturgical judgments which were made in the late 1960s, now regarded as Modernity's twilight years. The dominant academic consensus, with which Ratzinger is in strong accord, is that for liturgy to be liturgy it needs to be radically different from the everyday. Any attempted development which flows in the opposite direction is likely to be illegitimate. In *Principles of Catholic Theology*, Ratzinger writes that the human intellect manifests itself precisely in its transcendence of time and he defines tradition as the transcendence of time in both directions, that is, the direction of the past as well as the future.[42]

4. A Cosmic rather than Mundane Orientation

The attempt to correlate liturgical practices to the culture of modernity not only had the side effect of orienting practices away from the eternal to the present, but more generally away from the cosmic to the mundane— not just the present, but the commonplace present. In various works, including *The Spirit of the Liturgy*, *The Feast of Faith*, and *A New Song for the Lord*, Ratzinger is critical of celebrations of the Missal of 1969 that are self-centric and oriented toward the mundane. He observes that there has developed a fundamental way of looking at things in which the experience of togetherness and the fostering of community rank higher than the gift of the sacrament. Aidan Nichols calls this phenomenon the "de-railing of the theocentric act of worship onto sidelines of social edification and group psychological therapy."[43]

---

42. Ratzinger, *Principles of Catholic Theology*, 87.
43. Nichols, *Christendom Awake*, 31.

Ratzinger acknowledges that the experience of the community is more immediately accessible and more easily explained than the sacrament. However he adds that the result of placing the experience of the community above sacramental reality is momentous. The congregation is now celebrating itself and the church is reduced to being a vehicle for social purposes:

> Whoever elevates the community to the level of an end in itself is precisely the one who dissolves its foundations. What seems to be so pious and reasonable at the beginning is actually a radical inversion of the important concerns and categories in which we eventually achieve the opposite of what was intended. Only when the sacrament retains its unconditional character and its absolute priority over all communal purposes and all spiritually edifying intentions does it build community and "edify" humans.[44]

To illustrate his criticisms, Ratzinger drew an analogy between the self-centricity often found in suburban parish liturgies and the Old Testament narrative of the golden calf. He argued that the cult conducted by the high priest Aaron was not intended to serve any of the false gods of the heathen. Aaron knew that the golden calf was not God. The apostasy was more subtle:

> There is no obvious turning away from God to the false gods. Outwardly, the people remain attached to the same God. They want to glorify God who led Israel out of Egypt and believe that they may properly represent his mysterious power in the image of a bull calf. Everything seems to be in order. Presumably even the ritual is in complete conformity to the rubrics. And yet it is a falling away from the worship of God to idolatry. . . . Worship is no longer going up to God, but drawing God down into one's own world. . . . Man is using God, and in reality, even if it is not outwardly discernible, he is placing himself above God. . . . Worship becomes a feast that the community gives itself, a festival of self-affirmation. Instead of being worship of God, it becomes a circle closed in on itself. The dance around the golden calf is an image of this self-seeking worship. It is a kind of banal self-gratification.[45]

Alexandra Diriart summarizes Ratzinger's criticism of the mundane orientation in the principle that liturgical practices must be oriented from

---

44. Ratzinger, *New Song for the Lord*, 75.
45. Ratzinger, *Spirit of the Liturgy*, 22–23.

the visible to the invisible, from the world to God, from the temporal to the new city, the definitive Jerusalem.[46]

5. Different Principles for Post-Christian and Pre-Christian Cultures

In addition to the pastoral strategies of the 1960s and 1970s fostering a correlation of the church's liturgical practices to the culture of modernity, the Second Vatican Council's *Decree on the Church's Missionary Activity* allowed for "adaptations to the customs and cultic traditions of peoples." Here the church was not dealing so much with a rapidly post-Christian culture as with cultures which remained to some extent pre-Christian. In the context of pre-Christian cultures Ratzinger cautions that it is "not until a strong Christian identity has grown up in the mission countries can one begin to move, with great caution and on the basis of this identity, toward christening the indigenous forms by adopting them into the liturgy and allowing Christian realities to merge with the forms of everyday life."[47]

For an historical precedent which addresses precisely this problem of christening a pagan culture, Ratzinger (following the lead of Christian Gnilka), returns to St. Basil the Great's commentary on Isa 9:10. According to St. Basil,

> The sycamore is a tree that bears very plentiful fruit. But it is tasteless, unless one carefully slits it and allows its sap to run out, whereby it becomes flavourful. That is why, we believe, the sycamore is a symbol of the pagan world: it offers a surplus, yet at the same time it is insipid. This comes from living according to pagan customs. When one manages to slit them by means of the *Logos*, it [the pagan world] is transformed, becomes tasty and useful.[48]

Ratzinger adds that "the necessary intervention [of the *Logos* himself] requires understanding, familiarity with the fruit in the ripening process, experience and patience" and he emphasized that St. Basil really was talking

---

46. Diriart, "L'orientation liturgique de la sacramentaire de J. Ratzinger," 334. (The author is indebted to Dr. Oana Gotia for her English translation of this article).

47. Ibid., 82.

48. Ratzinger, *On the Way to Jesus Christ*, 46. See also Gnilka, *Chrêsis*. In a footnote Ratzinger acknowledges that the attribution of this commentary on Isaiah to St. Basil has been disputed but he follows Gnilka.

about entire cultures and not about the spiritual direction of individuals.[49] Specifically this means that "evangelization is not simply adaptation to the culture" or "dressing up the Gospel with elements of the culture, along the lines of a superficial notion of inculturation that supposes that, with modified figures of speech and a few new elements in the liturgy, the job is done."[50] Explicitly rejected is the notion that each individual national group might provide its own culture in which to wrap the faith and its liturgical expressions:

> One might think that the culture is the affair of the individual historical country while faith for its part is in search of cultural expression. The individual cultures would allocate, as it were, a cultural body to the faith. Accordingly, faith would always have to live from borrowed cultures, which remain in the end somehow external and capable of being cast off. . . . Such thinking is at root Manichean. Culture is debased, becoming a mere exchangeable shell and faith is reduced to a disincarnated spirit ultimately void of reality.[51]

In his address to the bishops of Asia, Ratzinger concludes that "if culture is more than a mere form or aesthetic principle, if it is rather the ordering of values in an historical living form and if it cannot prescind from the question of God, then we cannot circumvent the fact that the church is her own cultural subject for the faithful."[52] Moreover, he emphasized that this cultural subject "does not coincide with any of the individual historical subjects even in times of apparently full Christianization, as one thought one had attained in Europe."[53] Rather, the church maintains *her own* overarching form.

Notwithstanding his explicit eschewal of the suggestion that the church as a cultural subject must be European, Ratzinger has nonetheless been criticized for being Eurocentric and elitist. In a typical statement of this kind, Minlib Dallh has asserted that the majority of Catholics do not listen to Mozart or Beethoven, that is, to classical music, nor do they have any interest in classical Greek or Roman culture. He further claims that the Credo of the B Minor Mass by Bach is not holier or more beautiful than a Zulu dance during Christian liturgy.[54]

49. Ratzinger, *On the Way to Jesus Christ*, 47.
50. Ibid., 48.
51. Ratzinger, "Christ, Faith and the Challenge of Cultures."
52. Ibid.
53. Ibid.
54. Dallh, Review of *Ratzinger's Faith*, 177.

There is no doubt that Ratzinger is unapologetic about his love of elements of Catholic high culture that evolved in Europe. He has stated that the greatness of Western music from Gregorian chant to polyphony, to the Baroque age, to Bruckner and beyond is, for him, "the most immediate and the most evident verification that history has to offer of the Christian image of mankind and of the Christian dogma of redemption."[55] In response to Dallh however one might argue that if Ratzinger defends the European cultural expressions of Christianity so eloquently it is in part because they are *objectively beautiful* and one does not need to be born in Paris, Rome or Vienna to appreciate this. For Ratzinger chant, polyphony and the Credo of the B Minor Mass by Bach may be European cultural treasures but he sees no reason why they ought not to be shared with the rest of the world. He implicitly rejects the tendency of the nineteenth-century Romantics to tie culture to race and nationality and otherwise exalt particularity over universality.[56] He views the genius of the Catholic form, so to speak, as its ability to unite the particular with the universal in what he calls "the humanism of the Incarnation."

His general principle is that cultures grow organically and the more they are informed by Christian ideas, and the more their musicians and poets are informed by grace, the more splendid they are likely to be. The crucial element is some strong connection to Christ. In *Co-Workers of the Truth* Ratzinger writes that it is "from the humanism of the Incarnation that the uniqueness of Christian culture has evolved. All its specific characteristics are fundamentally rooted in the belief in the Incarnation and disintegrate when this belief is lost."[57] Similarly, Roger Scruton argues that "the high culture of Europe acquired the universality of the Church which had engendered it" and the art of European culture "bears witness to it, either by honoring or by defiling, the thought of God's incarnation."[58] Europe is special because of her long exposure to Christianity and for this same reason her neo-pagan apostasy is all the more tragic. For the past couple of centuries the European intellectual elite has been behaving like a rebellious teenager searching for a sense of self-identity unrelated to its Christian heritage. There has been the love affair with scientific rationality, then with the *Volk* and nationalism, then the free love movement of the 1960s followed by the economic rationalism of the 1980s. Now the 1980s generation of Bour-

---

55. Ratzinger, "Liturgy and Church Music."

56. These arguments have been presented in an earlier response to Minlib Dallh in *Conversations in Religion and Theology* 7 (2009) 178–83.

57. Ratzinger, *Co-workers of the Truth*, 18–19.

58. Scruton, *Philosopher on Dover Beach*, 123.

geois Bohemians is becoming bored with the idea of the state as a public utilities manager and Ratzinger/ Benedict XVI is appealing to their children who are unsure of what to make of this smorgasbord of lifestyle options not to be ashamed of their Christian heritage and its cultural achievements.

Thus, while Ratzinger affirms the *Decree on the Church's Missionary Activity* and in particular its allowance for "adaptations to the customs and cultic traditions of peoples," he cautions against any fabrication of liturgies by reference to nationalist criteria. He believes that only when Christianity has taken deep root in a culture may be it possible for Christians within that culture to discern which practices are capable of adaptation or "baptism" and which are not. (In this context it is interesting to note that it took centuries of Christian life in European societies for their liturgical treasures to be refined. It took monks at least four to five centuries to develop Gregorian chant, indeed some scholarly authorities place the development later in the ninth century at the time of Gregory II rather than in the sixth with Gregory the Great, and it was not until the sixteenth century that Giovanni Pierluigi da Palestrina came along with his polyphonic settings of the Mass and then another couple of centuries before the arrival of Bach, Mozart, and Beethoven).

Since it is grace and receptivity to the promptings of the Holy Spirit and the personal encounter with Christ that are the most important ingredients in cultural developments, they cannot be planned or "project-managed." This is the error of the mechanical rationalist. As David S. Yeago expresses the principle: "because the encounter of nature and grace is a meeting of contingencies in freedom, the encounter of theological reflection with human culture cannot be governed by any general method or forced a priori into an invariant theoretical framework."[59]

6. Excellence Not Pastoral Pragmatism

While the charge of Eurocentrism may be unfair, Ratzinger *is elitist* in the sense of believing that we should offer only our best, our most excellent, to God. In *The Feast of Faith*, he wrote,

> The Church must not settle down with what is merely comfortable and serviceable at the parish level, she must arouse the voice of the cosmos and, by glorifying the Creator, elicit the glory of the Cosmos itself, making it also glorious, beautiful, habitable and beloved. . . . The Church must maintain high standards, she

---

59. Yeago, "Literature in the Drama of Nature and Grace," 102.

must be a place where beauty can be at home; she must lead the struggle for that "spiritualisation" without which the world becomes "the first circle of hell."[60]

In various places Ratzinger describes the alternative view, that the merely comfortable and serviceable is acceptable for liturgical celebrations, as "pastoral pragmatism."[61] In *The Feast of Faith* he took issue with a commentary on *Sacrosantum concilium* by Karl Rahner and Herbert Vorgrimler in which they drew a contrast between utility music and what they called "esoteric church music" and in which they promoted the use of utility music, that is, music that is popular or pedagogically useful.[62] Central to this criticism of utility music and "Sacro-pop" (a common type of utility music) is a notion of spiritualization which is incarnational in the sense of involving bodily senses. In *The Feast of Faith* Ratzinger expressed his opposition to "utility music" and what in other places he has called "Sacro-pop," "emotional primitivism" and "parish tea-party liturgy" in the following terms:

> The movement of spiritualization in creation is understood properly as bringing creation into the mode of being of the Holy Spirit and its consequent transformation, exemplified in the crucified and resurrected Christ. In this sense, the taking up of music into the liturgy must be its taking up into the Spirit, a transformation which implies both death and resurrection. That is why the Church has had to be critical of all ethnic music; it could not be allowed untransformed into the sanctuary. The cultic music of pagan religions has a different status in human existence from the music which glorifies God in creation. Through rhythm and melody themselves, pagan music often endeavors to elicit an ecstasy of the senses, but without elevating the senses into the spirit; on the contrary, it attempts to swallow up the spirit in the senses as a means of release. This imbalance toward the senses recurs in modern popular music: the "God" found here, the salvation of man identified here, is quite different form the God of the Christian faith.[63]

While Ratzinger concedes that it is difficult to lay down a priori musical criteria for this process of spiritualization in the sense that it is easier

---

60. Ratzinger, *Feast of Faith*, 124.

61. For example, Ratzinger, *New Song for the Lord*, 107–9, and the Preface to Alcuin Reid's *Organic Development of the Liturgy*.

62. Rahner and Vorgrimler, *Kleines Konzilskompendium*, 48, quoted in Ratzinger, *Feast of Faith*, 97.

63. Ratzinger, *Feast of Faith*, 118–19.

to say what ought to be excluded, than what may be included, he is quite certain that all rock music should be excluded. This is because of its neo-Dionysian properties. Here he is referring to the distinction between Apollonian and Dionysian music associated with the classical Greek cults of the same name, with the Dionysian cult being synonymous with sensual excesses.[64] Dionysian music "drags man into the intoxication of the senses, crushes rationality and subjects the spirit to the senses."[65] It is precisely for this reason that Ratzinger regards rock concerts as pseudo-liturgies since they seek to offer the teenage fan an experience of self-transcendence or spiritual elevation and a sense of solidarity with a mass of other people.

In reaching these conclusions Ratzinger has been influenced by a number of German authors writing at the intersection of musicology and theology such as Hermann-Josef Burbach and Winfried Kurzschenkel.[66] He also recommends the work *Music and Ministry: A Biblical Counterpoint* by Calvin M. Johansson. According to Johansson liturgists have a tendency to oscillate between the poles of pragmatism and aestheticism. Aestheticism runs the risk of a preoccupation with beauty for its own sake; while pragmatism creates a false dichotomy between the medium and the message, the form and the content, so that each can go its own way without regard for the other.[67]

While Ratzinger opposes the idea of beauty for beauty's sake as it is construed by the nihilist wing of the Romantic movement, he nonetheless affirms a long tradition of Catholic theology which views beauty as a transcendental property of being. This tradition is particularly strong in the works of St. Augustine and St. Bonaventure and in the publications of Hans Urs von Balthasar. In *Sacramentum Caritatis*, as Pope Benedict XVI, he wrote that everything associated with the Eucharist must be marked by beauty:

> Like the rest of Christian Revelation, the liturgy is inherently linked to beauty: it is *veritatis splendor*. The liturgy is a radiant expression of the paschal mystery, in which Christ draws us to himself and calls us to communion. As Saint Bonaventure would say, in Jesus we contemplate beauty and splendor at their source. This is no mere aestheticism, but the concrete way in which the truth of God's love in Christ encounters us, attracts

---

64. Ibid., 119, and *New Song for the Lord*, 124.

65. Ratzinger, *Spirit of the Liturgy*, 150.

66. See, for example, Kurzschenkel, *Die theologische Bestimmung der Musik*; Fellerer, *Geschichte der katholischen Kirchenmusik*, vol. 1; and Burbach, *Studien zur Musikanschauung des Thomas von Aquin*.

67. Johansson, *Music and Ministry*, 55.

us and delights us, enabling us to emerge from ourselves and drawing us towards our true vocation, which is love.[68]

Moreover, *Sacramentum Caritatis* is authority for the position that the Eucharist contains something of that beauty which Peter, James and John beheld at the Transfiguration (cf. Mark 9:2) with the consequence that beauty "is not mere decoration, but rather an essential element of the liturgical action, since it is an attribute of God himself and his revelation."[69]

In an earlier publication, the famous *Ratzinger Report* of 1985, Ratzinger had stated that a "theologian who does not love art, poetry, music and nature can be dangerous" because "blindness and deafness toward the beautiful are not incidental: they necessarily are reflected in his theology."[70] He has also suggested that "the only really effective apologia for Christianity comes down to two arguments, namely, the *saints* the Church has produced and the *art* which has grown in her womb."[71] He has reiterated this statement in several interviews such as the following:

> I am convinced that the true apologetics for the Christian message, the most persuasive proof of its truth, offsetting everything that may appear negative, are the saints, on the one hand, and the beauty that the faith has generated, on the other. For faith to grow today, we must lead ourselves and the persons we meet to encounter the saints and to come into contact with the beautiful.[72]

This position is consistent with the theological interests of his friend and mentor Hans Urs von Balthasar and with the early influence of the German philosopher Josef Pieper on his intellectual formation, along with his description of himself as "in a certain sense, a Platonist." In particular he has acknowledged that early in his academic career he was influenced by what he called "the magnificent interpretation of Platonic eros" in essays by Pieper.[73] In *The Spirit of the Liturgy* he presents this account of Platonic *eros* in the following terms:

> For Plato, the category of the beautiful had been definitive. The beautiful and the good, ultimately the beautiful and God, coincide. Through the appearance of the beautiful we are wounded

68. Benedict XVI, *Sacramentum Caritatis*, para. 35.
69. Ibid.
70. Ratzinger, *Ratzinger Report*, 130.
71. Ibid., 129.
72. Ratzinger, *On the Way to Jesus*, 38.
73. Pieper, "Begeisterung und göttlicher Wahnsinn."

in our innermost being, and that wound grips us and takes us beyond ourselves; it stirs longing into flight and moves us toward the truly Beautiful, to the Good in itself.[74]

Ratzinger then acknowledged that Plato's conception of the beautiful and the good has been profoundly reshaped by the interconnection of creation, Christology and eschatology, and the material order as such has been given a new dignity and a new value. By virtue of the Incarnation the human senses now have the capacity to perceive something of the glory of the Incarnation. In this context, following the fourteenth-century Byzantine theologian Nicholas Cabasilas, Ratzinger distinguishes between two different kinds of knowledge: one is knowing through instruction, which remains second-hand and does not put the knower in contact with reality itself. The second kind of knowledge, in contrast, is through personal experience, through contact with the things themselves. Ratzinger acknowledges the importance of the first form of knowledge which he associated with the discipline of theology, but he adds that we must not despise the impact produced by the heart's encounter with beauty, or to reject it as a true form of knowledge. To do so, he says, would be "to dry up both faith and theology."[75] In one illustration of this principle he offered the example from his own life of sitting through a Bach concert conducted in Munich after the sudden death of Karl Richter:

> I was sitting next to the Lutheran Bishop Hanselmann. After the last note of one of the great Thomas Kantor cantatas triumphantly faded away, we looked at each other spontaneously and just as spontaneously said: "Anyone who has heard this knows that faith is true."[76]

According to Ratzinger the incarnation is rightly understood only when it is seen within the broad context of creation, history, and the new world: "Only then does it become clear that the senses belong to faith, that the new seeing does not abolish them, but leads them to their original purpose."[77] The problem he sees with those who stand opposed to beauty, or are at least skeptical of its positive theological value, is that they misunderstand the Incarnation. He suggests that the disposition of the iconoclast "rests ultimately on a one-sided apophatic theology, which recognizes only the Wholly Other-ness of the God beyond all images and words, a theol-

---

74. Ratzinger, *Spirit of the Liturgy*, 126–27.
75. Ratzinger, *On the Way to Jesus Christ*, 36.
76. Ratzinger, "The Feeling of Things."
77. Ratzinger, *Spirit of the Liturgy*, 123.

ogy that in the final analysis regards revelation as the inadequate human reflection of what is eternally imperceptible."[78] Ratzinger concludes that "what seems like the highest humility toward God turns into pride, allowing God no word and permitting him no real entry into history . . . matter is absolutized and thought of as completely impervious to God, as mere matter, and thus deprived of its dignity."[79] This has profound consequences for sacramental theology and remains a fundamental fault-line between Catholic and certain forms of Protestant theology which regard beauty as a Platonic and thus pagan concept from whose corruption Christianity needs to be purified.

Thus, one might conclude that for Ratzinger any attempted liturgical development which moves in the direction of pastoral pragmatism, of dumbing down the words and music and rubrics as part of a project of affirming the ordinary, is a move in the wrong direction. In *A New Song for the Lord* he acknowledged that an implication of this is that seminaries need to be a place of broad cultural formation. While he conceded that "no one can do everything," he nonetheless implored ecclesial leaders "not to surrender to philistinism," since liturgy is nothing less than "an encounter with the beautiful itself, with eternal love."[80]

Although the pro-beauty and excellence orientation may seem unduly demanding in a world of egalitarian enthusiasms, or in what von Balthasar called "a most unaristocratic age," Aidan Nichols, one of the foremost Anglophone authorities on the theology of Ratzinger, defends the need for such high standards in the following terms:

> The Liturgy as saving action is "catabatic" coming down from God to human beings. What by contrast is anabatic—going up to God—about the liturgy is the glorification of God by men. But notice that, while the catabatic aspect of the Liturgy must come first, it is to such anabatic glorification that the sanctifying divine action is ultimately directed. The example of our great High Priest tells us so. Christ's entire life and passion was directed chiefly to the glorification of the Father: even the salvation of the human race was subordinated to this goal. So also in the Liturgy the soteriological intent of the rite, aiming as it does, at our sanctification, is itself subordinated to its doxological purpose. This may seem an unnecessary exaltation of God at the expense of man, shades indeed, of a Feuerbachian nightmare. But we see that things cannot be otherwise, once we realize that

78. Ibid., 124.
79. Ibid.
80. Ratzinger, *New Song for the Lord*, 175.

our sanctification is nothing other than our incorporation into the glorification of God through Jesus Christ Our Lord.[81]

7. Liturgical Theology Must Not Be Severed from Dogmatic Theology

One of Ratzinger's favorite maxims, which he inherited from Romano Guardini, is that *logos* takes precedence over *ethos*. This means that the divine communication that ordered the world is real and alive and infiltrates the created world. The International Theological Commission under his leadership expressed the position in the following paragraph:

> In the last times inaugurated at Pentecost, the risen Christ, Alpha and Omega, enters into the history of peoples: from that moment, the sense of history and thus of culture is unsealed and the Holy Spirit reveals it by actualizing and communicating it to all. The Church is the sacrament of this revelation and its communication. It recenters every culture into which Christ is received, placing it in the axis of the world which is coming, and restores the union broken by the Prince of this world. Culture is thus eschatologically situated; it tends towards it completion in Christ, but it cannot be saved except by associating itself with the repudiation of evil.[82]

As a consequence, in different fields of theology, Ratzinger is always quick to reject the suggestion that doctrine either does not matter or is secondary to matters of practice. This is especially so in the context of his eucharistic theology. In a speech delivered at the Eucharistic Congress in the Diocese of Benevento in 2001, Ratzinger began by saying that in the early Church the Eucharist was often called *agape* or simply *pax*.[83] The Christians at that time sought to express the inseparable connection between the *mysterium* of the hidden presence of the Lord and the *praxis* of serving the cause of peace. No distinctions were made between orthodoxy and orthopraxis, between what today we call right doctrine and right practice. Contrary to the common contemporary interpretation, Ratzinger argued that orthodoxy means (and was understood by the early Christians to mean), the right way of worshipping and glorifying God. This is a much broader concept than

---

81. Nichols, "St. Thomas and the Sacramental Liturgy," 590.
82. International Theological Commission, "Faith and Inculturation," para. 28.
83. Ratzinger, *On the Way to Jesus Christ*, 107.

doctrinal precision. In effect it means that there is not a sharp dichotomy between belief and practice. Some liturgical practices, like some beliefs, are not orthodox, and one might add, practices which are formulated without any reference to doctrine (that is, *ethos* unrelated to *logos*) are unlikely to be orthodox, unless by some lucky coincidence.

In the Benevento Address Ratzinger focused his remarks on a particular doctrinal issue significant for liturgical practices—that of the sacrificial nature of the Mass. He acknowledges that some Protestants, following St. Paul's reference to the Supper of the Lord, prefer to speak of the Supper rather than the Eucharist. This usage disappeared in the second century but was revived by Luther and others in the sixteenth. Ratzinger rhetorically asks whether this change in usage from supper to *agape* or *pax* was a departure from the New Testament as Luther thought, or whether it had some other significance. He concludes:

> No doubt, the Lord had instituted his sacrament within the context of a meal, specifically, as part of the Jewish Passover meal, but the Lord had not ordered his disciples to repeat the Passover meal, which constituted the framework but was not *his* sacrament, not his new gift. . . . It was part of the essential development of the Church that she slowly detached the Lord's own gift, that which was new and everlasting, from the old context and gave it a distinctive form. This happened, on the one hand, because it was combined with the liturgy of the word, which has its model in the synagogue, and, on the other hand, because of the Lord's words of institution which formed the climax of the great prayer of thanksgiving and blessing (*berakha*) that was derived from the synagogue traditions.[84]

The early Christians thus recognized that the essential element of the Last Supper was the Eucharistic Prayer, not the meal which was merely the context in which this gift was first given to the world. Nonetheless Ratzinger observes that even among Catholics there has been a turn in recent times to a more Protestant understanding of the Mass and in particular to an emphasis on the meal aspect, rather than the sacrificial aspect. This phenomenon was particularly acute in the 1970s though remnants of it remain today. Ratzinger summarized the mentality in the following paragraph:

> The Church has reworked the whole thing into the Mass, turned it into another sacral cultic ritual; surrounded it with richly decorated cathedrals and with an imposing and sublime Liturgy, and has thus altered beyond recognition the simple nature of

---

84. Ibid, 110.

what Jesus commanded us to do . . . The Lord's supper should once more become a simple, human, everyday meal. And from that there followed for instance, the conclusion that it is not really right to have a church building, but rather we should have a multipurpose area so that the Lord's Supper can truly be held in an everyday setting and not be elevated into a cultic ritual. In the same way the demand emerged to do away with liturgical forms and vestments and the call to get back to the way we look in ordinary everyday life.[85]

Ratzinger concludes,

> Those attempts to tell us that we should "get back" to a simple profane meal, to multipurpose areas and so on, are a step back behind the turning point of the cross and the resurrection, that is, behind the essentials that are the basis for Christianity in its novelty. This is not restoring the original state, but abandoning the mystery of Easter and thereby the very center of the mystery of Christ.[86]

An equally strong defence of the sacrificial nature of the Eucharist can be found in another of Ratzinger's addresses delivered in 2001, in this instance at Fontgombault Abbey in the French region of Berry. In this address Ratzinger made it clear that he believes that each and every celebration of the Eucharist throughout history retains the original sacrificial dimension:

> This true sacrifice, which transforms us all into sacrifice, that is to say unites us to God, makes of us beings conformed to God, is indeed fixed and founded on an historical event, but is not situated as a thing in the past behind us, on the contrary, it becomes contemporary and accessible to us in the community of the believing and praying Church, in its sacrament: that is what is meant by the words sacrifice of the Mass.[87]

The call for the de-ritualization of the Eucharist and a renewed Protestant emphasis on the meal aspect has also fostered the idea that the Eucharist is a memorial of the meals Jesus had with sinners. In other words, the Eucharist becomes a sinner's banquet, Christ's "public gesture by which he invites everyone without exception," implying that "the Eucharist cannot be conditional on anything, not dependent on baptism or indeed any kind of

---

85. Ratzinger, *God Is Near Us*, 57.
86. Ibid., 65.
87. Ratzinger, Address at Fontgombault Abbey, July 22–24, 2001.

religious affiliation."[88] This notion has been particularly popular with liberation theologians. It first came to Ratzinger's attention in 1968 at the time of the student riots at the Sorbonne University in Paris. Marxist students who were picketing the lecture halls of the Sorbonne were given Communion by priests who were chaplains at the University. In his memoirs Ratzinger reflected that this was for him *the* single most disturbing event of 1968. He was more shocked by that than by student radicals claiming that Christ was a sadomasochist and that Christianity is a religion promoted by a hierarchical club of misogynists.

Ratzinger's response to the "sinner's banquet" theory is short and scriptural. He dismisses it in one sentence with the observation that the Last Supper was not held with publicans and sinners.[89] It was held with Christ's friends (although one was about to betray him). He adds that the Eucharist is not the sacrament of reconciliation but presupposes it. It is the sacrament of those who have already been reconciled. Consistent with this principle, in *Sacramentum Caritatis*, he reiterates the words of John Paul II in his encyclical *Ecclesia de Eucharistia* that the memorial of Christ is the "the supreme sacramental manifestation of communion in the Church."[90] He also notes that in *Lumen Gentium*, the Dogmatic Constitution on the Church, the church is defined as an "instrument for the redemption of all, sent forth into the whole world as the light of the world and the salt of the earth; and also as the sacrament (that is, efficacious sign and embodied form) by which Christ's mission is extended to include the whole of man, body and soul, and through that totality the whole of nature created by God."[91] Thus, as the mystical body of Christ, the church is "the instrument for God's plan to gather 'all things' (Ephesians 1:10) in Christ, as well as the eschatological form of redeemed creation." Nicholas Healy and David L. Schindler have expressed this archetypically *Communio* theology in the following terms:

> In the gift of the Eucharist Christ endows the Church with the "real presence" of his body and blood together with an inner participation in his mission to the world. If the mission of the Son is to redeem creation by means of an exchange in which he offers himself eucharistically to the world and receives the world as gift from the Father, then the Church is called to enter into Christ's life and mission by eucharistically receiving creation in its entirety as a gift that mediates and expresses the triune

88. Ratzinger, *God Is Near Us*, 59.
89. Ibid.
90. Benedict XVI, *Sacramentum Caritatis*, para. 36.
91. Ibid.

life—thereby confirming and fulfilling God's original plan for the world.[92]

Often these ideas are expressed in the language of the nuptial mystery, particularly in the works of Cardinal Angelo Scola of Milan and Cardinal Marc Ouellet, formerly of Quebec City but now the Prefect of the Congregation for Bishops.[93] Paragraph 27 of *Sacramentum Caritatis* offers an extensive presentation of the links between eucharistic theology and the nuptial mystery in the following terms:

> The Eucharist, as the sacrament of charity, has a particular relationship with the love of man and woman united in marriage. A deeper understanding of this relationship is needed at the present time. Pope John Paul II frequently spoke of the nuptial character of the Eucharist and its special relationship with the sacrament of Matrimony: "The Eucharist is the sacrament of our redemption. It is the sacrament of the Bridegroom and of the Bride." Moreover, "the entire Christian life bears the mark of the spousal love of Christ and the Church. Already Baptism, the entry into the People of God, is a nuptial mystery; it is so to speak the nuptial bath which precedes the wedding feast, the Eucharist" . . . Indeed, in the theology of Saint Paul, conjugal love is a sacramental sign of Christ's love for his Church, a love culminating in the Cross, the expression of his "marriage" with humanity and at the same time the origin and heart of the Eucharist.

This theology is light years away from the popularist reduction of the Eucharist to a symbol of human solidarity. It is this, but it is so much more. In *Sacramentum Caritatis* Benedict XVI summarized the high drama of the Eucharist in the following terms:

> The substantial conversion of bread and wine into His body and blood introduces within creation the principle of a radical change, a sort of "nuclear fission," which penetrates to the heart of all being, a change meant to set off a process which transforms reality, a process leading ultimately to the transfiguration of the entire world, to the point where God will be all in all (cf. 1 Cor 15:28).[94]

---

92. Healy and Schindler, "For the Life of the World," 51.
93. For example, Scola, *Nuptial Mystery*; Ouellet, *Divine Likeness*.
94. Benedict XVI, *Sacramentum Caritatis*, para. 11.

Thus the final in our list of principles is the idea that liturgical developments cannot proceed along their own course without reference to dogmatic theology and more generally the church's teachings in matters of sacramental theology. If indeed the Mass is a sacrifice which introduces a radical change within creation—a sort of "nuclear fission"—then one might be inclined to think twice about the propriety of utility music, "Sacro-pop," country 'n' western and other folksy accoutrements. However if it is only a memorial of something that happened centuries ago which has the effect of fostering community solidarity than there is clearly much less at stake in making injudicious judgments about music and symbolic gestures.

In an essay on Ratzinger's liturgical orientations Alexandra Diriart concludes that for Ratzinger (and here one could add de Lubac, Borella, Pickstock, and Dupré) an underlying problem (over and above the tendency in seminaries to teach liturgy and sacramental or dogmatic theology as completely unrelated subjects) has been so-called Modern Man's loss of a sacramental imagination. She noted that for Ratzinger the anti-sacramental attitude rests on a double anthropological error which finds its origin in the separation between matter and spirit inherited from Descartes. On the one hand is the idealist error, which ignores the importance of matter, and on the other hand there is a materialism which reduces things to purely functioning objects.[95] Diriart suggests that this gives rise to three interrelated problems for the understanding of sacramentality and hence, one could add, for the organic development of liturgy:

> I. The world, caught up in functionalism, became opaque. It stops at the outer surface of objects considered uniquely as objects and does not know anymore how to make room for this "symbolic transparency of reality" which opens up to the eternal, and which rests on the sacramental principle. Can sacraments be merely signs of the formation of a community, rituals which assure its cohesion and its good functioning?
>
> II. In the face of the fragmentation of the world based on what is fleeting, how does [the contemporary person] believe that a simple sacramental sign "could have a decisive relevance for his or her existence?" How is it possible to reconcile the definitive aspect of the sacrament with the feature of the openness of human existence, without being always subordinated to novelty and to movement?
>
> III. Influenced by the spiritualism of idealism, itself a heritage of Cartesian dualism, the modern man finds it difficult to believe

---

95. Diriart, "L'orientation liturgique de la sacramentaire de J. Ratzinger," 336.

that the spiritual could give itself through the material. Why should we connect the encounter with God to the existence of a sacrament, a limited material means? What could these few drops of water have to do with the relationship of man with God, with the meaning of his life, with his spiritual journey?[96]

Diriart's three problems may serve as a summary of Ratzinger's pathology report on "modern man's" loss of a sacramental imagination. She also notes that his treatment for the condition (which requires the reconnection of liturgy with faith and dogma) presupposes his interpretation of revelation and the relationship between scripture and tradition. A "snapshot" statement which encapsulates these links is Ratzinger's reflection that "evangelization is never merely intellectual communication [this is the error of the rationalist]; it is a process of experience, the purification and transformation of our lives, and for this to happen, company along the way is needed."[97] Hence, one might say, the need for a living tradition and a community which embodies that tradition, and the need for a cultic priesthood within that community without which no sacrament can be given or received.

Conclusion

For Joseph Ratzinger, now Pope Emeritus Benedict XVI, the Eucharist is not a folk reenactment of an evening of hospitality hosted by Jesus for friends and associates. It is a holy sacrifice offered on the altar of the world. It involves the participation of the Holy Trinity, as well as choirs of angels, archangels, cherubim and seraphim, priests who have been ordained forever in the Order of Melchizedek and the members of the Royal Priesthood, the friends of Christ, who, despite what some people may have thought in the 1960s, is actually a king, as well as a prophet and a priest.

Ratzinger's hermeneutic of continuity reaches back not merely before the era of Paul VI and the liturgical experiments of his pontificate, but before the Christian era itself, to the liturgy of the Old Testament. As Ratzinger noted, even Christ observed the principle of organic development by inserting the gift of the Eucharist into the Old Testament rite which was already waiting to receive it at a place which was appropriate for it.

While the enthusiasm for archeological excavation and mechanical rationalism has abated, the enthusiasm for utility music and a mundane

---

96. Ibid., 338–39.
97. Ratzinger, *On the Way to Jesus Christ*, 50.

orientation remains a barrier to any resuscitation of modern man's sacramental imagination. As Henri de Lubac wrote in 1980:

> There is nothing more demanding than the taste for mediocrity. Beneath its ever moderate appearance there is nothing more intemperate; nothing surer in its instinct; nothing more pitiless in its refusals. It suffers no greatness, shows beauty no mercy.[98]

It may well be that one of the legacies of the papacy of Benedict XVI will be a greater pastoral tolerance of a plurality of legitimate and mutually enriching rites, alongside a greater intolerance of pastoral pragmatism.

Bibliography

Borella, Jean. *The Sense of the Supernatural.* Translated G. John Champoux. Edinburgh: T. & T. Clark, 1998.
Benedict XVI, Pope. Address to the Pontifical Liturgical Institute, May 6, 2011. *Adoremus Bulletin* 17 (2011) 6.
———. *Sacramentum Caritatis.* Vatican City: Libreria editrice vaticana, 2007.
Burbach, Hermann-Josef. *Studien zur Musikanschauung des Thomas von Aquin.* Regensburg: G. Bosse, 1966.
Connerton, Paul. *How Societies Remember.* Cambridge: Cambridge University Press, 1989.
Dallh, Minlib. Review of *Ratzinger's Faith: The Theology of Benedict XVI*, by Tracey Rowland. *Conversations in Religion and Theology* 7 (2009) 172–78.
De Man, Paul. "Literary History and Literary Modernity." *Daedalus* 99 (1970) 384–404.
Diriart, Alexandra. "L'orientation liturgique de la sacramentaire de J. Ratzinger." *Anthropotes* 26 (2010) 319–51.
Dupré, Louis. *Symbols of the Sacred.* Grand Rapids: Eerdmans, 2000.
Edwards, Gareth. "Modern English in the Mass." *America*, October 22, 1966, 483–85.
Fellerer, K. G., ed. *Geschichte der katholischen Kirchenmusik.* Vol. 1. Kassel: Bärenreiter, 1972.
Florovsky, Georges. *On Church and Tradition: An Eastern Orthodox View.* La Cañada, CA: Holy Trinity Orthodox Mission, 2004.
George, Francis. *Inculturation and Ecclesial Communion: Culture and Church in the Teaching of John Paul II.* Rome: Urbaniana University Press, 1990.
Gnilka, Christian. *Chrêsis: Die Methode der Kirchenväter im Umgang mit der antiken Kultur.* Vol. 2, *Kultur und Conversion.* Basel: Schwabe, 1993.
Healy, Nicholas, and David L. Schindler. "For the Life of the World: Hans Urs von Balthasar on the Church as Eucharist." In *The Cambridge Companion to Von Balthasar*, 51–63. Cambridge: Cambridge University Press, 2004.
Hemming, Laurence Paul. *Worship as a Revelation.* London: Continuum, 2008.
International Theological Commission. "Faith and Inculturation" (1988). In vol. 2 of *The International Theological Commission: Texts and Documents.* San Francisco: Ignatius, 2009.

---

98. Lubac, *Three Jesuits Speak*, 55.

Johansson, Calvin M. *Music and Ministry: A Biblical Counterpoint.* Peabody, MA: Hendrickson, 1998.

Kaplan, Grant. *Answering the Enlightenment: The Catholic Recovery of Historical Revelation.* New York: Herder and Herder, 2006.

Kurzschenkel, Winfried. *Die theologische Bestimmung der Musik.* Trier: Paulinus, 1971.

Lubac, Henri de. *The Christian Faith: An Essay on the Structure of the Apostle's Creed.* Translated by Richard Arnandez. San Francisco: Ignatius, 1986.

———. *Three Jesuits Speak.* Translated by K. D. Whitehead. San Francisco: Ignatius, 1987.

Nichols, Aidan. *Christendom Awake.* London: T. & T. Clark, 1999.

———. "St. Thomas and the Sacramental Liturgy." *The Thomist* 72 (2008) 571–93.

O'Meara, Thomas F. *Church and Culture: German Catholic Theology, 1860–1914.* Notre Dame: University of Notre Dame Press: 1991.

Ouellet, Marc. *Divine Likeness: Toward a Trinitarian Anthropology of the Family.* Translated by Philip Milligan and Linda M. Cicone. Grand Rapids: Eerdmans, 2006.

Pickstock, Catherine. *After Writing: On the Liturgical Consummation of Philosophy.* Oxford: Blackwell, 1998.

———. "Liturgy and Modernity." *Telos* 113 (1998) 19–41.

———. "More than Immanent." *Sacred Music* 134 (2007) 63–72.

Pieper, Josef. "Begeisterung und göttlicher Wahnsinn: Über den platonischen Dialog Phairdros." In *Darstellung und Interpretationem: Platon,* edited by B. Wald. Hamburg: Meiner, 2002.

Rahner, Karl. "Towards a Fundamental Theological Interpretation of Vatican II." *Theological Studies* 40 (1979) 716–28.

Rahner, Karl, and Herbert Vorgrimler. *Kleines Konzilskompendium.* 2nd ed. Freiburg: Herder, 1967.

Ratzinger, Joseph. Address at Fontgombault Abbey, 22–24 July, 2001. *Oriens* 7 (2002). http://www.piercedhearts.org/benedict_xvi/Cardinal%20Ratzinger/theology_liturgy.htm.

———. "Christ, Faith and the Challenge of Cultures." Address given to the presidents of the Asian bishops' conferences, March 2–5, 1993, Hong Kong. http://www.catholicculture.org/culture/library/view.cfm?recnum=5179.

———. *Co-workers of the Truth: Meditations for Every Day of the Year.* Translated by Irene Grassl. San Francisco: Ignatius: 1992.

———. *The Feast of Faith.* Translated by Graham Harrison. San Francisco: Ignatius, 1986.

———. "The Feeling of Things: The Contemplation of Beauty." Message to the Communion and Liberation Meeting at Rimini, Italy, August 24–30, 2002.

———. *God Is Near Us: The Eucharist, the Heart of Life.* Edited by Stephan Horn and Vinzenz Pfnür. Translated by Henry Taylor. San Francisco: Ignatius, 2003.

———. "Liturgy and Church Music." *L'Osservatore Romano* 16 (1986) 6–8.

———. *A New Song for the Lord.* Translated by Martha M. Matesich. New York: Herder and Herder, 1996.

———. *On the Way to Jesus Christ.* Translated by Michael J. Miller. San Francisco: Ignatius, 2005.

———. Preface to Alcuin Reid's *The Organic Development of the Liturgy.* Farnborough: St. Michael's Abbey Press, 2004. Republished in *Adoremus Bulletin* 10.8 (November 2004) 3, 5.

———. *Principles of Catholic Theology*. Translated by Mary Frances McCarthy. San Francisco: Ignatius, 1982.
———. *The Spirit of the Liturgy*. Translated by John Saward. San Francisco: Ignatius, 2000.
———. "Theology of the Liturgy." Address at Fontgombault Abbey, July 22–24, 2001. Translated by Margaret McHugh and Fr. John Parsons. *Oriens* 7.2 (2002) 10–11.
Ratzinger, Joseph, with Vittorio Messori. *The Ratzinger Report*. Translated by Salvator Attanasio and Graham Harrison. San Francisco: Ignatius, 1985.
Reid, Scot M. P., ed. *A Bitter Trial: Evelyn Waugh and John Carmel Cardinal Heenan on the Liturgical Changes*. Farnborough: Saint Austin, 2000.
Schmitz, Kenneth L. "Postmodernism and the Catholic Tradition." *American Catholic Philosophical Quarterly* 73 (1999) 223–53.
Scola, Angelo. *The Nuptial Mystery*. Translated by Michelle K. Boras. Grand Rapids: Eerdmans, 2005.
Scruton, Roger. *The Philosopher on Dover Beach*. Manchester: Carcanet, 1990.
Yeago, David S. "Literature in the Drama of Nature and Grace: Hans Urs von Balthasar's Paradigm for a Theology of Culture." In *Glory, Grace, and Culture: The Work of Hans Urs von Balthasar*, edited by Ed Block Jr., 88–106. Mahwah, NJ: Paulist, 2005.

9

The Wound of Tradition

Jonathan Tran

> We have to learn what finding is, what it means that we are looking for something we have lost. And we have to learn what acceptance is, what it means that we have to find ourselves where we are, at each present, and accept that finding in our experiment, enter it in the account. That is what requires confidence.
>
> —Stanley Cavell, *The Senses of Walden*

What has become a Christian preoccupation with tradition might be better expressed in terms of lament, and the consternations regarding the flagging status of tradition a kind of salve on the wound of the church's many catastrophes. Otherwise, tradition becomes overconfident in its overdrawn rhetoric. To be sure, a vapid individualism poses a significant challenge to the church's ecclesial life, but too often churchly tradition-language forgets itself, swallowing up individuals in the process. And then the separateness of individuals gets subsumed within an account of tradition deployed for the sake of "tradition" as a counter-assertion. If in our response to secular individualism we deploy a monolithic tradition and if in the deployment of that monolith we overwhelm the separateness of each person, then we will have constructed an account of community at the cost of its benefits. Meaning, too many accounts of tradition are simply the far side of a false dichotomy between individual and community, as if the response to individuality as an assertion must take the form of community as an assertion. This seems to me an evasion of a serious problem, which has gotten lost. In relation to *this* problem, which Stanley Cavell characterizes as "the threat of skepticism," the false dichotomy of individual and community is a pedestrian issue. In the attempt to resolve that issue by way of a Hegelian subsumption of the individual, we have put forth something ugly.

When Alasdair MacIntyre emplots this dichotomy through valances like "emotivism" and "the failure of the Enlightenment moral project" his followers quite naturally conclude with tradition as the only viable rejoinder to "the new dark ages."[1] MacIntyre's work has profoundly shaped Christian (and Muslim) theology, so much so that we can now speak of tradition as a proper name. For example, the authors of the essays comprising *The Blackwell Companion to Christian Ethics* turn out creative exercises of this appropriation in a series of essays that repeat with little divergence the same formula Stanley Hauerwas made famous, where good liturgy = good people and bad liturgy = bad people, based on the equation that something's wrong with modern individualism and the church's eucharistic politics offers a liturgical alternative. You take this formula and cast it as a fix within the dystopic epic MacIntyre tells and you seemingly have a solution for all the troubles that beset us.[2] But a methodological issue troubles the narrative and its Christian appropriation: are things bad in this way, or are they simply cast in this way in order to give the claim to community traction? My misgiving here isn't with the indictment of secular individualism for its corrosive effects on ecclesial life (and otherwise) are readily evident. My initial concern is the way "tradition" gets pitched in order to champion a certain version while countenancing anything made to count as tradition. This I will refer to as a problem of overconfidence. My larger concern, which the first falls into, is the way the story misses the point and evades what is most central. And here I mean what first provoked the Idealists (all the way to MacIntyre) even if they could not long abide it: alienation as the sense of estrangement that can at best be acknowledged and never overcome. Addressing this is what takes up the bulk of Stanley Cavell's career, and something I hope to convey here as a sense of lament.

---

1. MacIntyre, *After Virtue*, 263.

2. *The Blackwell Companion* deals with everything from racism to cloning to war. I say this as a great admirer of the *Companion*, but I also sometimes worry about what I'm teaching when I teach it to undergraduate students. For better ways of stating these concerns, see Kelly Johnson's and Peter Dula's respective essays in *Unsettling Arguments*, 300–314 and 3–24.

My considerations follow two texts, each offering contrasting expressions of tradition. I begin with a historical critique of tradition's overconfidence. Theological appropriations of tradition have tended toward this overconfidence as a reaction to the arrogance of modernity. Overcompensating, these accounts of tradition employ suggestive rhetoric regarding tradition for the sake of offering the best account available, a tendency common for most Hegelian-bourn notions of history.[3] Through Willie Jennings' *The Christian Imagination*, I show how this rhetoric both results in excessive political warrants and turns a blind eye to those excesses. Following, I present, through Stanley Cavell's *The Senses of Walden*, a different kind of tradition. Cavell hardly speaks of tradition, but much of what he says about mutual attunement and maintenance intimate it. Cavell's ruminations on Thoreau's *Walden* present tradition as a wound suffered between despair and hope and I will argue that the church's many tradition-constituted wounds admonish lament as tradition's appropriate theological expression.

The Promise of Tradition

If tradition does as claimed, how do we explain José de Acosta Porres? Willie Jennings knows most Christian purveyors of tradition have never heard of Acosta, even though Acosta stands as one of the great exemplars of theological tradition, and Jennings thinks this is telling. In *The Christian Imagination: Theology and the Origins of Race* he chooses Acosta as his subject explicitly because Acosta fits the MacIntyrian bill on tradition-constituted moral formation so well and yet turns out so badly. Because Acosta receives and inhabits his predecessor culture as seamlessly as he does, rather than departing from it, because his education was so exacting, rather than vague, because he negotiated change so deftly, rather than ignoring or abdicating, because through him Christian moral inquiry progresses forward, rather than stalls, Acosta proves the ultimate test case. By relating Acosta's disastrous story, Jennings means to offer a counter-history to the one usually paraded by popular theological approbations of tradition, not because Acosta failed to live up to the Christian heritage, but because he realized it so splendidly.[4]

---

3. "Best account available" references Charles Taylor's *Sources of the Self*; I understand Taylor's work largely operating in this rubric. Consider for instance the fascinating similiarties between *Sources* and Taylor's *Hegel*.

4. Jennings, *Christian Imagination*. Hereafter page references will be made parenthetically.

Jennings begins with a straightforward reading of MacIntyre—a reading already put forth to great effect in this volume by Craig Hovey and one which readers interested in *MacIntyre* rather than *uses* of MacIntyre (my present concern) hopefully at this point presume. Jennings picks up on MacIntyre's account of "traditioned inquiry," drawing specifically from *Whose Justice? Which Rationality?*[5] His reading focuses on three aspects of MacIntyre's account: the ability of traditions to interpret the world, the critical juncture of re-interpretation, and the kinds of figures necessary for interpretation. Quoting MacIntyre, Jennings speaks of tradition as ongoing formation, such that respective traditions do not only form individuals, but also take on the character of temporal agency themselves:

> We are now in a position to contrast three stages in the initial development of a tradition: a first in which the relevant beliefs, texts, and authorities have not yet been put in question; a second in which inadequacies of various types have been identified, but not yet remedied; and a third in which response to those inadequacies has resulted in a set of reformulations, reevaluations, and new formulations and evaluations, designed to remedy inadequacies and overcome limitations. (69)

Over time, a MacIntyrian tradition gathers as a working body of "beliefs, texts, and authorities" cohere in response to identified challenges that arrive as inadequacies to a traditioned community's conceptual resources, resulting "in a set of reformulations, reevaluations, and new formulations and evaluations, designed to remedy inadequacies and overcome limitations." As new challenges mount within and outside a community, so the process begins anew (indeed, it never truly ends), emanating in a tradition that *lives* as such (with the implication that traditions unable to achieve each stage eventually die). Tradition takes on dynamic form for MacIntyre, foreclosing tradition as stale, static, or stolid. By construing tradition accordingly, MacIntyre offers a response to modern grievances with "religious tradition" that war against intellectual growth, with his most shocking conclusion painting modernity as itself a tradition. (In this sense, Jeffrey Stout's *Democracy and Tradition* is less the self-purported argument against MacIntyre and more an articulation of democracy on MacIntyrian terms. In a moment, I will look to Stout to fill a lacuna in MacIntyre.[6])

5. MacIntyre, *Whose Justice? Which Rationality?* As I am more interested here in what Jennings has to say about MacIntyre, I will reference Jennings' text, which quotes primarily from *Whose Justice? Which Rationality?*

6. Stout, *Democracy and Tradition*. For a depiction of Stout along these lines, see my "Laughing *With* the World: Possibilities of Hope in John Howard Yoder and Jeffrey Stout."

Underlining what has famously come to be known as "an epistemological crisis" Jennings quotes MacIntyre:

> At any point it may happen to any tradition-constituted enquiry that by its own standards of progress it ceases to make progress. Its hitherto trusted methods of enquiry have become sterile. Conflicts over rival answers to key questions can no longer be settled rationally. Moreover, it may indeed happen that the use of the methods of enquiry and of the forms of argument, by means of which rational progress have been achieved so far, begins to have the effect of increasingly disclosing new inadequacies, hitherto unrecognized incoherences, and new problems for the solution of which there seem to be insufficient or no resources within the established fabric of belief. This kind of dissolution of historically founded certitudes is the mark of an epistemological crisis. (70)

Such junctures arrive as forks in the road for MacIntyre's "tradition-constituted" community. At each juncture traditions can either stall and sooner or later die, or develop around new epistemes fomented by each respective juncture. Either way, the crisis functions as the very torsion of a tradition's development in time and communities able to receive crisis accordingly display the requisite vitality MacIntyre's account of tradition envisions. In true dialectic fashion, that which threatens to kill a tradition becomes the condition of possibility for its discursive survival.

MacIntyrian traditions are embodied in individuals able to carry on inquiry as a form of life. Not only do these traditions cultivate virtues created in the image of each respective moral community, those most thoroughly formed are able to carry on the work of the tradition itself, to imbibe its history in such a way that guides its future. Similar to what Hegel called "world-historical figures" these ones heroically survive the vicissitudes of epochal time and become microcosms of the entire dialectic (setting up MacIntyre's Thomas Aquinas to steal the show). As Jennings states, "A tradition is embodied both in a community and in its individual members.... The embodiment is not a matter of perfection, but of faithfulness and a constancy to working out the questions that face a tradition from within the *telos* of that tradition itself" (69).[7] The tradition's wholeness expresses itself in individuals able to hold together the various parts of the tradition's life in order to carry forth its existence. The Aristotelian formation of character matches the MacIntyrian progression of tradition, the former the neces-

---

7. Vis-à-vis Cavell's Emersonian perfectionism, I will return later to qualifications of perfection.

sary constituent for the latter and the latter embodied in the former. Again MacIntyre,

> It is only individuals . . . educated into the making of certain kinds of discrimination that enable them to order the expression of the passions in the light of an ordering of goods—something which in the first instance they will have to learn from their teachers. . . . For someone who lacked altogether the kind of training and development which Aquinas—and Aristotle—takes to be required would develop the expression of their desires in a piecemeal, uncoordinated way so that they would come to have in adult life desires which appeared essentially heterogeneous, aimed at goods independent of one another and without any overall ordering. (69)

Stout's consideration of tradition is instructive here, for it shows how MacIntyre's account of tradition underestimates the role of embodied individuals in precisely the way Jennings intends. According to Stout, MacIntyre, and those who follow him, construes exemplification without leaving space "between example and doctrine." However, without that space, MacIntyre's notion of exemplars, a central aspect of his Aristotelianism, can only do shallow work (or goes on holiday altogether). Yet, those (from transcendentalists to the black intellectual tradition) most central to the modernity MacIntyre critiques happen to typify the character and narrative MacIntyre requires, maintaining the indispensable space between "example and doctrine." The individual stands within this space between example and doctrine, mediating the distance by Stout's democratic revision of piety and bridging separation through the civic nation's dialogical life. Stout writes, "emulation can easily become a form of slavish idolatry, in which we are dazzled and bound by the person we admire. We must therefore take care to emulate also the excellence of self-trust, which consists in freedom from such subservience."[8] Between example and doctrine, between history and future, between knowing and being, stands the individual, allowing Stout to bring to conclusion MacIntyre's dialectic between idea and history, "opening up a space in which the ideal of democratic individuality and expressive freedom could be self-consciously pursued" toward intersubjectivity, or what Stout calls democracy.[9] Again, Stout's claim here attempts to advance, not undercut, the MacIntyrian concept of tradition; he only wants to properly recognize the individual as an essential facet of that conception. It is on the back of individuals that traditions go forth.

8. Stout, *Democracy and Tradition*, 172.
9. Ibid., 282.

Which is why Jennings' portrayal of MacIntyrian tradition features so prominently the Jesuit José de Acosta. After all, for Jennings, Acosta exemplifies not only his own medieval scholastic tradition but tradition-constituted inquiry as such, and Jennings means to make use of Acosta to show tradition's great promise and the glaring omissions such promise requires.

Acosta's context is significant for Jennings' case. Acosta was trained before the Reformation would split the church and hence represents a pre-Reformation, premodern point of reference, important given how most traditionalists want to locate their favored account of tradition in this period. For them, most that goes wrong occurs after this period and so the Reformation and modernity are to be blamed for the enervation of the church's pre-Reformation and premodern tradition. Second, Acosta was trained as a Jesuit, in the best of the Thomistic tradition, in the very form and content of the *habitus* so often espoused by followers of MacIntyre. It is precisely that Acosta epitomizes the tradition that interests Jennings and the outcome of Acosta's life, his Thomistic ecclesial formation, that Jennings thinks missing from these prevailing depictions of tradition. "By everyone's account this young man was exactly what the new emerging order, *La Compañía de Jesús*, the Society of Jesus, hoped for—a supremely trained, profoundly devout agent of ecclesial renewal who would foster in those he taught a learned piety" (65). The "tradition shaped Acosta" foreshadowed "the kind of *Bildung* (formation) that Hegel would envision two centuries later; yet with Hegel it would be without the deep Aristotelian and Thomist, that is, theological, underpinnings." Trained in "classic rhetoric and the study of classic languages," Acosta represented the very best the Jesuit order had to offer, which itself embodied "a mystical theology that bound learning to aggressive piety and inward examination and service. . . . The curricular goal, for the Jesuits, existed within the wider idea of the interpenetration of devotion and knowledge that was the hallmark of the formation desired by the order. The crucial foundation documents of the order, Ignatius's *Spiritual Exercises*, the *Formula*, the *Constitutions*, and *Autobiography*, all drew the Jesuit reader to desire both intellectual excellence and inward purity of soul established in obedience of Christ-centered spirituality and higher learning also the need for this synthesis to be embodied in Christian life and performed through service." In Acosta and the heritage that produced him, one finds the unity of the virtues and the aggregate discursive resources— "Thomist theology, moral philosophy, and Sacred Scripture...along with the other sources of theology in the church fathers and the councils, for the edification of the faithful"—espoused by MacIntyre as the rudiments of moral formation. For MacIntyre, Thomas Aquinas, the world-historical figure able to inherit and further two traditions (Augustine and Aristotle), not only exemplifies the content of Christian intellectual tradition but himself offers the form of MacIntyre's notion of tradition. To that end, Acosta fulfills the MacIntyrian vision of a Thomistically imbued moral education.

> His deepest theological sensibility was that of a Thomist, with a clear, precise doctrinal understanding and articulation joined to a conceptually clear vision of how the world is and ought to be ordered. As a Thomist, Acosta understood what the joining of Augustinian and Aristotelian logics meant for the rational articulation of Christian faith. His teachers understood that in Acosta they had one of the very best, very brightest students. (68)

Reflecting the account of MacIntyrian moral formation conveyed already, Jennings writes, "The kind of education MacIntyre described here and in many other important texts is *precisely* the kind of education and the kind of moral formation Acosta received" (69, emphasis added). In other words, whatever MacIntyre requires, Acosta provides. Hence, Jennings is keenly interested in watching how Acosta lives out what MacIntyre promises, and so puts MacIntyre, through Acosta, to the test. Not only does Acosta show what happens to tradition, but tradition as lived out, as Stout rightly showed, through the individual who stands "between example and doctrine." For MacIntyre, and therefore for Jennings in this instance, everything rests on Acosta and Acosta's ability, or inability, to carry forward the Christian theological tradition in a manner befitting MacIntyre and all his theological admirers.

The Complicated Distance between MacIntyre's Tradition and Christian Tradition

For Jennings, there is no better instance of a MacIntyrian epistemological challenge than Acosta's and European Christianity's "colonialist moment," which we know historically gets enunciated in the language of "Old World" and "New World" as if to bring MacIntyre's dialectic to sharp relief. Jennings follows Acosta along his missionary and colonial ventures and focuses on this point of engagement:

> He stepped onto the shores of Lima a theologian of the first rank, ready to do ministry. Not simply a Catholic theologian in the New World, he was one of the most important, if not the most important, bearer of theological tradition of Christianity to set foot in the New World in his time and arguably for at least

one hundred years after his arrival. *Indeed Acosta was the embodiment of theological tradition.* He was a traditioned Christian intellectual of the highest order who precisely, powerfully, and unrelentingly performed that tradition in the New World. (68, emphasis added)

And how did it turn out? Jennings put it simply: "when Acosta looked out onto the New World, the Christian habitus in which he had been shaped became the expression of a colonialist logic" (104). The historical incidence and consequence of European Christian colonization are well known and need not be rehearsed here; Jennings does well to encapsulate its hitherto unimaginable occurence using the Andean term *pachachuti* which means "world turned upside down" or "the turning about of time" (72). What we get in Jennings' *The Christian Imagination* is a much more complicated and even laden rendering of tradition, one that balks at MacIntyre's too easy account while resisting tradition's modern despisers, an account of tradition that continues MacIntyre's reasons for hope while also demonstrating how those hopes require what I will be inveighing as lament.

As quoted in part already, Jennings characterizes MacIntyre's account of tradition-constituted inquiry: "A tradition is embodied both in a community and in its individual members. In Acosta one can see this embodiment. The embodiment is not a matter of perfection, but of faithfulness and a constancy to working out the questions that face a tradition from within the *telos* of that tradition itself" (69). The succession of a tradition's development is a bit more complex than MacIntyre's overconfidence allows and involves discovery of a tradition's *telos*.[10] Because a *telos* cannot be known in advance, overconfidence becomes dangerous, blinding one to where a line of inquiry will lead and the consequences that follow (93). For Acosta, following the line of a theologically determined vision of creation entailed interpreting each historical incident within the terms of that vision, without allowing that engagement to critically trouble—or "judge" as Jennings' incisively puts it—the vision itself. The presumption that one's end will legitimate one's cause (a teleological certitude) results in an overconfidence endemic within dialectical projects.

Earlier, we had seen how for MacIntyre a tradition-constituted community utilizes historic resources to negotiate new challenges, overtime developing as a repertoire of engagements and modes of engagements with internal and external challenges to that repertoire. In a passage rich in MacIntyrian allusions, Jennings writes, "Acosta exhibits the stretching of

---

10. For a different rendering of this overconfidence, see Coles, "MacIntyre and the Confidence Trickster of Rivalish Tradition," in *Beyond Gated Politics*, 79–108.

theological speech in an attempt to make intelligible its vision of the world to the faithful of the Old World. This is a matter of coverage, of coherence, and of holding the entire world within theological sight" (89). Along the way, Jennings makes a provocative suggestion regarding the circularity of Acosta's rationale, the synthetic transitions of MacIntyre's stages of tradition, and the incessant expansion of capital:

> Acosta's efforts imitated the economic circuit that was quickly enfolding the expanding known world in cycles of production and consumption. The economic circuit's coherence was beautiful and constantly self-correcting. The economic circuit showed how merchants were able to adapt to newness, overcoming geographic barriers, transforming the inhospitable into livable habitation, and exacting goods and services from all it touched. The economic circuit was taking the New World and channeling it through the Old World and taking the Old World and performing it through the New World. (89; see also 224)

In Jennings' eyes, MacIntyre's pluralplastic tradition resembles how capital evolves and condescends to the various demands of each new engagement.

As if anticipating Stout's figuration of the individual, Acosta held no slavish allegiances to "tradition" (as moderns fear authority), just the opposite. While he was always careful to do so with delicacy, decorum and the appropriate deference, Acosta followed Thomistic form (again, MacIntyre's Thomas) in bringing along and then refashioning Aristotle and Augustine for his purposes. Given how deeply conscious (supremely in control) Acosta remained of the tradition he captained, Jennings portrays this subtle and careful appropriation and advancement as "Acosta's laugh" (85). Acosta was overwhelmed neither by past nor future. Instead Acosta's "powerful suturing of Scripture and tradition to this new space" enabled him to gamely transpose anything that came along through everything he already knew (105). An inherited schematics of divine providence portends the Spanish mission to the nations and assuages for the missional Christians both the Spanish fear of the unknown and the agony of the natives. A thoroughgoing doctrine of creation explains indigenous barbarism. A moral piety eases the distress Acosta encounters. A clever (one might say, MacIntyrian) shift in the narration of early church persecution requisitions suffering as an occasion for colonialists' forbearance. Through each of these maneuvers, theology culminates in a tradition-constituted set of conclusions: "God is responsible for colonial desire" (92).

Jennings argues that Acosta's colonialism stems from a defective Christology and cataclysmic supersessionism—"the most decisive and central theological distortion that exists in the church"—that blinded Christian colonial thinking from recognizing the catastrophe unfolding before its eyes and at its hands (113, 32). Since in its mind the Spanish church replaced Israel as God's favored, it continuously interposed itself as divinely chosen and its actions providential. This resulted in a replacement rationale that rapidly read its way forward. If it could have interpreted itself by way of a "simple Gentile remembrance," then it might have aligned itself more closely with the natives and allied itself to their fate (98). The supersessionist mistake led to hermeneutic disasters of astronomical moral and political magnitude.

Yet Jennings can make this critique only by tracing a central thread guiding Christian theology. Insofar as he inscribes before hand the telic structure of Christianity in these terms ("simple Gentile remembrance") does Jennings make this argument. His assessment of supersessionsim allows Jennings to attest that within the Christian theological tradition there existed resources to do otherwise than Acosta's colonialism (Jennings repeatedly raises the specter of humanism but leaves it undeveloped), even offering a counterexample in Bartolomé de las Casas' *In Defense of the Indians* (100–102). This is surely the right and necessary move for any Christian trying to find a theological way out of colonialism. But this doesn't let MacIntyre and especially theological appropriations of MacIntyre off the hook. One could retort that Acosta doesn't actually approximate MacIntyre's traditioned mode of inquiry just to the extent that he failed to carry out an incarnational and non-supersessionist version of it. But this begs the question. Because MacIntyre's traditioning articulates a form of inquiry without demanding any particular content, a MacIntyrian order of things would have to allow any number of possibilities (including Acosta's colonialism). What MacIntyre requires is a repertoire that allows the future to be read in terms of the past and the past to be corrected by future encounter. In both these ways Acosta completes the MacIntyrian line. To be sure, what Jennings so effectively describes as the colonialist moment "encases" Christian theology in just these ways, occluding its ability as a tradition "to question itself and generate principle-referential arguments that expose its own internal incoherence." Still, there is nothing in a MacIntyrian conception of tradition that guarantees internal incoherence be exposed as incoherence (as "internal," how could such a guarantee work?). Jennings' appeal for a theology resistant to Acosta's (European) Christianity obtains as a retrospective judgment on Acosta's catastrophes (107). In time, as MacIntyre does well to recognize, there is no way to know otherwise (and concomitantly, do otherwise). Las Casas' *supersessionist* (as Jennings concedes) generosity did otherwise; Acosta's supersessionism did not. The insistence of MacIntyre's contentless formulation (the threat of its open-ended form) reminds us that Jennings' anti-supersessionist Christology could go either way. Which is why something like lament is required.

The nature of MacIntyre's mode of traditioning, its tendencies for overconfidence, cannot ensure the kinds of adjudications Jennings thinks so crucial, nor can it safeguard against the kinds of judgments Acosta made standard. Lament does not guard against catastrophe, but it may guard against overconfidence. Lament is a sensibility resident (and I would argue, native) to Christianity (including one that too regularly breeds catastrophes like colonialism) and Christian appropriations of tradition should issue as lament so as to (among other things) guard against and respond to overconfidence. Jennings targets theological expropriations of MacIntyre that do not properly mind "the colonialist moment" as expression of Christian tradition. In this way, his argument is less with MacIntyre and more with theologians who seamlessly situate Christianity as a lived MacIntyrian tradition, specifically naming Herbert McCabe, David Burrell, and Stanley Hauerwas (71, 307). (Jennings could have included Radical Orthodoxy's *ressourcement* trends. Consider for example Yves Conger's rather paradigmatic description: "The very concept [of tradition] implies the delivery of an object from . . . one living being to another. It is *incorporated* into a *subject*, a *living* subject. A living subject necessarily puts something of himself into what he receives."[11]) And yet, as critical as his anti-supersessionism is, the way Jennings uses it against MacIntyre (vis-à-vis Acosta) feels similarly devised, once again overconfident (counting on right theology—like right tradition—to save us from ourselves, or the distance between us).[12]

Wound and Acknowledgment

Jennings calls "immoral" that theologians have claimed tradition a category of moral deliberation without adequately taking stock of how Christian tradition unfolded in catastrophes like colonialism. This disconnect is more than accidental for Jennings, and makes possible its deployment. The fact that most purveyors of tradition have left out any mention of tradition's overconfidence and the impressive violence it often unleashed is telling for the schemes that usually follow. Though some may pay lip service to the violence of tradition's overconfidence (embodied here in Acosta's theological imagination), more often than not, they do so, as Jennings says of

---

11. Congar, *Meaning of Tradition*, 112. Kim, "*Apatheia* and Atonement" apprised me of this passage.

12. Natalie Carnes helped me see this.

MacIntyre, to little effect. Hence, just as a "simple Gentile remembrance" might force (or invite) the care necessary for the moral judgments Jennings recommends, so a "simple Traditioned remembrance" might go a long way in helping us rethink theological conferrals of tradition. This is not to obviate theological uses of tradition (which is impossible) nor to extricate contemporary theology from MacIntyre's considerable influence (which is wrongheaded) but mainly to keep an eye on tradition's tendencies for overconfidence.

A simple remembrance would bid a different posture toward tradition (indeed, a different tradition), one which I am concerned to articulate in the second half of this essay. It would be to think of tradition in terms of lament, and to pay heed to a community's wounds and the disabilities of its moral vision given those wounds. This I understand to be the opposite of overconfidence, yet without kowtowing to tradition's modern despisers, offering an account of moral authority without allowing that authority to outstrip the good practices of attentive (honest) deliberation.

As a way into this concern, consider for a moment the fictional character Elizabeth Costello's mode of argument in a speech about "the lives of animals." In her discussion, Costello distances herself from certain sorts of arguments regarding animals, and instead turns to moral status as a point of departure.[13] Speaking of and likening herself to a monkey forced to demonstrate intellection, Costello says, "Red Peter was not an investigator of primate behavior but a branded, marked, wounded animal presenting himself as speaking testimony to a gathering of scholars. I am not a philosopher of mind but an animal exhibiting yet not exhibiting, to a gathering of scholars, a wound, which I cover up under my clothes but touch on in every word I speak."[14] What if the use of tradition as a moral strategy were conceived as displaying a wound, and the remembrance of wounding? I suspect this would offer a corrective of the kind Jennings thinks necessary though conveniently absent in most theological uses of tradition. Costello's speech argues for the good of animal life without embarking on arguments that both distance us from animal life and blunt the particular contours of humanness. The wound she mentions alludes to the traumas we each bear (because the things we do and the things done to us) and the intellectual tactics we employ in order to cope. Such strategies cover the distance and cover over the silences those wounds create. They overcompensate. Instead, Costello acknowledges the wound, and out of that acknowledgment makes

---

13. On the significance of moral status in ethical deliberation, see Wells, *Improvisation*, 87–102.

14. Coetzee, "Lives of Animals," 124.

a certain kind of argument (just like acknowledgment, as I mean to show, makes for a certain kind of tradition and use of tradition).

Acknowledgment is the key term here. In *The Claim of Reason*, Stanley Cavell revisits Wittgenstein's work on pain, pain behavior, and responses to pain. Cavell relates how philosophy since Descartes has been obsessed with epistemologically legitimizing (or delegitimizing) claims of pain. In a famous section of the *Investigations*, Wittgenstein raised questions about aspects of human existence (our relationships with one another) that elided the standard warrants. When it came to pain, how does one know another is in pain? Wittgenstein seemed to resolve this difficulty by suggesting that pain, like his metaphorical "beetle in the box," operated within a language game that precluded the question altogether, such that the presence of the beetle like the presence of pain became secondary to the forms of life linguistically coordinated around agreements about beetles and pain.[15] In other words, whether a beetle or pain was "in there" did not matter. This reading seemed to subjugate privacy to something Wittgenstein was thereafter associated with, the publicness of language. For Cavell, such publicness conferred a troubling disregard for (if not privacy) separateness, subsuming individuality in the name of community. In a remarkable passage, Cavell countered this reading by reclaiming Wittgenstein, and through that reclamation, the human:

> In Wittgenstein's work, as in skepticism, the human disappointment with human knowledge seems to take over the whole subject. While at the same time this work seems to give the impression, and often seems to some to assert, that nothing at all is wrong with the human capacity for knowledge, that there is no cause for disappointment, that our lives, and the everyday assertions sketched by them, are in order as they are. So some of Wittgenstein's readers are made impatient, as though the fluctuating humility and arrogance of his prose were a matter of style, and style were a matter of pose, so that these poses merely repudiate, not to say undermine, one another. To me this fluctuation reads as a continuous effort at balance, or longing for it, as to leave a tightrope. It seems an expression of that struggle of despair and hope that I can understand as a motivation to philosophical writing. I am led again to recognize, and again with no little astonishment, how at odds I find myself with those who understand Wittgenstein to begin with, or assert thesis-wise, the publicness of language, never seriously doubting it, and in that

---

15. Wittgenstein picks up these questions throughout *Philosophical Investigations*, but specifically I refer to §§243–326 and especially §293.

way to favor common sense. I might say that publicness is his goal. It would be like having sanity as one's goal. Then what state would one take oneself to be in?[16]

To Cavell, interpolating Wittgenstein as arguing for the publicness of language results in an empty argument, with the façade of having resolved philosophical skepticism in the name of publicness. Publicness on this score overrotates in response to the threat of skepticism, which Cavell thinks can (should) no more be resolved than humanness.[17] Rather the threat of skepticism, as rehearsed in what Cavell refers to as the Cartesian Recital (i.e., "how do I know . . ." in relation to other minds [i.e., Wittgenstein's boxed beetle] and external worlds [i.e., Austin's goldfinches]), should not press the question of epistemological certainty at all. Rather, the "truth of skepticism" brings to the surface a deep awareness of our separateness as persons, a separateness that cannot be overcome by way of certainty, epistemological or otherwise, and rather arrives as a claim on us: "The truth here is that we *are* separate, but not necessarily *separated* (*by* something); that we are, each of us, bodies, i.e., embodied. Each is this one and not that one, each here and not there, each now and not then . . . we are endlessly separate" and yet (and so) "we are answerable for everything that comes between us; if not for causing it then for continuing it; if not for denying it then for affirming it; if not for it then to it."[18] Here, Cavell introduces acknowledgment. If someone cries out in pain, and in answering her and her pain, we question the legitimacy of her cry (e.g., "Is pain *in* there?" or "Is pain *really* there?" just like, "Is the beetle *in* there?" or "Is there *really* a beetle in that box?"), then we will find ourselves relating to her in terms of legitimacy, as if her pain were a matter of analysis. And yet a cry of pain does not invite questions of legitimacy, and if they do for us, then no matter how we answer (e.g., "Yes, I believe you are in pain" or "No, you are not in pain") we will have transformed the moment (from companionship to something other, something diminished); we will have misunderstood the situation, what is being asked of us, or forgotten that something *is* being asked of us. Cries of pain invite acknowledgment, not certification. The question is one of personhood, which cannot be thought of in terms of certainty (what would it mean to be certain here?). Persons are to be acknowledged, not made certain of. Cavell is not so much denying the publicness of language as wondering why it is at issue. That philosophy seems bogged down by such issues demonstrates

---

16. Cavell, *Claim of Reason*, 44. See also Cavell, *Must We Mean What We Say?*, 1–72, 236–66.

17. Michael Tai helped me explain this as "overrotating."

18. Cavell, *Claim of Reason*, 369.

for Cavell its loss of humanity, a loss Cavell means to address by ordinary language philosophy's efforts to return words from their metaphysical to everyday use (metaphysical being questions like "How do I know you are in pain?" and everyday like "What is expected of me when someone cries out in pain?") as Wittgenstein says in §116 of the *Investigations*.[19]

It seems to me that something like acknowledgment is missing in how theologians have utilized tradition, "tradition" evading what is at stake in its invocation in the first place, that is, the wounds that Christianity suffers. Overcompensating it invokes tradition all the more as if greater exertion will somehow make the invocation right. And yet claiming tradition is like claiming publicness as one's goal; what could be truer; what would it mean to deny tradition? Claiming tradition occurs as making sanity one's goal, as if somehow tradition will ground one in the world (as if grounding a world one feels slipping away). From what I can tell, those claiming tradition suffer a wound (probably Christendom and the loss of Christendom and the many vestiges of that mistake and loss), and suffer it unacknowledged; in turn, they invoke tradition in ways that continue wounding and unacknowledgment.

Walden Pond and the Place of Lament

One of the voice-overs narrating Terrence Malick's film *The Tree of Life* intones, "Father, make me good . . . brave."[20] In *The Tree of Life* Malick, who studied under Cavell at Harvard (and who translated Heidegger under Gilbert Ryle at Oxford) before launching a critically acclaimed (though uncommonly bare) career as a film writer/director, puts forward a work of profound Cavellian sensibilities.[21] The entreaty for God/our forebears to bequeath to us our goodness comes with it the possibility of refusal. And so we require courage for whatever comes, and for the threat/truth of that ambivalence. I am concerned in what remains with speaking of tradition in terms of this sensibility, what might be called the constancy to abide the past in granting or withholding what we long for.

As quoted already, Cavell writes, "To me this fluctuation reads as a continuous effort at balance, or longing for it, as to leave a tightrope. It seems

---

19. Morgan, "Subjectivities of Possession" reminded me how and where Cavell and Wittgenstein respectively take up these issues.

20. *The Tree of Life* (Fox Searchlight, 2011). Of Malick's films, two explicitly deal with imperialism and colonization: *The Thin Red Line* (Fox, 1998) and especially *The New World* (New Line, 2005). For discussion of the latter, see Neer, "Terrence Malick's New World."

21. See Heidegger, *Essense of Reasons*.

an expression of that struggle of despair and hope that I can understand as a motivation to philosophical writing." He speaks of struggling to balance despair and hope and I think this gets at what is going on with theology's invocation of tradition, what is evading and being evaded in how tradition is schemed. Using MacIntyre to make sense of contemporary Christian existence is theology's attempt to settle its life between hope and despair, and I see this struggle motivating theological writing about tradition. In order to explain what I mean here, I turn to one of Cavell's texts that indirectly deals with tradition. I hope to illumine not only what he is doing, but what theological writing is too often not doing in its work on tradition.

In *The Senses of Walden*, Cavell focuses on Thoreau and his dismay with the received past.[22] This is a relationship of hope and despair and Cavell stresses how hope and despair best name the tensions/promises of tradition. Cavell tells us "The writer is aligning himself with the major tradition of English poetry, whose most ambitious progeny, at least since Milton, had been haunted by the call of a modern epic, for a heroic book which was at once a renewed instruction of the nation in its ideals, and a standing proof of its resources of poetry" (6). Thoreau, in Cavell's reading, inhabits a legacy that both demands adherence and makes clear the unlikeliness of that adherence. Tradition here is austere and finds its fullest expression in what Cavell calls elsewhere "this new yet unapproachable America."[23] The question before Thoreau is whether the nation can live up to its own best hopes and if it doesn't, what its true patriots are to do (24). For Thoreau, the answer lies at Walden Pond, which is both an escape from and a step into the hopes and demands that constitute American life. Writing becomes the chief task of this vocation because America is best understood as literary in shape, an epic that bequeaths to Thoreau's generation Romanticism's revolutionary promise and the despair those promises visit upon the generations that followed, "the whole hope of it in their adolescence, and the scattered hopes in their maturity" (Ibid.). Because in "Thoreau's adolescence, the call for the creation of an American literature was still at its height: it was to be the final proof of the nation's maturity," the great endeavor now falls to Thoreau and his cohort to script America (its past and future, the meanings of its past and future). Thoreau's responsibility comes as a textual enterprise insofar as the whole experience of America can be summed up, even recapitulated, in Thoreau's Walden Pond notes (13, 22).

22. Cavell, *Senses of Walden*. References will be made parenthetically.

23. Cavell, *This New Yet Unapproachable America*. Cavell portrays themes of engagement and estrangement most readily in his stunning essay "A Cover Letter to Molière's *Misanthope*," which Cavell describes as "a love letter to America," in Cavell, *Themes Out of School*, 104.

In his turn, reading *Walden* engrafts Cavell into the very tradition he comments on, and yet ensconcing that tradition does not grant him bearings but the opposite—"vertiginous" Cavell calls it:

> How far off a final reading is, is something I hope I have already suggested. Every major term I have used or will use in describing *Walden* is a term that is itself in play within the book, part of its subject—e.g., migration, settling, distance, neighborhood, improvement, departure, news, obscurity, clearing, writing, reading, etc. And the next terms we will need in order to explain the first ones will in turn be found subjected to examination in Thoreau's experiment. The book's power of dialectic, of self-comment and self-placement, in the portion and in the whole of it, is as instilled as in Marx or Kierkegaard or Nietzsche, with an equally vertiginous spiraling of idea, irony, wrath, and revulsion. Once on it, there seems no end; as soon as you have one word to cling to, it fractions or expands into others. (12–13)

Notice for Cavell, self-comment follows emplacing oneself in the story one tells, lending to a "vertiginous spiraling of idea, irony, wrath, and revulsion," and again, "Once in it, there seems no end." Those claiming what Cavell names "an epic ambition" ought to pay heed to the type of drama at play; the movement speaks as much to the respective individual's movement within a tradition (the continual production of tradition as a heuristic of the self's relations) as the respective tradition's movement in history. Much like Foucault's self-care, Cavell admonishes cultivation of virtue, but virtue of a specific kind.[24] Quoting Thoreau, "I said to myself, I will not plant beans and corn with so much industry another summer, but such seeds, if the seed is not lost, as sincerity, truth, simplicity, faith, innocence, and the like, and see if they will not grow in this soil, even with less toil and manurance, and sustain me, for surely it has not been exhausted for these crops" (25); and yet the tending of virtue comes back empty, or returns to Thoreau unexpected (unwanted) fruit: "Alas, I said this to myself; but now another summer is gone, and another, and another, and I am obligated to say to you, Reader, that the seeds which I planted, if indeed they were seeds of those virtues, were wormeaten or had lost their vitality, and so did not come up" (24–25, quoting from *Walden*, VII, 15). The promise now results not in a requiting of expectation but the revelation of its endlessness: "Walden shows that the we are there; every tongue has confessed what it can; we have heard everything there is to hear. There were prophets, but there is no Zion; knowing that, Jesus fulfilled them, but the kingdom of heaven is not entered into; knowing

---

24. For Cavell's and Foucault's similarities, see my *Foucault and Theology*, 125–59.

that, the Founding Fathers brought both testaments to this soil, and there is no America; knowing that, Jonathan Edwards helped bring forth a Great Awakening, and we are not awake." Within this vein the challenge of patriotism arrives as the remittance of utterances like, "What is left to us is the accounting. Not a recounting, of tales or news; but a document, with each word a warning and a teaching; a deed, and each word an act" (30).

Cavell speaks of lament in terms of mourning (as moulting) and morning, which comes to greatest intensity in the middle of *Senses of Walden*.

> The writer comes from a sense of loss.... Everything he can list he is putting in his book; it is a record of losses. Not that he has failed to make some gains and have his finds; but they are gone now. He is not present to them now. Or, he is trying to put them behind him, to complete the crisis by writing his way out of it. It is a gain to grow, but humanly it is always a loss of something, a departure. Like any grownup, he has lost his childhood; like any American, he has lost a nation and with it the God of the fathers. He has lost Walden; call it Paradise; it is everything there is to lose. The object of faith hides itself from him. Not that he has given it up, and the hope for it; he is on the track. He knows where it is to be found, in the true acceptance of loss, the refusal of any substitute for true recovery. (51–52)

Cavell goes on to explicate loss variously in senses I am trying to use to touch on tradition as loss, wound, and lament: "The first step in attending to our education is to observe the strangeness of our lives, our estrangement from ourselves, the lack of necessity in what we profess to be necessary. The second step is to grasp the true necessity of human strangeness as such, the opportunity of outwardness" (55); "That life on earth is a test and a sojourn is hardly news. We merely sometimes forget what a land of pilgrims means, or forget to discover it. It is not the writer's invention to be peregrine is to be a stranger, any more than it is his fancy that perdition is the loss of something" (52); "The writer of Walden suffers this gladly, and uses the loon to exemplify the book's theme of insanity" (42).

Elsewhere Cavell encourages "we become ashamed in a particular way of ourselves, of our present stance, and that the Emersonian Nietzsche requires, a sign of consecration to the next self, that we hate ourselves."[25] Harkening back to themes that comprise the Cavellian universe, he imagines the self thrown off and into a world that continuously takes and returns. Here the relations travel between Thoreau and himself as writer at Walden, between Thoreau and his readers, between Thoreau and Cavell,

---

25. Cavell, *Conditions Handsome and Unhandsome*, 16.

and between Cavell and us; in other words between the text, the traditions within which it stands (or does not stand) and the varied selves granted: "Here the writer fully identifies his audience as lost to it. The fate of having a self—of being human—is one in which the self is always to be found; fated to be sought, or not; recognized, or not. My self is something, apparently, toward which I can stand in various relations, one in which I can stand to other selves, named by the same terms, e.g., love, hate, disgust, acceptance, knowledge, ignorance, faith, pride, shame" (53).[26] Tradition can be figured in these tones, and at its most honest, theology too, something of "a phenomenological description of finding the self, or faith of it, is one of trailing and recovery; elsewhere it is voyaging and discovery" and most critically in terms of intellectually strategic yet disingenuous deployments of tradition, Cavell offers a contrast: "[Thoreau's] descriptions emphasize that this is a continuous activity, not something we may think of as an intellectual preoccupation. It is placing ourselves in the world. That you do not know beforehand what you will find is the reason the quest is an experiment or an exploration" (53).[27] Thence, "The very awareness of time compromises presentness; the succession of words is itself a rebuke. There never is but one opportunity of a kind. That is the threat, but also the promise. To go on, untransformed, unchaste so far as you know, means that you have not been divided by the fact and concluded your mortal career. But to learn to await, in the way you write, and therewith in every action, is to learn not to despair of opportunity unforeseen. That was always the knack of faith" (61). Here one comes to grips with the critical insight offered in Cavell's use of "morning" within the landscape of Thoreau's imagery. The unraveling of the self is also its recovery, and so with the world and the traditions that place oneself into the world. For Cavell, hope endures—*Senses of Walden* says regularly that we are "perched" "on the verge of something"—and the trick is to not allow the self's unraveling and tradition's lubricity to unlink one from the expectation that tradition will give one the world.[28] Without

---

26. Cary Wolfe helpfully comments upon Cavell's notion of the loss of self and its connection to "the thing-in-itself" (95): "[for Cavell] we find ourselves in a position that is not just odd but in fact profoundly unsettling, for philosophy in a fundamental sense then fails precisely insofar as it succeeds. We gain knowledge, but only to lose the world." Wolfe, "Exposures," 4.

27. Consider Cavell's splendid autobiographical reflections on his dissertation topic prior to coming under the influence of Austin: "what dissatisfied me was . . . it, or my use of it, was mechanical, that I was repeatedly arriving at conclusions that I already knew. I could not take myself by surprise, and, or therefore, I could not say whether I was losing faith in the pertinence of the ideas or losing interest in what I had to tell about them." Cavell, *Little Did I Know*, 320.

28. On "lubricity" see Cavell, *Conditions Handsome and Unhandsome*, 38.

hope, our various realisms will not only infect the world, but fail to give it to us at all: "we despair ourselves and let our despair dictate what we call reality."[29] This, Cavell calls "a sort of a disease of the imagination, both of the private imagination we may call religion and of the public imagination we may call politics" (72, 73).

For Cavell, politics is properly an issue of maintenance, the responsibilities we hold because of mutual attunement in language. His correction of what Peter Dula pines as the "rush to community" is not meant to undermine political life but show it to be all-important, too important to leave as an epistemic issue.[30] Cavell says, "Knowing oneself is the capacity for placing-oneself-in-the-world."[31] All of his efforts in the service of skepticism is meant to shift one toward another kind of confidence, one he believes there along (residing in our speaking, it could be no nearer) yet disparaged in our quest for a cheap certainty. (Recall Wittgenstein: "The aspects of things that are most important for us are hidden because of their simplicity and familiarity.... we fail to be struck by what, once seen, is most striking and most powerful."[32]) In seeking goodness and foisting staid conceptions of tradition as its conveyance, we have lost the courage necessary to receive the goodness we desire, and so have traded genuine goodness for lesser versions.[33] Much of Cavell is present in theological reflection on tradition, but tends to get lost, and so, comes to no effect. (How does the tradition-constituted history Jennings relates effectuate how we understand tradition and whether our conception of tradition allows us to receive truthfully that history?)

In *The Claim of Reason*, Cavell showed how in speaking one claims community (what *we* ordinarily mean, not what is metaphysically given us), which is to say, in speaking, one speaks for others, and it is "we," not some others who are "fully authoritative in this struggle," who confer the meaning of our words.[34] Hence in claiming a tradition one claims belonging with a

---

29. With characteristic insight and aplomb, Stanley Hauerwas considers these matters in his Society of Christian Ethics 2012 Presidential Address, "Bearing Reality."

30. Dula, *Cavell, Companionship, and Christian Theology*, 42. Also see *Modern Theology* 27.3 (2011), which focused on Cavell's work, with Cavell in response.

31. Cavell, *Claim of Reason*, 108.

32. Wittgenstein, *Philosophical Investigations*, §129.

33. Nowhere does Cavell portray this more powerfully than in the remarkable final part of *Claim of Reason*, "Between Acknowledgement and Avoidance," where he moves among automatons who think themselves humans, humans who think themselves automatons, slave masters who think of their slaves as human, and Othello's drive to possess Desdemona.

34. Cavell, *Claim of Reason*, 17–36. If "disagreement persists, there is no appeal beyond us, or if beyond us two, then to beyond some eventual us" (19). Cavell borrows from one of his favorite passages in the *Investigations*, §217, where Wittgenstein, his

tradition as a discursive community that houses space for belonging and companionship. To speak for a tradition is to belong to it, to others who speak thus. This is why for Cavell acknowledgment is so important, just as why for him the threat of skepticism bespeaks duty (and the disavowal of it, shirking duty). What Cavell says about sharing language can also be said of those sharing a tradition, the sharing of which is achieved by nothing more than the claiming of it: "Wittgenstein's appeal to criteria is meant, one might say, exactly to call to consciousness the astonishing fact of the astonishing extent to which we do agree in judgment; eliciting criteria goes to show therefore that our judgments *are* public, that is shared. What makes this astonishing, what partly motivates this philosophizing on the subject, is that the extent of agreement is so intimate and pervasive."[35] One of *The Claim of Reason*'s chief points, drawing on the *Investigations* §373, is that judgments are based on criteria about identity not essence, and, hence, our common judgments are shared agreements in what *we* say a thing is versus what that thing is. *Senses of Walden* reiterates this point, "Writing—heroic writing, the writing of a nation's scripture—must assume the conditions of language as such; re-experience, as it were, the fact that there is such a thing as language at all and assume responsibility for it" (33). The claim of tradition here takes on something like choosing moulting and habitation, dwelling within a community-constituted tradition—"Our faithfulness to our language repeats our faithfulness to all our shared commitments" (66)—and the purposeful choices necessary to prune over-confidence, especially an overconfidence that will naturally avoid moulting: "What I have to work out is still my salvation, and still in fear and trembling (cf. Philippians 2:12). The crisis is still mine to spend" (44). Here, Cavell speaks of "the idea of morning and of moulting" and these notions name for him a posture of habitation, of the patriot who truly loves and seeks/speaks the nation's best while doing so knowing full well that such seeking and speaking can only be done engaged with despair and hope.

> [Thoreau's] problem—at once philosophical, religious, literary, and I will argue, political—is to get us to ask the questions, and then to show us that we do not know what we are asking, and then to show us that we have the answer. The fiction is that some unknown people have asked him these prompting questions: Where does the book begin, the bulk of whose pages he wrote in the woods? That is, at what point do we realize the "I" of the

---

reasons having run out, resolves, "This is simply what I do." See also *Senses of Walden*, 85–86.

35. Ibid., 31. Emphasis original. See also *Senses of Walden*'s discussion of the "truth of skepticism" in the extended note on 106–7.

first paragraph, the second word of the book, has merged with the "I" the book is about? . . . To get us to ask the questions. That means to fox us into opening our mouths. (47)

For Cavell this brings us closest to our traditions, that is, ourselves, but this intimacy requires courage, a prayer for bravery, because "To maintain nextness to ourselves, we require new, or newly conceived, capacities for constancy and change" (109). This "neighboring of the self" Cavell refers to as "the self's companionability" (108). In *Conditions Handsome and Unhandsome*, Cavell relates this dynamic between self, other, and language in terms of perfectionism, the endless process of "absolute responsibility of the self to make itself intelligible, without falsifying itself."[36] Working out his most sustained engagement with political theory, Cavell favors an account of democratic life likened to marriage and re-marriage, rather than the chastened account of constitutional democracy received through Rawlsian political liberalism. For Cavell, political engagement is less about negotiating one's rights and obligations in relation to competing rights and obligations (i.e., justice) but rather the allowances for the self's growth within a context where one is allowed and called upon to speak for another, and how the self and society (what he calls the good soul and the good city) require and bequeath the other's possibility.[37] The problem with Rawls' admirable account of politics is that it fails to take stock of how society endangers the soul, which follows Cavell's regular themes of estrangement and personhood (what is at issue for Thoreau in *Walden*). So Cavell attempts to work out a politics that rightly situates the goods of self and society, similar to how tradition might be envisaged to the benefit of those inhabiting them. As such, Cavell's portrayal of politics is a bit more perilous than Rawls', but that's largely the point. In speaking of perfectionism, Cavell imagines nothing less than what MacIntyre conveys as a basic rudiment of tradition, "an outlook or dimension of thought embodied and developed in a set of texts spanning the range of Western culture . . ."[38] Participating in a tradition, like participating in a society, then, takes place like marriage as the ongoing call for acknowledgment.[39] The metaphor of marriage Cavell utilizes to represent democratic life helps theology's uses of tradition better attend to its own wounds, to acknowledge them, since after all, marriage is not primarily about justice (not that it is not about justice) but the ability to register one another's pain, including the pains suffered in marriage. In other

---

36. Cavell, *Conditions Handsome and Unhandsome*, xxvii.
37. See ibid., 24–32.
38. Ibid., 4.
39. Ibid., 105–6.

words, as Cavell says, marriage requires and allows forgiveness. Forgiveness may be the final difference between MacIntyre's tradition and its Christian expression.

Christian Tradition

My goal in this essay hasn't been to argue that good traditions and their liturgies do not form good people, but simply to show how good traditions produce people like Acosta and possess limited ability to see beyond the linguistic possibilities of those productions; by extension I have tried to shed light on why the Christian preoccupation with tradition remains unable (unwilling) to see this. That goodness doesn't always replicate itself (or that badness sometimes yields goodness) is not a strike against the moral significance of tradition (as if the point is to make traditions more efficient, as if the goal is the replication of persons) but only a feature of humanness, which theology may ride roughshod over in its rush to tradition. Jordan Rowan Fannin makes just this point by offering a Cavellian account of tradition through John Howard Yoder's "looping back." Yoder proves especially apropos here because as a pacifist, he requires something like tradition in order to affirm continuity to the church's peace witness while resisting certain methodological injunctions about tradition. Fannin employs Cavell's terminology to explicate how for Yoder tradition cannot be conceived monolithically and shows what negotiating faithfulness amongst multiple claims to authority ("tradition") requires, perceptively concluding that the claim of tradition largely functions as what Cavell calls (as I have already reviewed) criteria:

> The question of the authority of tradition, as I take it, can be cast as a question of how and why to name faithfulness and unfaithfulness. This question will encounter the fact of the presence of multiple Christian traditions (small *t*, plural) and may still affirm the search for Christian unity without being led astray by either. . . . The presence of contradictory claims to faithfulness undermines not only the truth of the gospel's claims but also *real* Christian unity. Therefore, those claims ought to be submitted to scrutiny and found to be either faithful reformulations of the tradition or unfaithful deviations from it. These are matters of both truth and of reconciliation. I take this to be a problem of criteria. What "counts as" faithful reformulations and extensions of our common tradition, and on what grounds do we classify something as a "falling away" from that tradition or as

an unfaithful translation of it (say, syncretism)? In this view, tradition is not a thing but a process—one which Yoder calls "traditioning." As a verb (at least a gerund) the nature of this tradition[ing] is growth; yet, for Yoder, this is not the growth of a tree—whose origins can be pointed to and clearly marked. It is a vine whose growth is marked by constant interruption and regular pruning, which demands a constant looping back. This image of promoting "new growth" that is closer to its source, and thus its vitality, is reminiscent of Adolf von Harnack's disdain for accretions and desire for the original spring, but also differs in important ways. Yoder's is not a search for an essence of Christianity to which we can appeal for our judgments of "faithful" and "unfaithful." While von Harnack's appeal is to a kernel, Yoder's is to a "confession"—an agreement. It is not an appeal to an "it" but to a "we." It is not an appeal to a foundational truth, but to a process (perhaps to the community of witnesses?) that—importantly—is also always reaching back. We do not have direct access to a set of propositions, but rather, the "heart of our tradition" is not the Christ event itself, but a set of memories of and testimony to that event.[40]

Fannin's comparison to von Harnack is reminiscent of how ordinary language philosophy seeks to return language from metaphysical to everyday use. In her reading, Yoder sets as the criteria for truthfulness that which is granted by those who speak, the we granted in speech. Nothing lies outside (or inside vis-à-vis von Harnack's kernel) us that can certify our judgments. This is the force of Cavell's claim that criteria bespeak agreements of identity (what *we* say a thing is) not essence (what that thing *is*). The temporal image of "looping back" countenances the only other available to us, that is, what we have said in and about the past. Jennings is able to charge Acosta's colonialism with supersessionism by first retrieving a prior ecclesial judgment about God's covenant promise to Israel (from which the charge of supersessionism gains intelligibility). It is important to acknowledge that Acosta too had historical options; that he did not figure to use them as Jennings would have liked means he did not understand them useful in the ways Jennings thinks critical. We are forced to admit—this, the "threat" of the truth of skepticism—that it was not incumbent upon Acosta to read church history other than how he did; that he read it as he did, and that such a reading carried it the moral force of the claim to tradition, was also what allowed him to both choose colonialism and be confident in that choice.

---

40. Fannin, "A Yoderian/Wittgensteinian Possibility for Conversation," 6–7. Fannin references Yoder, *Priestly Kingdom*, 66–70.

This is what I have called tradition's tendency for overconfidence. Nor does it follow that a non-supersessionist position would have necessarily precluded Acosta's colonialism. One can imagine any number of warrants in the tradition that would have resulted in the same historical occurrence (I suspect with Foucault that linguistic accretions gather as matters of accident with greater regularity than genealogies like Jennings' appreciate), just as one can witness, through Las Casas, a supersessionist repudiation of the same colonialist logic. All that is required is a looping back. And all that is available is a looping back, and the communities of discourse that require and make available looping back. If we can accommodate ourselves to these conditions, we might be able to avoid forgetting that tradition works like this. Fannin encourages Yoder's confession, and I encourage Cavellian lament. Accommodating ourselves to these conditions means accepting humanness. Cavell characterizes the opposite of this acceptance the denial of the human, which he believes may be the most human (given human attunement in language, its diaphanous certainty and solidity) of human tendencies. The virtues Cavell finds in Thoreau's tending are ones of manurance, necessary in fields where hope and despair struggle together, which is how I have tried to portray Christian tradition.

Bibliography

Cavell, Stanley. *The Claim of Reason: Wittgenstein, Skepticism, Morality, and Tragedy.* Oxford: Oxford University Press, 1979.

———. *Conditions Handsome and Unhandsome: The Constitution of Emersonian Perfectionism.* Chicago: University of Chicago Press, 1990.

———. *Little Did I Know: Excerpts from Memory.* Stanford: Stanford University Press, 2010.

———. *Must We Mean What We Say? A Book of Essays.* Cambridge: Cambridge University Press, 1976.

———. *The Senses of Walden.* Chicago: University of Chicago Press, 1981.

———. *Themes Out of School: Effects and Causes.* San Francisco: North Point, 1984.

———. *This New Yet Unapproachable America: Lectures after Emerson and Wittgenstein.* Albuquerque: Living Batch, 1989.

Coetzee, J. M. "The Lives of Animals." The Tanner Lectures of Human Values. Delivered at Princeton University, October 15–16, 1997. http://tannerlectures.utah.edu/_documents/a-to-z/c/Coetzee99.pdf.

Coles, Romand. *Beyond Gated Politics: Reflections for the Possibility of Democracy.* Minneapolis: University of Minnesota Press, 2005.

Congar, Yves. *The Meaning of Tradition.* Translated by A. N. Woodrow. San Francisco: Ignatius, 2004.

Dula, Peter. *Cavell, Companionship, and Christian Theology.* New York: Oxford University Press, 2010.

———. "Wittgenstein Among the Theologians." In *Unsettling Arguments: A Festschrift on the Occasion of Stanley Hauerwas's 70th Birthday*, edited by Charles R. Pinches, Kelly S. Johnson, and Charles M. Collier, 3–24. Eugene: Cascade, 2010.

Fannin, Jordan Rowan. "A Yoderian/Wittgensteinian Possibility for Conversation: Embracing Particularity, Relinquishing Universality, and Naming Error in Inter- and Intra-Community Dialogue." Unpublished essay, Spring 2011.

Hauerwas, Stanley. "Bearing Reality." Presidential Address given at the annual meeting of the Society of Christian Ethics, Washington, DC, January 4–8, 2012.

Hauerwas, Stanley, and Samuel Wells, eds. *The Blackwell Companion to Christian Ethics*. Blackwell Companions to Religion. Oxford: Blackwell, 2004.

Heidegger, Martin. *The Essense of Reasons*. Translated by Terrence Malick. Evanston: Northwestern University Press, 1969.

Jennings, Willie James. *The Christian Imagination: Theology and the Origins of Race*. New Haven: Yale University Press, 2010.

Johnson, Kelly. "Worshipping in Spirit and Truth." In *Unsettling Arguments: A Festschrift on the Occasion of Stanley Hauerwas's 70th Birthday*, edited by Charles R. Pinches, Kelly S. Johnson, and Charles M. Collier, 300–314. Eugene: Cascade, 2010.

Kim, Paul. "*Apatheia* and Atonement: Grammar and Salvation for Contemporary Christian Theology." PhD diss., Baylor University, 2011.

MacIntyre, Alasdair. *After Virtue: A Study in Moral Theory*. Notre Dame: University of Notre Dame Press, 1984.

———. *Whose Justice? Which Rationality?* Notre Dame: University of Notre Dame Press, 1989.

Morgan, Brandon Lee. "Subjectivities of Possession: A Wittgensteinian Politics of Memory and Self-Education." Unpublished.

Neer, Richard. "Terrence Malick's New World." http://nonsite.org/issue-2/terrence-malicks-new-world.

Stout, Jeffery. *Democracy and Tradition*. Princeton: Princeton University Press, 2004.

Taylor, Charles. *Hegel*. Cambridge: Cambridge University Press, 1977.

———. *Sources of the Self: The Making of Modern Identity*. Cambridge: Harvard University Press, 1992.

Tran, Jonathan. *Foucault and Theology*. London: T. & T. Clark, 2011.

———. "Laughing *With* the World: Possibilities of Hope in John Howard Yoder and Jeffrey Stout." In *The New Yoder*, edited by Peter Dula and Chris Huebner, 253–70. Eugene, OR: Cascade, 2009.

Wells, Samuel. *Improvisation: The Drama of Christian Ethics*. Grand Rapids: Brazos, 2004.

Wittgenstein, Ludwig. *Philosophical Investigations*. Edited by P. M. S. Hacker and Joachim Schulte. Translated by P. M. S. Hacker, Joachim Schulte, and G. E. M. Anscombe. Oxford: Wiley-Blackwell, 2009.

Wolfe, Cary. "Exposures." In *Philosophy and Animal Life*, edited by Stanley Cavell et al., 43–89. New York: Columbia University Press, 2008.

Yoder, John Howard. *The Priestly Kingdom: Social Ethics as Gospel*. Notre Dame: University of Notre Dame Press, 1985.

www.ingramcontent.com/pod-product-compliance
Lightning Source LLC
Chambersburg PA
CBHW030615230426
43661CB00053B/1993